Introducing Charlotte Charke

Introducing

Charlotte Charke

Actress, Author, Enigma

Edited by
Philip E. Baruth

Afterword by
Felicity A. Nussbaum

University of Illinois Press

Urbana and Chicago

© 1998 by the Board of Trustees of the University of Illinois
Manufactured in the United States of America
1 2 3 4 5 C P 5 4 3 2 1

This book is printed on acid-free paper.

Frontispiece: "Mrs. Charlotte Charke." Artist unknown. Frontispiece
to *A Narrative of the Life of Mrs. Charlotte Charke* (1755). Courtesy of
the Honnold Library, Claremont College.

Library of Congress Cataloging-in-Publication Data
Introducing Charlotte Charke : actress, author, enigma /
edited by Philip E. Baruth ; afterword by Felicity A. Nussbaum.
    p.   cm.
Includes bibliographical references (p.   ) and index.
ISBN 0-252-02415-x (acid-free paper)
ISBN 0-252-06723-1 (pbk. : acid-free paper)
1. Charke, Charlotte, 1713–1760—Criticism and interpretation.
I. Baruth, Philip E. (Philip Edward)
PN2598.C28X158   1998
792'.028'092—ddc21   98-8907

CIP

Contents

Acknowledgments

More than anyone or anything else, I would like to thank my department at the University of Vermont for its humane and forward-looking policies for junior faculty; the junior sabbatical leave I was granted during the spring of 1996 was crucial to my work on this text. Two individuals deserve special thanks in this context—Tony Bradley and Alan Broughton. As chairmen, both Tony and Alan were instrumental in securing this valuable time for their hard-pressed junior colleagues.

I would like to acknowledge the English Department at the University of Illinois, Urbana-Champaign, as I wrote the bulk of the text while living in Champaign and was granted free use of university facilities through the department's intervention. Among the faculty at Urbana-Champaign who deserve my particular thanks: Liz Bohls, David Hirsch, and Richard Powers. I issue blanket thanks to the librarians and support workers in the many libraries of Urbana-Champaign.

I mention Robert Folkenflik in my dedication, but will acknowledge again his value as mentor during my time at the University of California, Irvine, and beyond. Final thanks to my readers—Joseph Chaney, Kristina Straub—and to Karen Hewitt and Veronica Scrol, my editors at the University of Illinois Press, for having perceived the value in scholarly work on this truly unaccountable historical figure. Thanks also to Heather Marcovitch, my editorial assistant at the University of Vermont, for her help and computer savvy. And to Louis Simon, a very canny copyeditor.

This book is dedicated to two exceptional individuals, Robert Folkenflik and Melissa Tedrowe: Bob first introduced me to Charke's work in the late 1980s, and Melissa supported me unfailingly and unstintingly throughout the writing and editing process. Thank you both.

Introducing Charlotte Charke

Introduction

Philip E. Baruth

I first read Charlotte Charke's *Narrative* of her own life in the form of a second-generation Xerox copy—that is, a copy of a copy of the 1969 facsimile edition of her 1755 autobiography. Nearly everyone I knew who had read her work (and a growing number had in 1987) had read it in this form—a historical footnote that has much to say about the ways that personal information technology has worked to disable traditional canonical structures. Architects have long honored the principle that paths should lead where people wish to walk; that is, architects have been forced to honor this principle by people creating paths as they need them, necessitating that concrete be poured into the resulting muddy ruts. In a similar fashion, computer text and Xerox copies have allowed academics to set about reviving and recirculating previously maligned authors, whether or not publishers have chosen initially to follow their lead. In Charke's case, fortunately, the time between Xerox-critical mass and republication of her text has not been overly long: a newly edited paperback version of the *Narrative* should be available as you read these lines.

A companion problem to that of her central text's availability has always been the lack of sufficient critical work to accompany it. One biography of Charke exists, Fidelis Morgan's useful but somewhat fragmentary work *The Well-Known Troublemaker* (1988). But while scholarly articles and book chapters on Charke now surface with some regularity—and while these disparate critical essays have laid the groundwork for a more sustained approach—there has been no book-length critical study of her life and work. It is this particular void that I see being filled by *Introducing Charlotte Charke*.

The volume's task is undeniably a schizophrenic one: as the only comparable critical text available, it should serve the needs both of scholars in the field who have already digested the little extant work on Charke and seek new approaches, and the needs of students approaching Charke and the eighteenth-century stage perhaps for the first time. For this reason, I've structured the text in three parts, with the first designed as a substantial introduction to the historical and critical essentials of Charke's life. This introduction I see as most useful for those at the initial stages of inquiry about Charke; I attempt to present, at each stage of Charke's career, a detailed overview of those mid-century institutions with which she was most intimately and inextricably connected—the loosely organized strolling companies and circuits, for example. Still, I would like to believe that there is much for the Charke scholar in this introductory section as well: among other lines of argument, I present an extended consideration of the impact the Licensing Act of 1737 had on Charke's career and on English dramatic freedoms as well. If only as a counter to traditional readings of Charke—which disparage her as shiftless or devoid of skill as an actress—I would recommend these pages, where she appears rather as a bona fide talent, for whom the Licensing Act proved cruelly effective in everyday practice.

Part 2 functions as something of a synechdoche for the recent critical work on Charke. Much of that work has centered on her idiosyncratic methods of subject-formation, and how these various practices ironically depend upon the highly public nature of Charke's theatrical family. Only through the mediation of her family's reputation can Charke conceive, construct, and disperse an arguably independent version of herself: a subjectivity, with the possibilities for social and political agency which that term implies. Two of the essays in this section, those by Sidonie Smith and Kristina Straub, have been highly influential in the formation of thought on Charke and are here reprinted as a convenient resource for the reader; they are reprinted as well for the economy with which they suggest a spectrum of recent critical opinion I detail at much greater length in chapter 1. Sidonie Smith's "The Transgressive Daughter and the Masquerade of Self-Representation" characterizes Charke as something of a "failed" feminist in spite of momentary subversions of the dominant political order; Charke wishes, in some real sense, to *be* her father (that is, a man) rather than simply to imitate him. Straub, for her part, argues that Charke's refusal to settle into either the role of heterosexual actress or lesbian cross-dresser is itself subversive, in that it holds open the possibilty of other, divergent sexualities and social roles for women. Like Smith's article, Straub's "The Guilty Pleasures of Female Theatrical Cross-Dressing" does not credit Charke with conscious rebellion, but it is reflective of the opposing wing of existing Charke criticism, in which her career is seen as fruitful political resistance.

The other essay in this section, a new piece by Jean Marsden titled "Charlotte Charke and the Cibbers: Private Life as Public Spectacle," carefully chronicles the way that Colley Cibber's *Apology* "begets" his son Theophilus's *Serio-Comic Apology* and his daughter Charlotte's *Narrative*. Cibber's children take his obsession with rendering the private public to a vertiginous extreme; Marsden asserts that the son and daughter completely collapse the distinction between public and private, life and theater, text and performance, and in this way preserve no self behind the mask—they turn themselves through aggressive self-publication into "stock figures out of dramatic texts, texts staged within the confines of the personal narrative."

Part 3 of *Introducing Charlotte Charke,* "Re-Contextualizing Charke," is in some ways the volume's most forward-looking contribution. Anyone who familiarizes him- or herself with the existing scholarship will notice that it tends to investigate a relatively focused and concentrated range of related critical questions, usually within the scope of Charke's own texts. It is a logical development, given the practical concern that until recently each critic writing on Charke assumed the responsibility of describing her singular life and of commenting on the political implications of those life choices. Hence, few scholars to date have placed her work in broader contexts, broader historically, socially, and generically.

The four essays in this third section seek to examine Charke's relevance in striking new ways. Perhaps most fundamental (and literal) in its questioning of existing representations of Charke is Robert Folkenflik's "Charlotte Charke: Images and Afterimages." Folkenflik examines the relatively small number of images traditionally associated with Charke and arrives, through painstaking deduction and analysis, at some surprising conclusions. The attractive and widely circulated figure of Charke engraved by L. P. Boitard, for example, is quite probably *not* Charke at all—at least "there is no reason to believe" that it is, as Folkenflik carefully words it. This iconographic vetting serves to separate the images of Charke into three camps, those certainly her, those probably her, and those most probably another model altogether. From this reorganization comes a conclusion consistent with my own findings in chapter 1 of this text: although Charke's image "has been linked to such artists as Dandridge, Boitard, Gravelot, Van Loo, and Hogarth," in the years following the Licensing Act of 1737 Charke was in fact "reduced to being depicted by provincial artists, and the only true portrait of her is by an unknown and dubious hand."

Madeleine Kahn's "Teaching Charlotte Charke: Feminism, Pedagogy, and the Construction of the Self" examines a less concrete set of representations. Located firmly in Kahn's own first-person experience as a late-twentieth-century instructor at a small women's college, this essay details the way in which Kahn's students' sophisticated yet "wishful" approaches to Charke have inflected her own interpretation of the *Narrative*. Along with its perspectives on Charke, the essay offers a thoughtful re-evaluation of the place feminism has assumed in contemporary pedagogy. In this sense Charke becomes for Kahn—and for Kahn's readers—an instructive reflection of the culture she and her students inhabit, one in which women have made great gains but continue to search energetically for self-definition in the women's literature they read.

Hans Turley's contribution, "'A Masculine Turn of Mind': Charlotte Charke and the Periodical Press," breaks new ground in a similar fashion, providing the first detailed inquiry into Charke's reception by the mainstream press of the mid-1750s. Possibly more eye-opening than any other single statement in this volume is the fact with which Turley begins his argument: In 1755 the *Gentleman's Magazine* devoted more space to Charke's *Narrative* than to any other of the year's productions, which included such works as Johnson's *Dictionary* and Voltaire's *History and State of Europe*. While Johnson's masterwork received just six pages in the April number, Charke's work appeared in a fifteen-page summary with commentary, these pages spaced out over three consecutive months. Turley makes the case that more space was devoted to the *Narrative* because, in a sense, it *mattered* more. Charke represented a more pressing ideological problem: her blurring of gender and sexual boundaries, boundaries otherwise increasingly visible in the century, represented a distinct threat that the *Magazine* evidently felt bound to confront.

The last essay in this section seeks to extend the limited work that has been done on Charke's movements within and between various genres. Joseph Chaney's "Turning to Men: Genres of Cross-Dressing in Charke's *Narrative* and Shakespeare's *The Merchant of Venice*" focuses on the obvious but previously unexplored connection between these two authors. Shakespeare's work is a lens through which Charke constantly demands that she be viewed; one of her very first male roles was Roderigo in *Othello*, and the *Narrative* is strewn with allusions to *Hamlet* and other popular Shakespeare plays. Approaching this connection from the standpoint of genre theory, Chaney seeks to demonstrate that both Charke's autobiography and Shakespeare's comedy present "a similar obstacle to the critic who seeks to isolate within them a subversive moment in the history of gender configurations: the teleological genre governing each text threatens to obscure, under an ideological veil of obvious meanings, whatever subversion we might hope to find there." The working out of the generic form, in each case, necessitates a formal denial of gender subversion, although, as Chaney argues, this denial can be rendered visible or told as a meta-generic "secret." Thus cross-dressing becomes more than simply an individual life's choice—it becomes an apt metaphor for this complicated process of generic cloaking. Yet, like Smith, Chaney sees Charke as something less than a self-conscious rebel, one whose text is ultimately subservient to the popular needs of her genre rather than triumphant over them.

As I've said above, the essays in this section advance the study of Charke and take it in unprecedented directions, possibly the surest proof that Charke criticism has left the initial stage at which much of the argument concerned the relevence of the subject herself. Kahn's essay *assumes* that Charke will be taught, a state of affairs that the *Gentleman's Magazine* (as Turley shows) would have found profoundly disturbing, and that assumption testifies to the very clear success of those critics whose essays have preceded this volume.

PART 1

Discovering Charlotte Charke

1

Who Is Charlotte Charke?

Philip E. Baruth

In his 1907 text on eighteenth-century actresses, *Comedy Queens of the Georgian Era,* John Fyvie begins the chapter on Charlotte Charke as follows: "Colley Cibber, poet-laureate, popular actor, sparkling dramatist, successful manager, and—by virtue of his *Apology* for his own life (which needed none)—author of the most entertaining book in all theatrical literature, was the father of twelve children . . ." (Fyvie 42).[1] Fyvie, like most critics up to the present day, would quite clearly prefer to be discussing the father rather than the father's youngest daughter, Cibber rather than Charke née Cibber. Fyvie's answer, then, is that Charlotte Charke (1713–60) was a forgettable actress brought to the English stage through her renowned father's influence.

Continuing in the same grudging strain, Fyvie notes that additionally Charlotte, "who inherited some measure of her father's literary faculty," published in 1755 a narrative of her "singular career." This narrative—*A Narrative of the Life of Mrs. Charlotte Charke, Written by Herself*—Fyvie dubs "one of the queerest bits of autobiography extant" (Fyvie 42). It is a descriptive phrase that comes into its full ironic character only in our own times: Charlotte Charke was also a "notorious" cross-dresser, a woman who dressed as a man both on stage and in real life, who lived with one "Mrs. Brown" as "Mr. Charles Brown" for nearly a decade of her life.

While little of the early work on Charke deals directly with this aspect of her life, nearly all of the current criticism highlights it, tracing intriguing connections between sexuality, autobiography, and subject-formation. The *Narrative* of her life she addressed generally to her father and published in installments, the first of which begged him to forgive her transgressive lifestyle ("my Folly") and take her back into the domestic and financial security of the Cibber family; the unspoken threat was that as long as forgiveness was withheld, installments—installments brimming with "Folly"—would be forthcoming. In this way, the serial text enacts a very complex set of functions, signaling loyalty through imitation (of her father's *Apology*), independence through revelation of "Mad Pranks," and a willingness to form a self before the eyes of a scrutinizing public.

The narrative installments record a life of masquerade, during which Charlotte doggedly tried her hand at a host of explicitly male trades. She was a grocer, a groom, a butler, a pastry maker, a sausage higgler, a publican, a puppet-show proprietor. She was a novelist, who produced four fictional works: *The Mercer* (n.d.), *The History of Henry Dumont, Esq., and Miss Charlotte Evelyn* (1756), *The Lover's Treat: or, Unnatural Hatred* (1758), and *The History of Charley and Patty* (n.d.). She was a dramatist and producer, with the authorship of three plays to her credit: *The Carnival* (1735), *Tit for Tat; or, Comedy and Tragedy at War* (1743), and *The Art of Management* (1735), the only one of the three to be published. But most consistently and definitively she was a strolling actress—not in her father's London sphere, but in the ill-attended and ill-paying "productions" staged in barns and halls across the English countryside.

Charke's *Narrative* is her father's *Apology* seen through a glass very darkly: where Cibber describes London high-life and a class of actor socially venerated by the early 1700s, Charke tells of the hazards of the road, being thrown in jail as a vagabond, being robbed by managers, and hissed by illiterate audiences. As a record of those experiences, the *Narrative of the Life of Mrs. Charlotte Charke* is invaluable; but further it provides evidence that women did live out lives of their own making in the age of Richardson's *Clarissa* and in the heyday of the conduct manual. Charke, typically, dedicates her autobiography to herself, and makes it clear that self-discovery is one of her primary motivations: "If, by your approbation, the World may be perswaded into a tolerable Opinion of my Labours, I shall . . . venture for once to call you, FRIEND; a Name, I own, I never *as yet have known you by*" (14).

In 1907 the answer to the question of Charke's identity was her father's prominence, his position as poet laureate and author. Today, the answers are quite different and quite characteristically multiple: she was a very early female autobiographer and novelist, she was a historian of low- and middle-culture among a wide swath of the English populace, and she was a woman who made a life's work of transgressing dramatic, social, and sexual boundaries. As such,

Charke seems a figure who should have been—by the year 1998—rediscovered and made the subject of serious critical inquiry. As yet, she has been only partially recognized. Erin Mackie renders the critical paradox neatly: "The constitution of women's lives in the eighteenth century, the relationship between autobiography and fiction, the significance and nature of eighteenth-century cross-dressing, the hermeneutics of travesty, life on the margins of society and gender—it seems inevitable that the current cultivation of these topics would have brought the narratives of the life of Charlotte Charke into thorough and perspicacious assessment. However, much of the work on Charke is incomplete" (Mackie 841).

In the following pages I attempt to begin filling the critical gap Mackie describes. Beginning with Charke's *Narrative* in the year 1755—the touchstone for all students of Charke's life—I try to place her sometimes confusing record in a useful historical perspective, by clarifying the legal and social proscriptions against which she struggled. From 1755, when Charke was middle-aged, I move back to her earliest and most successful moments on the stage; in this way, I hope to illustrate the direct confluence between the troubled history of the eighteenth-century stage and Charke's personal history of rapidly shifting occupations and wandering. Finally, I look at the controversies surrounding Charke's "infamous" lifestyle, questions of her sexuality, and how those questions feed into the more general and ongoing considerations of Charke as an early feminist author. It is my own feeling that Charke has been treated with notable unfairness for nearly all of the last two and a half centuries, due to a discomfort with her cross-dressing and a concerted attempt on the part of Cibber's biographers to absolve the father through the casual defamation of his children, primarily Charke. In light of this, I try throughout to engage the tradition of Charke criticism, in an effort to alert current students of her autobiography to unwarranted characterizations of her that continue to dominate most of the "authoritative" reference works they will encounter.

Historical Contexts of Charke's Life

The Context of Charke's *Narrative*

On the last Saturday of April, 1755, Charlotte Cibber Charke Sacheverell—a forty-two-year-old actress who, in spite of the greater notoriety of her first and third surnames, most often styled herself Charlotte Charke—published the first installment of her "singular" autobiography. She was extraordinarily tired for a forty-two-year-old repertory actress. She had spent the previous eighteen years dodging a legal system determined to keep her from the stage, as well as feuding with her own infamous family, who were now by and large indifferent to her. The last nine of those eighteen years she passed in effective exile from London,[2] as a strolling actress, moving from makeshift company to company and traveling chaotically between small, often parochial English manufacturing towns and rough seaside ports and back again, at the whim of incompetent managers.

She had been imprisoned for debt, and harassed as a "vagabond" under an unpopular amendment to the Act of Queen Anne. There had been moments of success, in Bath and other fashionable watering holes, but these were short-lived and followed always by months or years in inept rural companies. "I have had the Mortification of hearing the Characters of *Hamlet, Varanes, Othello*, and many more Capitals, rent in Pieces by a Figure no higher than two Six-penny Loaves, and a Disonancy of Voice, which conveyed to me a strong Idea of a Cat in Labour" (153).

Charlotte had returned to London from these "peregrinations" in December 1755, of the bitter opinion that "going a Strolling is engaging in a little, dirty Kind of War, in which I have been obliged to fight so many Battles, I have resolutely determined to throw down my Commission: And to say Truth, I am not only sick, but heartily ashamed of it, as I have had nine Years Experience of its being a very contemptible life" (152). As the daughter of England's relatively wealthy poet laureate, she had known much better, earlier in life, and she was simply tired of exile. "When I set my foot upon *London* Streets, though with only a single Penny in my Pocket, I was more transported with Joy, than for all the Height of Happiness I had, in former and at different Times, possessed" (213).

She desired nothing more than to remain in the city, and—in typically hyperactive fashion—had decided on four or five different ways to do that. She was close to finishing her first novel, *The History of Henry Dumont, Esq., and Miss Charlotte Evelyn,* and was certain her readers would find it to their tastes (210); she would open an "oratorical academy, for the instruction of those who have any Hopes, from Genius and Figure, of appearing on either of the *London* Stages" (214); she would obtain a special Grant from the Lord Chamberlain for a Benefit at the Hay-Market Theater of "ONE NIGHT ONLY," and so tiptoe back into the good graces of the acting establishment (57). But her pet project was a narrative of her own life, and it represented the most intricate and successful of her strategies.

"When I first came to town," she later insisted, "I had no design of giving any Account of my Life, farther than a trifling Sketch, introduced in the preface, to Mr. DUMONT'S History" (214). But being "positively and strongly" urged by friends (one of the few acceptable excuses for autobiography in the eighteenth century), she began to write an account of her own life calculated to succeed in one of several ways.

First, both the book's text and its advertisement were written with an eye toward exploiting the more infamous aspects of Charke's life—chiefly her predilection not simply for men's clothing, but for assuming male roles both on- and offstage for much of her life. Accordingly, the frontispiece promised "Her adventures in Mens Cloaths, and being belov'd by a Lady of great fortune, who intended to marry her" (12). Having spent her life testing her audience's response to gender switching, Charlotte neatly walked the line between overt titillation and acceptable morality. (Despite the advertisement's hinting, the "Lady" is very quickly disabused, and Charke turns the incident into an emblem of proper heterosexual conduct.)

Key to this brand of acceptable sensationalism was Charke's representation of herself as a penitent, one who had given up "travesty" and "adventuring" for good—and as has been suggested above, this was probably more true than false. There is a note of sincerity in many of her declarations, and throughout her text Charke refers to her days in "breeches" as "mad Pranks" (12), "my former Madness" (20), and "little follies of prattling Infancy" (101). She stoutly denies a report that she had recently slipped from her good resolutions: "That I designed to forsake my Sex again, and that I positively was seen in the Street in Breeches. . . . This I solemnly avow to be an impertinent Falshood, which was brought to *London* and spread itself, much to my Disadvantage, in my own family" (206).

This outraged mention of her family gets to the heart of the second strategy at work in the *Narrative:* Charlotte had decided to reconcile, if not with her entire family, then with her father. The financial motives for this, while certainly operative, should not be seen as all-encompassing; Charke clearly hoped to start over with her father, and through his pardon to be relieved of the black-sheep stigma she felt had burdened her for the whole of her adult life. Still, Cibber was easily capable of supporting her financially or of restoring her to respectability in the London theaters, and in this way her emotional and practical impulses were likely inseparable. Whether she sought to avoid her older sister's expected interference or whether she sought to appeal to Cibber's own sense of the dramatic, Charke selected the highly public method of her serialized autobiography to make her case to her father.

Her attempt to elevate this filial purpose above all others she marked typographically. Typically, in speaking of her father or their rift, the text reverts to upper-case, developing a sort of running super-text imbued with its own particular importance and solemnity: "But I dare confidently affirm, MUCH PAINS

has been taken to AGGRAVATE MY FAULTS, and STRENGTHEN his Anger
..." (24). She paid her father the compliment of alluding several times to his
own infamous autobiography, referring, for instance, to her text as the "brat of
my brain" (15), a metaphor Cibber had developed in his *Apology* (Cibber 2).[3]

And she invoked, with neat irony, the biblical narrative of the Prodigal Son:
"The Prodigal, according to Holy Writ, was joyfully received by the offended
Father: Nay, MERCY has even been extended itself at the Place of Execution ..."
(100). The public format allowed her to draw on sentimental convention, to
involve her father in a drama already well in motion by the time the printed
installment came to his hand:

> Nor was I exempted from an equal share in my Father's Heart; yet, partly thro' my
> own Indiscretion (and, I am too well convinc'd, from the cruel Censure of false and
> evil Tongues) since my Maturity, I Lost that Blessing: Which, if strongest Compunc-
> tion and uninterrupted Hours of Anguish, blended with Self-conviction and filial
> Love, can move his Heart to Pity and Forgiveness, I shall, with Pride and unutter-
> able Transport, throw myself at his Feet, to implore the only Benefit I desire or ex-
> pect, his BLESSING, and his PARDON.
>
> But of that, more hereafter—And I hope, ere this small Treatise is finish'd, to have
> it in my Power to inform my Readers, my painful Separation from my once tender
> Father will be more than amply repaid, by a happy Interview. (17–18)

As this last short paragraph evidences, Charke's second strategy of paternal
reconciliation was backed up by a third—by publishing her combined auto-
biography/appeal in *serial* form, she could greatly increase the pressure on her
father to take her back into the family. Those Londoners who read the initial
installment expecting lurid tales of Charke's cross-dressing had the added pleasure of peering into the current, circuitous affairs of the Cibber family. They
were made an audience to the reconciliation attempt, in fact as well as figure.
At a stroke Charke increased her leverage with her father and her pool of paying customers.

When the first week's installment had been shipped to the bookseller's
stands, Charke wrote Cibber a personal letter, stressing her own fault in their
estrangement but also hinting at the pressures of public scrutiny: "I doubt not
but you are sensible I last Saturday published the First Number of a Narrative
of my Life, in which I made a proper concession in regard to those unhappy
Miscarriages which have for many Years justly deprived me of a Father's Fondness. *As I am conscious of my Errors, I thought I could not be too publick in su-
ing for your Blessing and Pardon*" (99, emphasis mine).

Whether intended or not, the set-up carried a faint whiff of blackmail: should Cibber fail to reconcile with her, more installments would follow and these would be filled with the same sort of cross-dressing "pranks" he had always warned his daughter against. He would be forced to relive in turn each of his daughter's disgraces and missteps. Worse, the reading audience would be informed, by the very appearance of each new number, of his continuing hard-heartedness. Cibber, whether he liked it or not, had become a character in his daughter's highly public "Prodigal" drama. The only choice left him was whether he would play the Father-as-Hero or the Father-as-Villain.

Not surprisingly, he chose the latter. Cibber had a reputation, after all, for treating his family with spectacular indifference. In his own autobiography, *An Apology for the Life of Colley Cibber* (1740), Cibber had made direct reference to his wife only once, by way of joking that he had produced as many plays as she children, and thus they were quits as far as productivity (Cibber 146). A famous letter of the period, written by Charles Johnson, publicly accused him of gambling away his children's inheritance, while "his daughter very bare in clothes" [Charlotte herself] looked on (Morgan 25). And as butt of Fielding's *Pasquin* and the supreme butt of Pope's *Dunciad,* Cibber was quite accustomed to weathering attacks.

For whatever reasons, he saw fit to refuse her. Whereas some ten years before he had responded to a request for money with a few ornate lines—"The strange career which you have run for some years (a career not always unmarked by evil) debars my affording you that succour which otherwise would naturally have been extended to you as my daughter" (Morgan 124)—Cibber now responded by returning her letter enclosed in a blank sheet of paper. As a deliberately cutting gesture, it foreshadowed Charke's legacy in her father's will (he was to die two years later): "five pounds and no more" (Morgan 184).

But the beauty of Charke's rhetorical design was that it anticipated Cibber's abrupt snub, and then took it *en passant.* She simply incorporated the new material into the ongoing dramatic narrative:

> I shall now give a full Account of, I think, one of the most tragical Occurrences of my Life, which but last Week happened to me. The reader may remember, in the First Number of my Narrative I made a publick Confession of my faults; and, pleased with the fond Imagination of being restored to my Father's Favour, Flattered myself, ere this Treatise could be ended, to ease the Hearts of every humane Breast, with an Account of a Reconciliation.
>
> But how FRUITLESS WAS MY ATTEMPT! I wrote, and have thought it necessary, in Justification of my own Character, to print the Letter I sent my father. . . . Can I then be blamed for saying with the expiring *Romeo,*

> "—*Fathers have flinty Hearts! No tears*
> *Will move 'em!—Children must be wretched!?*"

This SHOCKING CIRCUMSTANCE! has since confined me to my Bed; and has been cruelly aggravated by the terrible Reflection of being empowered to say, with *Charles* in *The Fop's Fortune,* "I'M SORRY THAT I'VE LOST A FATHER." (98)

It is melodrama very calculatingly done, and demonstrates that Charke even five years from the end of her life was hardly the pitiful and witless wretch painted by Samuel Whyte in his "ACCOUNT OF A VISIT TO MRS. CHARKE" (221, printed following the text of the Ashley edition of the *Narrative*). Note the way that Charke blends the new real-life material with the dramatized summary of events from the previous number: "The reader may remember, in the First Number of my Narrative. . . ." She guides the reader's reactions through selected references to established drama, again—in what now seems both delicious and deliberate irony—invoking famous *male* characters whose dilemmas parallel her own. And she makes perhaps unwittingly clear that she views herself, in spite of the pose of incapacitation, as the final victor in the game of morals her father (and London itself) had always insisted she play. She is "empowered," that is to say, rather than mortified or chastened, to say that she has lost a father. The audience has been recruited emotionally and morally to her cause; Charke's desires are mirrored in the "Hearts of every humane Breast."

And the best part of it all was that even Cibber's returning the letter in a blank could not end the spectacle, or the low-level tension. The reader could always assume that one of the future installments would persuade or shame or gall him into renewed participation. Charke, for her part, continued to assert the possiblity as the size and the notoriety of the work grew.

In this sense, the *Narrative* was not only Charke's most successful extended work in prose, but her most successful drama. It had all of the best elements of mainstream eighteenth-century comedy, raised somehow out of the stuff of real-life London: a stormy father-figure, a woman in and then out of "breeches," the titillating spectacle justified by frequent moralizing, and a run as long as Charke—both author and stage-manager—saw fit. The public certainly continued to ask for more. "The instalments [*sic*] sold so well that they were published as a book, which went into two editions before the end of the year" (Morgan 182). The success of the *Narrative* paved the way for Charke to act in London again, albeit with her brother Theophilus's (still illicit) Haymarket Company, and to publish three short didactic novels. And while none of these things made her a rich woman, she accomplished her purpose of remaining in London and acting there, if only sporadically, until her death in April of 1760. It was very much the right version of Charke's life at the right time.

Charke, Theatrical Freedom, and the Licensing Act of 1737

Perhaps no other single event changed the character of Charke's life so dramatically as the passage of the Licensing Act of 1737. Combined with her own tempestuous relations with London's patent theaters, Covent Garden and Drury Lane, the Act (and the patent system as a whole) all but guaranteed the obscurity she labored in for most of her life. Like many players, including her older brother Theophilus, Charke saw her extremely bright prospects dim rapidly with the Government's wholesale repeal of traditional theatrical freedoms in that year.

The year 1730—the same year in which her father was designated laureate— was a momentous one for Charlotte Charke. In February, at the age of seventeen, she married the composer and dancing master Richard Charke, an employee of her father's at Drury Lane Theater. In December she gave birth to their only child, Catherine. But more important than either of these events, judging by means of space accorded them in the *Narrative,* was Charke's debut on the London stage.

At the urging of the celebrated actress Anne Oldfield, Charke moved up the date of her first appearance a season in order to debut in Oldfield's own benefit performance—a mark of the intimacy and advantage then Charlotte Cibber enjoyed early in life, even as an unknown, with the Drury Lane Company. The accelerated debut was a move her father approved, though he took the caution of protecting her name (and his own) in the event of a botched performance—the playbill for *The Provok'd Wife* credited the part of Mademoiselle only to "a young Gentlewoman, who had never appeared on any Stage before" (50). Charke, however, aquitted herself admirably. She was in fact chosen to play the same role again about three weeks later, this time billed by name (Morgan 51).[4] Her closest critics—Oldfield and Cibber Senior himself— showed their "Approbation" of her talents, but if we can believe Charke's own reports, the town as a whole was more than merely supportive. Charke is candid about her own self-absorption at the time, and makes it clear that she actively sought out public reaction under the cloak of anonymity. Nothing but positive comments seemed to be making the rounds: "Nor do I believe it cost me less, in Shoes and Coaches, than two or three Guineas, to gratify the extravagant Delight I had, not only in reading the [play]Bills, but sometimes hearing myself spoken of, which luckily was to my Advantage; nor can I answer for the strange Effect a contrary Report might have wrought, on a Mind so giddily loaded with conceited Transport" (51).

From 1730 onward Charke's career continued to pick up steam. With a modesty for which she has never been given sufficient credit, she relates a string of successes in the following two seasons. In 1731 she played Alicia in Rowe's tragedy *Jane Shore,* a demanding role ordinarily played by the well-known Mary Porter; yet the young actress "found the audience not less indulgent than before" (52). Even in "Capital" or leading characters, she "escaped with Life" (52). She began, as a result, to gain respect within the Drury Lane Company and was selected as "Stock-Reader to the Theatre" or general understudy (53). It was not a company task lightly assigned or given merely through favoritism. The stock-reader had to be prepared to fill a number of complex roles, "Capital" as well as supporting, at the last possible instant. Charke was called upon in the summer of 1731, for instance, to play Cleopatra only "at the second music." In this capacity the stock-reader would have had to display general competence, in both tragedy and comedy, as well as recognized "genius" in certain individual roles. Charke had begun to make her mark. "Beginning to make Acting my Business as well as my Pleasure," she recalls, "the Success I had . . . raised me from Twenty to Thirty Shillings per Week" (53).

At this point in time, even minor revolutions couldn't alter her prospects. In 1733, her father abruptly decided to retire from theatrical management and sold his share in the royal patent of Drury Lane Theatre to one John Highmore. The shift in power greatly displeased Charke's brother Theophilus, who had been managing the company for their father for some time and who expected to be next in line for ownership. Almost immediately, a theatrical war broke out, with the majority of the Drury Lane actors defecting to one of several technically illicit theaters to the west of central London—the "Little Theater" in the Haymarket. Charke jumped ships too: "My Brother being principally concerned, I also made a Decampment; and was, by Agreement, raised from Thirty Shillings to Three Pounds, had a very good share of parts . . ." (54). Although actors' salaries were often quickly bumped up in times of competition between theaters, it is safe to assume (if only from her liberty to choose roles) that Charke was viewed as one of the ersatz company's stronger players.

It is telling to note that the *Oxford Companion to the Theatre,* like nearly every other theatrical encyclopedia, mentions nothing of Charke's early, solid success (in fact it has no entry for Charke, ranging her under her father's name). "Married at 16 to Richard Charke, a violinist at Drury Lane," the *Companion* entry reads, "and widowed in 1737 . . . she went on the stage, quarreled with the managers, and ran away, communicating with her family from time to time in order to borrow money from them" (Hartnoll 178). The year 1733 does mark the beginning of Charke's serious quarrels with London's patentee managers, but what is most notable—and little noted—about this period is that Charke, for all of her moments of caprice, was enough in demand to be able to move freely between the handful of working theaters, all but two of which operated in defiance of the patent tradition. Her greatest successes coincide with the years of most freedom for the theaters in and around London. On November 12, 1733, John Highmore—still smarting from his old company's rebellion and current good fortune—had one of the Little Haymarket company arrested on a charge of vagrancy; a two-decades-old statute (12 Anne 2, ch. 23) declared a wide range of players and strollers to be "Rogues and Vagabonds" (Liesenfeld 18). The legal action was in keeping with the patentees' traditionally fierce response to anyone or anything challenging their effective monopoly on dramatic performance. As Cibber notes, patentees had often in the past defended their turf by exploiting personal connections with the Lord Chamberlain, and procuring orders to silence any upstart theater. In this case, surprisingly, the courts found in favor of the actor John Harper, because he owned a house in Westminster, and could not therefore be classed a vagrant.

It was a satisfying victory for Charke, Theophilus, and their company, but more generally it was a victory for the free market in actors, which kept salaries high and managerial tyranny low. "Drury Lane and Covent Garden continued to be the strongest houses, but the power of their managers was held in check by the possibility that their actors could leave for another theater" (Liesenfeld 22). In addition to the two traditionally licensed theaters, several other "new wave" theaters were given indirect leave to stand by the decision in the Harper case.[5]

When Highmore finally sold his contested share in the theater's management to Charles Fleetwood, the rebel players (including Charke) returned to Drury Lane, where business continued with "great industry" and "proportionable Success," even "super-extraordinary Success" (54). Charke grew so confident of her prospects, in fact, that following her first quarrel with Fleetwood, she "without the least Patience or Consideration, took a *French* Leave of him, and was idle enough to conceive I had done a very meritorious Thing" (54–55). Compounding the effect of a move she soon regretted, she wrote, staged, and acted in a farce directed squarely at her old Drury Lane manager called *The Art of Management*. This piece of very broad satire, performed at one of the new theaters in York Buildings, Villiers Street, certainly widened the rift between Charke and the patentees at Drury Lane. But it also greatly pleased audiences: a review of the first night highlighted Charke's tragic abilities, which "drew tears from the whole audience," and the success of the farce, itself "very much applauded" (Morgan 56). And although Fleetwood apparently packed the audience with young clerks to damn it, and although he attempted to buy up the small print run of *The Art of Management,* he was unsuccessful on both counts. Charke continued to free-lance among the "new wave" theaters (and even occasionally at the patent theaters, in off seasons or in particular productions), and even managed a Haymarket company herself during the 1734 summer season.

Between 1734 and 1737, the increasing freedom of the theater, the growth of Charke's own personal success, and the growth of her own opinion of her own personal success all reached their high-water mark. In 1735, due to the intervention of Charke's father, the patentees at Drury Lane (primarily the disgruntled Fleetwood) agreed to restore Charke to her "former station" (55). As Covent Garden and Drury Lane remained the two most popular houses, as well as the two firmly protected by the Crown, it was a sensible move for her to return. But her former station was a relatively lowly one, given that she had become accustomed while at the new theaters to selecting choice roles and occasionally directing the company as a whole. The patent theaters were notoriously hierarchical, with established players fiercely defending a range of popular roles as their own. As Colley Cibber notes of his own early success, it "could not recommend me to any new Trials of my Capacity; not a Step farther could I get, 'till the Company was again divided; when the Desertion of the best Actors left a clear Stage, for younger Champions to mount, and shew their best Pretensions to favour" (Cibber 104–5).

For whatever reasons, Charke left Fleetwood and Drury Lane after only two months, returning to the Haymarket Theater, now managed by one of her father's sworn enemies, the playwright and novelist Henry Fielding. Unfortunately for Charke, it proved precisely the wrong alliance at precisely the wrong time.

The Licensing Act of 1737   By the 1730s, the new, nontraditional companies had come to relish their role as gadfly to both the dramatic and political rulers of the kingdom. Henry Fielding's Little Haymarket Company in particular rejoiced in the fact that the patent system, with its traditional overtones of censorship, had been revealed as toothless. Even the active disapproval of the king apparently meant nothing: "If a manager wished to operate a theater without the sanction of letters patent, and even under the disapproval of the Lord Chamberlain, there was no remedy at law available to the Crown or to others who opposed him" (Liesenfeld 16). Fielding and his company embarked on a course of relentless and biting political satire, and drew the town in droves. His New Theater in the Haymarket was a stripped-down operation—"cheaply constructed and cheaply equipped," and with "no manager in the usual sense" (Battestin 83)—allowing for greater experimentation and rapid response to political developments.

Vincent J. Liesenfeld's *Licensing Act of 1737* demonstrates quite vividly the way in which Fielding exploited unpopular policies of George II and the Walpole administration, and in turn the way that Walpole interpreted the Haymarket's many successes as signs of imminent insurrection. In 1736, for example, Parliament passed the Gin Act, a bill aimed at the problem of common drunkenness; London of the eighteenth century was notorious for its gin consumption, as dramatized by Hogarth and others, and the new bill sought to limit the number of gin shops (which reportedly numbered over six thousand prior to the bill's taking effect). The means for limiting gin consumption were purely economic: the bill increased "the fee for a liquor retailer's license from £20 to £50, and the tax on a gallon of gin from 5s. to £1" (Liesenfeld 62–65). It was a regressive measure, aimed at preventing the common worker from drinking while doing little or nothing to curtail the consumption of the wealthy or the growing middle class of tradesmen and manufacturers. The bill was passed in the spring and scheduled to take effect in September, leaving several months for the city to stew over the news.

Accordingly, during this charged interval, Fielding's company presented an anonymous farce entitled *The Deposing and Death of Queen Gin*. The play was the first of a number of public spectacles damning the Gin Act before and after it took effect. "London began to take on the appearances of an occupied city. When Michaelmas arrived (29 September), retailers of liquor draped their signs with black and organized mock lyings-in-state and funeral processions for 'Madam Geneva,' re-creating publicly the action of the farce performed at the Little Theater in Haymarket almost two months earlier" (Liesenfeld 64). By the following month, mobs were rioting sporadically, some shouting, "No gin, no King." The protest over the Gin Act began to meld with protest over turnpikes and the Jacobite dream of a restored Stuart succession. Royal horse and guards were called out into the streets.

In this instance, Fielding's production reflected—and in a circular fashion both spurred and focused—a growing discontent with George II's policies, his lavish spending, and his prolonged absences from England. The Haymarket company provided an abbreviated visual language for political protest. They continued producing direct, successful, and dangerous political satire into late 1736 (including *The Fall of Bob, Alias Gin*), when Charke joined the company.

As her staunchly conservative father later put it, in writing Fielding's dramatic epitaph, "He produc'd several frank, and free Farces, that seem'd to knock
all Distinctions of Mankind on the Head: Religion, Laws, Government, Priests,
Judges, and Ministers, were all laid flat, at the Feet of this *Herculean* Satyrist!"
(Cibber 156). Cibber's cold irony very accurately reflects the strength of the
backlash engendered by Fielding's new style of political comedy.

The Court and Parliament were not Fielding's only targets. As mentioned
above, he, like many other prominent authors of the day, took particular exception to the fact that a second-rate poet—Colley Cibber himself—had been made
poet laureate primarily on the strength of his comedic powers, his flattery, and
his political ductility. Fielding, who had had several of his early plays flatly rejected by Cibber at Drury Lane, lampooned his former critic in every genre available to him. "When Cibber had been announced Poet Laureat[e] . . . Fielding
inserted a new scene, *The Battle of the Poets* (featuring Sir Fopling Fribble, alias
Cibber), into his satire *Tom Thumb*" (Morgan 59). Fielding's *Shamela* and *Joseph Andrews* both contain satire on Cibber's ego and his lack of classical training; *Shamela* in particular ridicules Cibber's *Apology* as the product of an egoist. With the exception of Alexander Pope, Fielding had wounded Cibber perhaps
more than any other single writer.

His company's acquisition of Charke was a godsend. Not only could he give
center stage to a daughter who had so recently offended her father and the London theatrical establishment,[6] thus ensuring further embarrassment for the
laureate, but due to Charke's fondness for and ability in male roles, he could
use her to strike more directly at Cibber. Charke presents the story of her first
role for Fielding, Lord Place in *Pasquin,* as the logical outcome of chance circumstance:

> What further aggravates my Folly and Ingratitude, I made, even then, but a short
> Stay with him, and joined the late *Henry Fielding,* Esq.; who, at that Time was Man-
> ager at the *Haymarket* Theatre, and running his Play called, *Pasquin,* the eleventh
> Night of which I played the Part of Lord *Place;* which, 'till then, had been performed
> by Mr. *Richard Yates:* But as he had other Parts in that Piece, Mr. *Fielding* begged the
> Favour of him to spare that to make room for me, and I was accordingly engaged at
> Four Guineas *per* Week, with an Indulgence in Point of Charges at my Benefit, by
> which I cleared Sixty Guineas. (55–56)

Pasquin, of course, satirized Colley Cibber among others—Lord Place was in
fact the play's heavily caricatured version of Cibber. No wonder, then, that
Fielding "begged" Richard Yates to give up a choice part to a newcomer. The
chance to have Cibber's daughter animate his caricature of the laureate was

one Fielding could not resist, as further indicated by the quite favorable terms of Charke's employment. (The manager rarely suspended "Charges"—a percentage of the gross receipts—during an actor's benefit.) Among other absurdities, Lord Place bribes election officials and, in an infamous passage, offers a reluctant voter the job of poet-laureate:

> *Voter.* I don't care much what it is, provided I wear fine clothes, and have something to do in the kitchen, or the cellar. I own I should like the cellar, for I am a devilish lover of sack [wine].
> *Lord Place.* Sack, say you? Odso, you shall be poet-laureate.
> *Voter.* Poet! no, my lord, I am no poet; I can't make verses.
> *Lord Place.* No matter for that; you'll be able to make odes.
> *Voter.* Odes, my Lord! what are those?
> *Lord Place.* Faith, sir, I can't tell what they are; but I know you may be qualified for the place without being a poet.[7]

Still, for all Charke's innocence here, she could not have been ignorant of the implications of playing in *Pasquin,* in that particular role and for that particular manager. But apparently the opportunity was one she, for her own reasons, could not resist. In some ways it was the realization of a childhood ambition: her *Narrative* opens, after all, on a now-famous scene in which Charlotte at age four uses her father's "enormous bushy Tie-wig," waistcoat, sword, and hat to give the neighborhood an impromptu impersonation of him (20). In any event, it was a performance the town too could not resist. "*Pasquin* was a huge hit, and ran, tagged with a selection of afterpieces, until May" (Morgan 60). According to one Fielding biographer, "The play was still being discussed as a topical event a year after the opening night" (Donald Thomas 127). It was enough to legitimize a company perceived only weeks before as upstarts. As Fidelis Morgan notes, this turn of events was probably the "final straw" for Cibber, and may have produced a short but heartfelt letter from father to daughter: "Why do you not dissociate yourself from that worthless scoundrel, and then your relatives might try and aid you. You will never be any good while you adhere to him, and you most certainly will not receive what otherwise you might from your father." (Morgan 86–87).[8]

Still Charke chose to cast her lot with Fielding, and for a final few months she was well rewarded for it. In 1737, Fielding continued his remarkable string of hits with a farcical review of the year's events titled *The Historical Register for the Year 1736. The Historical Register* combined all of Fielding's satirical talents and targets: in addition to a final scene which "represents Walpole's bribery of members of Parliament," the play managed to satirize Colley Cibber for

his alterations of Shakespeare (through the character Ground-Ivy) and Theophilus Cibber (Pistol) who leads a mob and "thinks himself a Great Man" (Liesenfeld 101–2). Charke played an auctioneer, Christopher Hen, based on a famous Covent Garden auctioneer, Christopher Cock; the name change was
rendered, of course, more humorous by the audience's knowledge that the male
part was being played by a woman. She presides over an auction attended by
bargain-hunting and promiscuous gentry, offering among other articles "a very
considerable quantity of interest at Court," which everyone wants, and a "small
quantity of 'true French' modesty, warranted not to change the colour of a lady's complexion on any provocation," this time to "no bidder, modesty being
'out of fashion'" (Dudden 198–99). Her auction scene in act II was generally
regarded as one of the "centerpieces" of the show (Donald Thomas 131).[9]

The response was tremendous. The *Daily Advertiser* reported that it "received
the greatest Applause ever shown at the Theatre"; to make matters worse for
its real-life targets, "Through the remainder of the season it was performed
on thirty-five of the thirty-nine evenings the Haymarket was open, holding
the stage without interruption (except for Wednesdays and Fridays during
Lent, and Passion Week) until the first week in May" (Liesenfeld 103–4). In the
repertory world of eighteenth-century theater, where a run of two weeks constituted a hit, Fielding's *Historical Register* was all but unprecedented.

But Prime Minister Robert Walpole had not been idle during Fielding and
Charke's bravura season. Thwarted in its efforts two years earlier to halt what
it considered seditious performances, his administration took a new tack in 1737.
Three days following the first performance of *The Historical Register,* on March
21, the House of Commons took up consideration of a bill aimed at prohibiting dramatic performances in the university towns of Oxford and Cambridge.
Ostensibly this measure was designed to restore the university officials' traditional authority to protect students from immoral influences, but clearly the
timing of the Cambridge theater bill suited the Walpole administration.

> The action of the House on the universities' bill early in May marked a turning point
> in the history of theater law: meeting as a committee with Robert Walpole in the chair,
> it approved legislation that would directly prohibit the performance of any plays in
> the vicinities of the two universities. Such a proscription, had it been first proposed
> for London or for the nation in general, would probably have provoked . . . a flood of
> petitions and substantial opposition in the House. But the bill for Cambridge and
> Oxford was limited both geographically and politically. (Liesenfeld 113)

In this way, Walpole used the universities' traditional legal status—acting in *loco
parentis* to matriculating students—to bypass libertarian arguments, and thus

establish a legal precedent otherwise difficult or impossible to come by. (Much the same argument has been made by civil libertarians in the United States, especially those concerned with the issues of drug-testing in high schools and censorship of television and the Internet: In both cases, critics contend that an invasive government is using the unique case of minors as an entering wedge for a general limitation of liberty.) Again the timing supports the idea that Walpole was pushing a two-step strategy of censoring performance: On May 20, only one day after the passage of the universities theater bill, Parliament began to consider a much more sweeping piece of legislation—the Licensing Act.

The Licensing Act was in the form of an amendment to the Act of Queen Anne relating to rogues and vagabonds, entitled "An Act for reducing the Laws relating to Rogues, Vagabonds, Sturdy Beggars and Vagrants, into One Act of Parliament; and for the more effectual punishing such Rogues . . . and sending them whither they ought to be sent." The Act of 1737 merely extended the existing laws against vagrants to players of all sorts, excepting those specifically licensed by the Lord Chamberlain. It also provided for a review of all new and old plays by the Chamberlain, with fees to be paid for each individual permission granted. Of course, in order to effect this scrutiny, the Lord Chamberlain would need to create a small bureaucracy dedicated to censoring writing for the stage: "Either he [the Lord Chamberlain] would require help or he would assign someone to do the job for him. Grafton took the latter course and so the offices of Examiner and Deputy Examiner of Plays were created in 1738" (Conolly 15). All play-writing, at least all writing destined for the stage, would thereafter be subject to more active government censorship. Further, the new act closed the loophole that had previously allowed John Harper to escape prosecution, stating explicitly that performing was enough to be judged a vagrant, whether one was also a householder or not. Sybil Rosenfeld makes clear the implications for actors in the provinces:

> Then, in a later clause, it stated that no person was to be authorized by the King's patent or by licence of the Chamberlain to act for hire, gain or reward in any part of Great Britain except the City of Westminster or where the King was residing. In other words, playing in the provinces had no legal authority, and provincial players were therefore subject to be treated as vagrants. On the oath of a creditable witness, or on his own confession, an offender was to be sentenced to a fine . . . [or] committed to prison, without bail, and with hard labor, for a period not exceeding six months. Informers were encouraged by a reward of half the fine, and the other half was to go to the poor of the parish. (Rosenfeld 7–8)

One other little discussed consequence of the act—although it was eloquent-

ly expressed by Lord Chesterfield in an impassioned speech against passage—
was that it would have the curious effect of politicizing the stage all the more,
although the discourse would be decidedly one-sided:

> This Bill will be so far from preventing the Stage's meddling with Politics, that I fear
> it will be the Occasion of its meddling with nothing else; but then it will be a polit-
> ical Stage *Ex Parte*.—It will be made subservient to the Politics and Schemes of the
> Court only.—The Licentiousness of the Stage will be encouraged instead of being
> restrained. . . . Whatever Man, whatever Party opposes the Court, in any their most
> destructive Schemes, will, upon the Stage, be represented in the most ridiculous Light
> the Hirelings of a Court can contrive.[10]

Chesterfield points out that the Walpole administration's proposed legislation
would not only silence dissent and raise large sums of money for permission to
produce standard as well as new plays, it would also convert the entire dramatic
apparatus of Westminster into an unwilling but effective propaganda corps.

Several factors contributed to the ultimate passage of the Licensing Act. First,
Walpole could count on a certain amount of sympathy to the bill from tradesmen and citizens who opposed the theaters for religious reasons. Theaters, like
casinos or X-rated cinemas in our own time, were thought by many to lead to
a neighborhood's certain degradation, driving industrious working people to
turn lazy or to move to other areas. "Physical and economic symptoms of the
spiritual pollution they allegedly spread became an important element in attacks against theaters in the mid-thirties, when there were frequent efforts to
correct problems of crime and urban decay in London" (Liesenfeld 25). Second, as Prime Minister, he could orchestrate the timing of the bill for best effect. In the case of the Licensing Act, debate began in May and the final votes
fell in June, "when most MPs had already left town" (Morgan 63). And third,
Fielding and others had provided Walpole with perfect material to persuade
reluctant MPs that the theater had tilted too far toward sedition and engen-
dering disrespect toward the monarchy.

As if *The Historical Register* weren't enough, at a key point in the debate
Walpole produced the manuscript of a play entitled *The Golden Rump*. Based
on a piece that had appeared earlier that year in *Common Sense*—a publication linking itself explicitly with "the social and political ridicule which had
been so effective on the stage of the Little Theatre in the Haymarket" (Liesenfeld 92)—*The Golden Rump* was a somewhat scatalogical satire in the tradition of *Gulliver's Travels*. The manuscript has never been recovered. In the
original magazine piece, however, the king was portrayed as a figure with goat's

legs and feet, and a very prominent gold posterior, part of an elaborate play on the king's real-life illness: "an excruciating case of the piles complicated by a fistula in the same area" (Liesenfeld 96). The Queen and Walpole were also made sport of, depicted as having to insert a bellows-like contraption into the area of complaint to relieve their leader. Walpole seized on the play, using it to his own parliamentary advantage and attributing it to Fielding; Fielding for his part accused Walpole of having it written specifically to sway the debate over the Licensing Act.[11]

It mattered little who penned the manuscript. If Fielding didn't write that particular piece of satire, he authored others nearly as outrageous to a Parliament only newly accustomed to seeing political events and personages mocked on the stage. It was Cibber, Fielding's nemesis, who best summarized one of the most ingenious rationales for the Walpole administration's attempts at censorship—again, one familiar to students of the censorship question in the late twentieth century: "The Eye is much more affecting, and strikes deeper into the Memory, than the Ear: Besides, upon the Stage, both the Senses are in Conjunction. . . . Thus a dramatic Abuse is rivetted, in the Audience. . . . For these Reasons, I humbly conceive, the Stage stands in need of a great deal of Discipline and Restraint" (Cibber 157).

With the passage of the Licensing Act, the Crown gained complete control over theatrical representation in the kingdom. The prohibition was so sweeping that the common practice of ad libbing was technically outlawed, as authorities would be unable to review beforehand what words would be spoken.[12] Where before managers had felt free to defy royal orders to silence their theaters, following the summer of 1737 the threats were too real to ignore. One of Henry Fielding's actors, attempting to find a loophole in the Act, was sent to Bridewell Prison. Fielding left the theater altogether. Within days only the two patent Theaters Royal were offering plays to a public that had been used to choosing among as many as seven theaters. The "new wave" of London theater was dead.

One of the greatest losers was Charlotte Charke. Having burned her bridges both to her father and to the company at Drury Lane, she found herself unable to work in London and legally barred from playing anywhere else. It was a paradox that would quite literally determine the remaining half of her life. But her *Narrative* puts a characteristically positive spin on the bleak outlook for 1738. She mentions nothing about the coercive effects of the Licensing Act. "I took it into my head," she writes with perfect nonchalance, "to dive into Trade" (60).

The Years Following 1737: Evading the Licensing Act

Fidelis Morgan has written quite convincingly of Charke's value as an active
agent in the fight against the Licensing Act. "Charlotte Charke's theatrical work
did not make her a star, but her lifelong fight with the Licensing Act was a real
achievement, and her methods are still in use today" (Morgan 210). Charke's
other lifelong struggle, against an entire taxonomy of gendered behaviors, these
in turn serving and naturalizing the discourse of male-centered heterosexuality, seems never to have been brought entirely to consciousness. As I will
discuss in a later section, Charke's discomfort with the *praxis* of gendered sexuality finds expression in a great number of ways, but primarily in a sort of
carnivalesque risk-taking she rarely examines. In her evasion and subversion
of the Licensing Act, though, Charke displays a pattern of small-scale yet concerted effort. It is a pattern that marks the years 1738 to 1755, age twenty-five
to forty-two for Charke, and it is indicative of the strength of both her political will and her call to the stage.

While Charke never wrote at any length about the Licensing Act—as I've
noted, the *Narrative* conspicuously and decorously avoids the subject—her
brother Theophilus did pen an angry anti-censorship manifesto in 1756, the
year after Charke's autobiography appeared.[13] At the risk of conflating the
brother and the sister, who lived very separate and distinct lives, I would argue that Theophilus's remarks may cast some useful light on Charke's thoughts
about the Act. For one thing, Cibber's *Two Dissertations on the Theatres* captures the general spirit of frustration and rebellion that must have predomi-
nated among "unpatented" players at mid-century. But further, Charlotte and
Theophilus did work closely together occasionally, as indeed they did only
months before Theophilus published *Two Dissertations* (in September 1755 they
undertook together one of the last in a long line of attempts to stage a play
around the specific provisions of the Act). It seems likely that Charke would
have agreed with the general drift and tenor of Theophilus's remarks, although
her own rhetorical stance in the *Narrative* would have prevented her from similarly expressing herself.[14] My purpose in quoting *Two Dissertations,* then, is
to attempt to demonstrate the politicized thought—again, common among
players in the out-of-favor cohort—that would have given some shape and
direction to a life that can only strike the casual reader as flighty or anarchic.

It is interesting to note that Theophilus in his tract is as careful of his father's
persona as his sister. He says nothing of Cibber's support of the Act, nor of
the way that his father sold out his interest in Drury Lane Theatre to John
Highmore. Instead, he reserves all of his rhetorical fire for the current paten-

tees of 1756. The pamphlet begins with general lament, "How hard the present Condition of an Actor! If not the Favourite or Flatterer of a Patentee, how deplorable may be his State!" (T. Cibber 20, First Diss.), but it moves rather quickly to an activist pitch: "As there is Room for Reformation (which begins more and more to be called for) I shall not fear, with the Spirit of a free-born *Englishman*, to attack these powerful mock Princes, in Behalf of the Actors in general, who may be call'd the Limbs of the Theatrical Body" (T. Cibber 63, First Diss.). The language is both violent and familiar from the political arena—the patentees are represented as "Princes" who have supressed the native liberties of their fearless subjects. (In a later passage, this phrase is replaced with "Patentee Potentates," a nicely alliterative bit of ridicule.) The standard trope of the body politic is transformed into the "Theatrical Body," and in this way Cibber manages to retain the sense that overwhelming strength and normalcy reside in the oppressed actors. And, of course, if the actors are the limbs, presumably the patentees would serve as the "head" of this sleeping body: the suggestion of beheading is implicit, drawing the reader's memory back to Charles I. "Free-born" Englishmen have revolted before, Cibber implies, with dire consequences for those who seemed to enjoy absolute power.

Working a related vein, Cibber carefully appropriates the rhetorical force of the abolitionist argument: "It is a melancholy Reflection for poor *English* Comedians, in a free Kingdom, to consider, they are the only Slaves of that Country; but, too true it is" (T. Cibber 21, Appendix). As the previous section attempted to illustrate, the comparison was not inappropriate; although, in the sense that only the patented actors and managers were permitted to "slave" for the pecuniary and political benefit of the Crown, it was almost too sunny a metaphor. But Cibber does not criticize without finally providing his own considered solution:

> As People will have their Amusements—(and a well conducted Dramatic Entertainment, is allow'd to be the most rational one,) as the pleasurable Money expended throughout this Kingdom Amounts to a Vast Sum.—Would it be absurd to propose, that at least, four theatres, fix'd at different Quarters of *London,* and *Westminster,* should be again allowed?—And that a certain Number of traveling Companies of Comedians should be appointed, thro' the several Circuits of the Kingdom, and allotted their different Towns to play in, at different Seasons of the Year? (T. Cibber 73)

The proposal is that the Crown continue to license but at least do so in *quantity.* More than anything, it was the limitation of legality to two theaters that rankled with actors of the period. Cibber cannot imagine large sections of the kingdom without drama, a world without traveling companies; the proliferation of companies he envisions has a flavor of inevitability to it, even a moral imperative.

In all, *Two Dissertations* demonstrates a good deal of rhetorical savvy, and provides some excellent clues to the general mind-set of the "unauthorized" mid-century player. The flexible use of political and military language reflects the moral dualism that was certainly at work: the people wanted and needed the "rational" education of drama, and tyrants were denying them this suste- nance. Of course, Cibber's pamphlet represents the unpatented actor's argu- ment at an advanced stage of development. By 1756, he had had nineteen years to cull points for and against from the newspapers, to discuss the issue with peers, and to submit petition after petition to the Lord Chamberlain for per- mission to open a third patent theater. In fact, Cibber's Appendix is a compi- lation of each begging letter, formal petition, legal memorial, and public ap- peal he wrote over the years in a futile attempt to sway the Crown. It is a Kafka-like production. It shows Cibber expending his life in a futile enterprise, with no reward or success save the evidence he produces of that very futility. It is also an emblem for Charke's eighteen years of persistent, illicit perfor- mance. She too experienced her own years of strolling as futile, yet, in addi- tion to bringing drama to those who would otherwise have been deprived of it, she left a record of resistance that exhibits its own unique authority.

Charke on a Makeshift Stage   As Charke's lone book-length biographer puts it, Charke took "a few months to think through the theatrical problem" once the Licensing Act showed its legal bite (Morgan 63). Like many others, Charke's impulse was to find technically legal ways to continue acting—but perhaps unlike others, she was possessed of an admittedly singular and exhibitionist approach to the problem. The first two "schemes" she developed, and put into practice in the winter and spring of 1738, give the flavor of an alternating pat- tern she was to repeat for a number of years to come.

The first of the schemes, as I've noted earlier, involved turning to trade: "To that End, I took a Shop in *Long-Acre,* and turn'd Oil-woman and Grocer" (60). This initial turn at mercantilism proves a striking scene, one that comes to- gether in a manner that proves increasingly familiar as the *Narrative* progresses. Above all, Charke strives to make clear that this was no serious run at busi- ness, no thought-through proposition. She goes out of her way to indicate that it was a "Whim," and that contrary to shopkeepers truly hoping to succeed, her own "Stock did not exceed ten or a dozen Pounds at a Time of each Sort" of tea and sugar (60–61). The goods, as she further intimates, are not designed so much to bring her profit as to "furnish [her] with as much Discourse, as if

I had the whole Lading of a Ship in my Shop" (61). Charke makes it abundantly clear, then, that serious trade could not have been further from her mind. Instead, at least as she construes her own experience in hindsight, she was *playing* at trade, acting the Oil-woman. This interpretation she implicitly but resolutely insists upon: "This new Whim proved very successful, for every Soul of my Acquaintance, of which I have a numerous share, came in Turn to see my mercantile Face" (61). She speaks, as well, of playing the "Character of Grocer" (62). Her "mercantile Face" she fleshes out with nonstop "discourse" about her trade, and in the way that eighteenth-century comic figures often betray only a single concern or ruling passion (a tradition brought to its fruition by Jane Austen), she produces laughter by talking of nothing else:

> The Rise and Fall of Sugars was my constant Topick; and Trading, Abroad and at Home, was as frequent in my Mouth as my Meals. To compleat the ridiculous Scene, I constantly took in the Papers to see how Matters went at *Bear-Key;* what Ships were come in, or lost; who, in our Trade, was broke; or who advertized Teas at the lowest Prices: Ending with a Comment upon those Dealers, who were endeavouring to under-sell us; shrewdly prognosticating their never being quiet, 'till they had rendered the Article of Tea a meer Drug; and THAT I, AND MANY MORE OF THE BUSINESS, should be obliged entirely to give it up. An Injury to Traffic in general! that must be allowed. (61)

That she herself, as an older woman looking back, views the "ridiculous Scene" *as a scene* and not as a business is obvious, but I would suggest something more: that Charke even at the time had no real intention of setting up a thriving business in sugars and oils. Rather, she set up a sort of storefront theater, to which the town was invited to watch her strut and thunder in satirical imitation of the average London shopkeeper.[15] Note the way that her description of her old oil-shop "discourse" is finally overrun by that discourse; the uppercase emphasis and the impassioned non sequitur ("An Injury to Traffic in general!") give a taste of the sort of bombastic performance visitors of her shop could hope to see. It was performance art, in the postmodern sense of the term: ephemeral, metadramatic, and constituted both as critique and as collaborative performance—the "piece" could not exist, after all, without her "Acquaintance" coming to see it and agreeing to "act" as customers. And like most late-twentieth-century performance art, it was on at least one level *political* theater. Not only was Charke taking off the London merchant, but part of the point was that her comedic talents were being wasted. By "div[ing] into Trade," Charke could most publicly register a form of absurdist protest. Thus, when she writes that at her oil-shop, "I carried on the Farce" (61), we might understand this in two ways: she staged a farcical performance intended to delight her customers, and she was visibly and all but intentionally poor at her trade, a further means of dramatizing her predicament as an unlicensed actress.

I don't mean to suggest that Charke's every move was governed by such highly developed rhetorical and political motives; certainly some of her impulse to make her living by trade was simple economic need coupled with a misplaced faith in her own business skills. Still, each of Charke's separate business ventures seems constructed according to the same plan, to entertain (and perhaps instruct) and then spin theatrically out of control.

But let me turn to the second "scheme" Charke developed following passage of the Act. Immediately after the failure of the oil-shop, she "positively threw it up, at a Hundred Pounds Stock, all paid for, to keep a grand Puppet Show over the Tennis-Court, in James Street, which is licenced, and which is the only one in this Kingdom that has had the good fortune to obtain so advantageous a Grant" (65). It was a capital irony: Charke became in effect the only "patented" puppeteer in England, and briefly enjoyed the sort of monopoly that was strangling her own acting career—but she was, of course, limited to the puppets themselves and could not herself come before the audiences.

Even so, the puppet theater became a much more direct satirical weapon than her oil-shop theater. As Scott Cutler Shershow demonstrates in *Puppets and "Popular" Culture,* Charke's puppet theater allowed her to "embody in miniature the complex dynamics of class, gender, and culture which her whole difficult career can otherwise be seen to illuminate" (154). Shershow's book also corrects a common twentieth-century misconception of the puppet tradition, the tendency to believe that the genre was (in the eighteenth century, for instance) primarily for children, and thus an infantile artistic medium. In fact, the puppet theater was popular and "accessible to the broadest possible range of spectators—not only in terms of social class but even in terms of age. Indeed, across an extended historical period, puppet theater has gradually moved toward its present status as a mode of performance primarily for children as though the diminutive theatrical object recreated its audience in its own image" (Shershow 3).

Charke's puppet theater, like others in the long English tradition, went in for broad comedy as well as varied bits of satire, but it also would have presented the viewer in 1738 with a running set of allusions to the theatrical politics of the previous year. First, Charke hit upon the strategy of "reproducing in miniature a conventional theatrical season of the period," and then "reminding her audience that the plays were to be performed by puppets while announcing them exactly as if they were to be acted by actors: 'The part of the

Mock Doctor by Punch . . .'" (Morgan 64). This bit of whimsy had the added effect of "reminding" the audience that real actors were currently forbidden to play the popular selections she was presenting. Second, by playing Fielding's recent works, including *Covent Garden Tragedy,* and by playing them so close to the Haymarket theater ("virtually next door"), Charke was able to keep alive in the minds of the audience the memory of the Haymarket Company's smash successes and its place as symbol of the opposition. Again, she was out to show that the independents were not dead and would continue to crop up in unlikely places: "Charke's puppet shows, in their deliberate invocation of her own theatrical notoriety, their incongruous mix of carnivalesque comedy and the fashionable, must have offered a particular theatrical charge to an audience otherwise now limited to the two patent houses" (Shershow 156–57).

It is interesting to note that Charke has occasionally, and somewhat inexplicably, been accorded as much or more respect for her brief stint at puppeteering than for her lifelong work on the human stage—which isn't saying as much as it might. Consider this mixed review from one puppet historian, writing originally in 1955:

> In our portrait gallery of puppeteers Charlotte Charke takes an obvious and important place for her eccentricity. She has, too, provided us with the unique documentation of her autobiography. This fascinating book is neither literature nor history, but the inconsequent and madly egocentric memories of an aging and desperate woman, a glimpse into a twisted and distraught human soul. Modern psycho-analysis would, no doubt, neatly label Mrs. Charke as a psychopathic lesbian, but we need not here peer too far into the deep well of loneliness from which this unhappy woman drew her inspiration. We may remember her as a plucky girl in her early twenties, who found in her company of wooden players a loyalty and devotion that she could never command from human actors; and we may salute her as a puppet showman of unusual intelligence, taste, and courage. (Speaight, *History,* 107–8)

Suffice it to say that literary criticism has solidly repudiated much if not all of this genuinely bigoted and splenetic characterization of Charke. I quote it primarily to show the distinction drawn between Charke-as-actress-author and Charke-as-puppeteer, because in this way a subsection of literary criticism has replicated the stance of the Walpole bureaucracy, that Charke was dangerous and unacceptable on the stage, but showed "taste" and "courage" and "pluck" while moving figures from behind it.[16]

These two fairly different ventures—that of the oil-shop and the puppet theater—suggest the outline of a pattern I mentioned earlier: following 1737, Charke alternates between "trade" ventures and more directly theatrical evasions of the Act. It is as though she cycles between more direct longing to return to performance (as well as more direct desire to protest her legal inability to do so), and periods of more indirect response to her situation. In 1742, for example, Charke decided to earn her living as a "higgler," or dealer in sausages and other meat products. As with the oil-shop, she has an audience that shows her a solid core of support: "Instead of being despised by those who had served me in my utmost Exigencies, I was rather applauded. Some were tender enough to mingle their pitying Tears, with their Approbation of my endeavouring as an honest Livelihood, as I did not prostitute my person" (115). All of the familiar elements are here: the substitution of theater terms for trade terms—she is "applauded" in her performance as tradeswoman—and the "tender" tragedy of her wasted career, a concertedly didactic aspect I have discussed above. And at least one contemporary account indicates that Charke's attempts to "perform" the desperateness of her situation, and so direct the public discourse, were at least partially successful. In *Sawney and Colley, a Poetical Dialogue,* a contemporary publication satirizing Cibber's quarrel with Pope, Charke is referred to as a successful actress, one whose current "trade" life is just another humorous role: "she play'd . . . to the high Recreation of many Audiences: And has since chose to communicate herself to the Publick by Daylight in Men's Cloaths. The *Part* she is said to excel in at present, is that of crying *Black-Puddings, Sheep's Trotters, & c.*" (*Sawney* 4). But for its unmistakable air of sarcasm, this is just the sort of attention that Charke seems to have sought.

But later in 1742, after a "hungry Cur" ate the last of her stock of pork, Charke turned in desperation back to actual stage work, although in the form of technically illegal and temporary engagements. She played for a man named Yeates at the New Wells; she played at Bartholomew Fair for several days in a booth-stage; and several months later she played with a "Master of Legerdemain" who once he had Charke in his employ "commenced Manager and . . . tragedized in a Place called *Petticoat-Lane,* near *white-Chapel*" (121). But this notoriety put her in legal danger, not just for playing without a licence, but from her creditors, who were given to assuming that her salary was much higher than it was in reality. She turned again back to trade, or rather her own dramatic rendering of trade, and her reason for doing so seems relatively straightforward: "I soon grew tired of leading such a Life of Fear, and resolved to make Trial of a Friendship of my late Uncle . . . to give me as much Money as would be necessary to set me up in a Publick House" (122).

This scheme again matches the requirements of the "trade performed as protest" scenario. Charke "precipitately took the first House" where she saw a For-Lease sign, evidently anxious to have it because it was located in Drury

Lane, near the patent theater from which she was now barred. Most notably, one of her primary reasons for going out of business was "the Happiness of the unprofitable Custom of several Strolling-Actors, who were unfortunately out of business; and, tho' they had no Money, I thought it incumbent on me, as they stil'd themselves Comedians, to credit them 'till they got something to do" (126). Not only does Charke make clear that her "Publick" house is a sanctuary to the "out of business" actor, but she manages to publicize their predicament (and hence her own) through this affectionate poke at their penniless condition. Charke's two-track life, then, might more profitably be seen as a single extended attempt to earn a living and lodge a faint public protest, albeit a single attempt with two distinct levels of risk.

Of the many tricks devised to evade the Licensing Act, Charke either used or had a hand in shaping most of them. She performed paid concerts of music, and during the intermission performed tragedy ostensibly for free; she, along with her brother, worked the "rehearsal" ploy, in which the performance was technically a rehearsal of students in an oratorical academy; and, as Fidelis Morgan points out, she originated the device of selling ale and throwing in entertainment at no charge—a device still in use today (Morgan 127). But none of these tricks, in and of itself, was very successful. Theophilus's "Academy" was regularly closed down. The truth of the matter was that only influence could protect one, as the popular Samuel Foote's successful evasion of the Act in 1747 proves.[17] The younger Cibbers, of course, had no true influence by the 1740s, and their father for his own reasons refused to take their part. But it is fair to say that their unstinting attempts to evade and protest the unpopular Act helped to foster a climate in which greater leniency toward the stage seemed a prudent political course. It is interesting to note that as early as 1976 Charke was beginning to be recognized for her role in opposing the Act. Conolly, in *The Censorship of English Drama,* refers casually to "a succession of wily actors and managers—James Lacy, Charlotte Charke, Tony Aston, Henry Giffard, Charles Macklin, Theophilus Cibber, Samuel Foote" who "found ways of performing legitimate drama in one way or another outside the confines of Covent Garden and Drury Lane" (Conolly 13). Significantly, Conolly mentions only one woman—Charke—and in this way refers indirectly to her preeminence as a female participant historian of this chaotic time and place.

The ban on provincial companies was the first to fall. As Lawhon and Smith note, "seven royal patents were awarded to provincial theatres in the years between 1768 and 1779 alone" (145). More than likely, the government realized it could not prevent strolling and touring companies from playing and decided to attempt to control, and tax, the practice through licensing certain troupes (exactly what Theophilus Cibber had proposed some years earlier in *Two Dissertations on the Theatres*). In this way, the Crown was later to tacitly admit what Charke realized in late 1746, that although the provinces were brutish to a Londoner born to the Theatre Royal, they were also ironically the winter quarters of theatrical freedom in England.

The Life of the Strolling Player: The Provinces, Mid-Century

If there was a fresh new bureaucracy in London, dedicated to scrutinizing the patent theaters and the productions of the London playwrights, the country provinces rarely felt its reach. Alvin Thaler makes the point that strolling companies were in a perfect position to flout copyright law, for example, and that simply by attempting to use the latest and most attractive material, they brought new drama to the provinces very quickly—sometimes within the space of a month or less. The practice of stealing hit plays was so well established that as "late as 1795 the London managers could win no redress in the courts when they sued certain provincial managers for stealing their plays" (Thaler 271). The relative freedom enjoyed by the strolling player is typified by Charke's experiences in the market town of Tiverton. There, she and her company played *The Beaux' Stratagem* to "a Range of drunken Butchers, some of whom soon entertained us with the inharmonious Musick of their Nostrils" (164). Disgusted with the quality of the audience, Charke and her fellow actress Mrs. Elrington began to alter the play at will, introducing actions and characters completely at odds with the established text:

> This absurdity led us into several more, for we both took a Wild-goose Chace through all the dramatic Authors we could recollect, taking particular Care not to let any single Speech bear in the Answer the least Affinity; and, while I was making Love from *Jaffier*, she tenderly approved my Passion with the Soliloquy of *Cato*.
>
> In this incoherent Manner we finished the Night's Entertainment. Mrs. *Sullen,* instead of *Archer,* concluding the Play with *Jane Shore's* Tag, at the End of the first Act of that Tragedy, to the universal Satisfaction of that Part of the Audience who were awake, and were the reeling Conductors of those who only *Dreamt* of what they should have *seen.* (165–66)

Of course, this complete freedom in dramatic representation was matched by the near-complete indifference and boorishness of the audience—no one cared to exercise control over the country play because there was nothing at stake. There was little or no money to be made; following this performance, Charke records that, "For some Time we drag'd on our unsuccessful Lives, without the least Prospect of an Alteration, that I at last gave up all Hopes and Expectations of ever enjoying a happy Moment" (166). There was no real sense of dramatic illusion to maintain, and no threat that the audience would hold the actors to a London standard. In fact, at least once Charke recalls having a member of the audience *ask* that she mix speeches from different plays together, a request with which she happily complies (168). The provincial haven of dramatic freedom, then, was also and more categorically a player's purgatory, a world of insignificance and social stigma, poverty, cold, dirt, and degraded artistic standards.

Yet, as Thaler also nicely observes, "in Post-Restoration times as well as during the Elizabethan period there were greater and lesser strollers" (246). In general, the better companies were those supplied by actors from the patent houses of London, and they tended to make targeted tours of locations where they could be assured of quality fixtures and audiences, as well as sufficient receipts to pay their greater expenses and salaries. Norwich and Ipswich both had permanent theaters by 1758; Bath apparently had a new theater in 1750. (Bath was a case unto itself, with royalty in the audience and authors coaching the companies—Gay came in 1728, for example, to rehearse the Bath Comediens in his wildly popular *Beggar's Opera*.) And towns within a day's ride of London, such as Richmond, were treated to weekend visits by the most famous stage personalities. These higher-toned companies often went out of their way to distinguish between themselves and the "lesser" sort of strollers. Joseph Austin's company, for instance, which played a lucrative circuit in the north of England, lived by a set of numbered contractual articles obviously designed to maintain a visible difference between themselves and strollers of the general stripe: there were articles against drunkenness and asking the manager for advances, as well as the admonition that "if any person's dog appears on the stage at rehearsal, the person to whom such dog belongs shall forfeit one shilling" (David Thomas 241). Similarly, as the lower sorts of companies entered a town beating a large drum, some of the better companies advertised in playbills the fact that they did *not* use a drum (Thaler 265).

As one might expect, a player out of favor with the patent houses would be out of favor in their touring companies as well. In general, Charlotte Charke spent little time with the "greater" sort of touring company. Even during her stint as a prompter/manager for the Bath Company, she was barred from the stage by the other actors, the result of jealousy or perhaps of the stigma attaching to those who had spent too much time playing in the provinces (204). Her nine years of on-and-off strolling were spent for the most part with the poorest sorts of companies, those that lived on credit and all too often carried scenery on their backs from town to town.

A "Little Dirty Kind of War": Daily Realities   Charke's almost constant poverty has been treated by many of her critics as proof of either laziness or lack of talent. It has been seen as a personal rather than an occupational hazard. But the "lesser" strolling economy, structured around the sharing system, was as a whole an impoverished one, and for those unlucky enough to have no other means of support, it could involve them in a morass of slowly increasing debt. To understand the bleak quality of the stroller's life, it is necessary first to understand the mere trickle of funding that kept them at subsistence level or, indeed, below it.

Typically the take for a small strolling company was low to begin with. Whereas a well-known touring company from London's Covent Garden Theater could afford to dismiss an audience in 1779 because "there were but thirty shillings in the house," the lesser country companies played as often as possible for nearly half that sum.[18] Charke writes that during her stretch with the Elrington Company in 1749 they played a "little Market-Town, called Columpton," and there the take "never amounted to more than Twenty Shillings at the fullest House" (161). Except in times of exceptional audiences—for instance, when a company could arrange their performances to coincide with regional races or country wakes, or carnivals—the pool of incoming funds was limited at best. And that small pool was funneled through the sharing system before it reached the actors themselves: "Company managers offered their employees a specified share in the profits of the company (both money and goods) rather than a salary: if a given performance produced no profits, there was no money to be shared" (David Thomas 256). Under this sharing tradition actors even divided the unburned ends of candles when the night was finished, a measure of how jealously profits were watched.

In and of itself, this system of pooled funds and shared profits seems more or less equitable, but in practice it led to massive abuse. For one thing, all members of the company received equal recompense, so that a nine-year-old daughter of the manager, playing a waiting maid with few lines, would receive the same share as the lead or capital players. The manager took not one share but as many as six, one for his own acting, one for watching the funds, and four "dead shares" designed to cover expenses and the general running of the company. Shares could also be divided in complex ways, or bought and sold, and managers often controlled shares they did not own outright.

And there were other unscrupulous techniques a manager could put into practice. They were guaranteed by custom a place for any of their children in the company; more than one managerial couple was accused of enlarging their family to enlarge their take. A manager with three children, and whose wife acted as well, could rake off as many as ten shares. And, in addition, there was the matter of the stock debt.

> In fact rascally managers could, and no doubt did, cheat their companies by trumping up what was known as the stock debt. The stock debt was the accumulation of big bills that the management owed. Sometimes the manager would discharge these out of his own pocket at the conclusion of a season and would then assume the right to take the money from future successful nights. This was fair enough if the manager played fair, but it became proverbial that the stock debt was never paid. Ryley knew of a company where the stock debt had been £400 for years, though he was convinced that it had been paid off over and over again. (Rosenfeld 29)

Certainly it was Charke's experience that, although players were left to gape like "so many hungry Magpies" (161), the provincial manager "never fails in all Companies, to eat, as *Bombardinian* says, 'Tho' all Mankind shou'd starve'" (160).

The player's only relief from the sharing system, if it can justly be called relief, was the tradition of benefit nights. During a benefit night, once a season, a given actor selected the play to be performed, as well as his or her role in it; he or she then received all proceeds from the door, excepting of course deductions for "expenses" tallied by the manager. The only exception was the "clear benefit," ordinarily reserved for stars who the management would otherwise have had trouble keeping; in such cases the actor received the entire take, although at least one stroller, Tate Wilkinson, records a scene with a manager who pretended later never to have promised to waive expenses (Grice 24). Benefits could be lucrative, if the audience were large and particularly if the player could come up with some attraction to bait the crowd; Charke's own debut, of course, came at the urging of a Drury Lane actress looking to add novelty to her own benefit night. Typically a player was allowed the unburnt candles from his or her own benefit.

And benefits worked on a player's vanity, always symbolizing the amount they *could* be making if freed from the other sharers and given the spotlight. As S. W. Ryley writes in *The Itinerant,* a strolling memoir glossed with novelistic touches, "I had no great opinion of *sharing;* but with that partiality to my own abilities, which is no where more prevalent than on the stage, I conceived that there would be little doubt of the benefits proving lucrative, for I should have an opportunity of exercising my talents to advantage" (197). Soon, as one might expect, Ryley is in debt like all of the other players, and in this way he exemplifies not only the lure of benefits, but the characteristic disappointment players experienced in them.

The final straw with regard to the benefit was that the player, man or woman, was expected to pre-sell tickets to their own night, resulting in an exhausting door-to-door search for patronage. As country towns could be spread over some area, an actor might walk several miles to the home of a single well-to-do family. "The whole benefit system put the actor in a position of inferiority and dependence. He had to go begging from door to door, visiting the gentry for the favour of their patronage . . . Templeton once distributed nine hundred bills for his benefit" (Rosenfeld 31). One way to decrease one's labor, though at the expense of increasing one's dependence, was to beg that a given member of the gentry "bespeak" the play, or fund the performance alone by buying all of the tickets and distributing them free to friends. In any event, tradition required that a player return the morning after the benefit to give thanks to all patrons, tramping the same long miles—preferably with spouse and attractively theatrical children in tow. It did not do to offend the local gentry, as often their good will was the only thing that stood between the actors and an "information" that would force the local constable to bring them in under the Licensing Act. Even in York, the manager of the prosperous York theater was subject to peremptory commands to scuttle a play that the local gentry or militia found objectionable (Fyvie 17).

In all, the benefit tradition, at least as it fell out in the country, was a haphazard and degrading practice that rarely kept the strolling players above the poverty line. Combined with the sharing system, it meant living on credit for several months, more often than not, and making just enough (or just less than enough) to pay off those bills at season's end. Among others, John Bernard speaks caustically of "the usual prospect of playing six weeks for my amusement, and taking a benefit at the end for the remuneration of my butcher and baker" (Grice 24).

In light of this general lack of funds, much of Charke's experience seems more economically determined, and general to the strolling world. Inasmuch as players had barely enough to live on, and managers rarely reinvested all the money they collected in "dead shares," the troupe's costumes, props, and stage sets were all infamously shabby. Charke recalls seeing an actress take the stage and play a Spanish queen without any stockings at all under her dress, "though I must do the Person Justice to say, it proceeded from an unprecedented Instance of even a superfluity of good Nature, which was excited by her Majesty's observing *Torrismond* [the male lead] to have a dirty Pair of Yard Stockings, with above twenty Holes in Sight; and, as she thought her Legs not so much exposed to View, kindly strips them of a fine Pair of Cotton, and lends them to the Hero" (150). Lest anyone accuse Charke of embellishing the poverty of her company, John Fyvie produces a very similar instance from the memoirs of Elizabeth Farren, in which an actor waits with bare legs behind the scenes in a theater barn because "the man's wife was then on, using the stockings, and that . . . he was waiting till she took them off in order to his putting them on" (Fyvie 25). The literature of the strolling stage is replete with instances of actors and actresses appearing in filthy and worn remnants of once gaudy costumes. This state of affairs was not helped by the fact that many strollers drank heavily, and walked from show to show along roads that were often little more than muddy ruts, or "ponds of liquid mud," as Arthur Young wrote of the early English turnpikes (Grice 35). The spectacle of flamboyant yet threadbare costuming defined the strolling company in the public mind. Charke at one point notes that, upon entering the town of Tiverton, "a good-looking Farmer met us, by our Appearance guess'd what we were, and ask'd if we were not Comedians?" (164). While the bright rags symbolized for moralists the fallen and corrupting nature of the players themselves, more generally they became another advertisement for the gay and uncaring diversions the company desperately promised:

> Usually the troupe would have some bright distinction in their dress to mark them off from ordinary mortals. At Newby Bridge Ryley's eye was caught by a band of itinerants: one was adorned with a gold-laced cocked hat and long ruffles, another wore scarlet, all had tarnished gold on their waistcoats and silk stockings. . . . We hear, too, of a bill deliverer sporting a suit of blue and gold, with a gold-laced hat and a gold-headed cane. Even when the company were reduced to tatters, some remnants of gold or lace usually remained on their clothes. (Rosenfeld 20)

By the end of the century, the tattered clothes combined with a devil-may-care attitude had become a characterization invoked in overtly sentimental terms, not unlike portrayals of traveling circus performers in the United States. In fact, the cliché of "running away to join the circus" derives from English memoirs like Charke's, in which well-to-do young men and women leave their families to travel with flashy but ultimately unstable rural companies. S. W. Ryley describes just such a scene in *The Itinerant*. A young man with an inheritance promised and a career as a cloth-manufacturer under way, he is drawn to seek out the manager of a roving company of actors:

> In a remote corner of the room, and near the window, stood the great man himself—not in buff, though nearly so—without coat or waistcoat. He wore a garment that once bore the name of shirt, and still gave that idea, from the dirty ruffles that hung over his still more dirty hands; black velvet small clothes, somewhat rusty; no stockings, but old *red morocco slippers,* bound *with tarnished gold . . .*

I now accosted him, and, after apologising for his deshabille, he entered into conversation, with a degree of wit and spirit neither his appearance nor circumstances seemed to warrant.

"You see, sir, though an actor, I am a *holy man*"—pointing to his shirt. "Permit me to pun upon my own poverty. We players are a set of merry, undone dogs, and though we often want the means of *life*, we are seldom without the means of *mirth*. We are philosophers, sir, and laugh at misfortune; even the ridiculous situations we are sometimes placed in are more generally the cause of *mirth* than *misery*." (Ryley 83–84)

The manager here, in good novelistic fashion, eloquently summarizes the strolling comedians' best and only defense of their wardrobe: the rags are a badge of honor, the mark of a certain style of homespun philosopher, rather than evidence of reduced circumstances. In spite of the cultural sentimentalization of the stroller's poverty, however, the reality was that actual play-going audiences responded favorably to more convincing spectacle. Companies and individual players knew that better costumes meant more money, and hence, more and better costumes, and so on. In one recorded instance, a company hired a young actress who came to them seeking employment, Mary Sumbel, and then abruptly hired her mother as well when it turned out that the mother had a trunk stuffed with usable gowns (Fyvie 317).

Much the same can be said of a given company's properties and sets. Charke more than once finds herself playing in a company whose physical effects, rather than providing a convincing illusion, merely signal the absence of one. When she manages the Elringtons' company, for instance, she soon finds that "One Scene and a Curtain, with some of the worst of their Wardrobe, made up the *Paraphanalia* of the Stage, of which I was Prime Minister" (167). Such rudimentary equipment strained the ingenuity of the company. In the case of Charke's single backdrop, more than likely it was painted with some scenery and some form of building, so that where a player stood could at least suggest indoors or outdoors. But even so, the audience was called upon to imagine a great deal, including, occasionally, that one player was two or more of the principal characters. Charke's "doubling" anecdote—in which Mrs. Elrington takes over for a drunk actress and plays both Lucy and Polly in *The Beggar's Opera* (161)—is relatively common in the literature of the period. In addition to players playing opposite themselves in the same scene, they were often required to double or triple up jobs offstage, such as printing playbills (as Charke does in Bath), prompting, snuffing candles, and playing musical accompaniment. When Ryley attended a strolling performance of *Hamlet*, the manager was also the ticket-taker, dressed in some shreds of armor to play the ghost of the murdered king when the moment came (Ryley 98).

And all of this improvisation took place in highly improvised surroundings—a small playhouse or theatrical booth, in the event that a country town had such a thing, but more often than not a barn on the outskirts of town, or failing that a relatively large room at an inn. Often it was a question of what the local authorities would allow: the Licensing Act, while not ordinarily enforced in the provinces, was always a lurking threat. Newly arrived managers engaged in a prudent set of negotiations, which, together with the flamboyant entry of the company behind the drum, was called "taking the town."

> Managers of touring companies practiced obsequious routines to win over the mayor and magistrates of the town in which they hoped to find quarter. They sent forward their most presentable member to ask permission to play in a barn or booth or inn yard. In a climate of suspicion and intolerance, however, respectability was a hard-won thing. . . . It was as likely to depend on whether the magistrate had had a good lunch, on his whim, as much as on whether the petitioning players could boast aristocratic backing. (Grice 14–15)

Charke's experience in Minchin-Hampton (169), where she and two of her company were locked up under the provisions of the Act, stands out as atypical: they had in fact been invited by one of the local nobility to play in the area, but were still imprisoned in what seems to have been a scheme to extort money indirectly from the nobleman. The incident demonstrates the far-reaching power the Licensing Act exerted over less well-connected players regardless of their location in England. A thinking manager took the town carefully and in accordance with local custom, settling more often than not on renting a barn from a willing farmer, a barn some distance from the town's center.[19] In this way, dealings with town officials were kept to a minimum.

But what the barn setting gained in legal discretion, it lost in aesthetics and general safety. Temporary galleries sometimes collapsed, fires occasionally broke out in a hayloft, people were occasionally trampled in a press to see a particularly anticipated play or traveling puppet-show (Thaler 273). It is interesting to note that such disasters were routinely interpreted and used rhetorically by anti-theatrical religious groups; such groups would cast the calamity as divine retribution, leveled against the actors for corrupting the morals of the country. Among such groups were the Methodists, led by the Reverend John Wesley and his brother Charles. Charke's anti-Methodist diatribe near the end of her *Narrative* (201–3) becomes somewhat more understandable in light of this long-standing enmity between the dramatic and religious elements. And of course, in addition to being at ideological odds, the two groups competed for audience share: Thomas Snagg, another memoir-writing stroller, records that in Manchester he lost his entire crowd to an unexpected appearance by John Wesley, who preached in the open air for free (Grice 20).

As she was acting in such impoverished conditions, in little better than rags, before audiences whose tastes encouraged the "Buffoonery in Comedy, and Bellowing in Tragedy" (168) that authors including Charke and Goldsmith satirized, it is easy to see how and why Charke would have been prone to leave one acting position on the spur of the moment to take another that promised better. Indeed, such quick moves were an accepted part of the profession.[20] It is also easy to see why, at the end of her "nine Years Peregrination" (12), Charke was so glad to return to London, and why she would set about attempting to mend fences with her father and the comparatively posh theatrical world he represented. Her last movements before returning to London are particularly painful, full of suddenly disintegrating companies and forced marches "through intricate Roads and terrible Showers of Rain" (209).

Unlike many participant historians of the rural stage, Charke does not indulge in sentimentality or nostalgia when recounting her years as a stroller. She is blunt, even bitter in her denunciations of managers, players, and provincial audiences alike. "Thank Heaven," she writes, "I have not, nor ever intend to have, any farther Commerce with them, but will apply myself closely to my Pen" (214). It is, certainly, the remark of a woman who has failed to regain the prominence she enjoyed at twenty-one through the indirect route of rural theater. It has a tang of sour grapes. But more to the point, it is the remark of a woman who had experienced firsthand the privations of a system that most often involved players in a spiral of increasing debt and increasing fear of arrest for debt. And finally, it reflects the experience of a woman whose dangers as a stroller were different from and greater than those faced by men like Ryley or Wilkinson. When she and Mrs. Brown tramp from one job in Wiltshire to another in Hampshire, ordinarily a distance of forty miles, they are forced to walk twenty miles out of their way to avoid the dangers involved in that "long, solitary walk" (208).

Charke's decision upon returning to London to apply herself to her pen is ironic in light of this history of risk as a woman stroller. As the first sentence of her *Narrative* makes clear, the literary world was if anything more hazardous for a woman than the dark roads of the provinces: "As the following History is the Product of a Female Pen, I tremble for the terrible Hazard it must run in ven-

turing into the World, as it may possibly suffer, in many Opinions, without perusing it" (15). It is entirely characteristic of Charke that she ran the risk anyway.

Charke and Critical Controversy:
Feminism, Cross-Dressing, and Sexuality

Early on in her *Narrative,* Charke tells a childhood anecdote in which a woman—"one of my Mother's straitlac'd, old-fashioned Neighbours"—convinces
Charke's mother to take away her daughter's gun, thus preventing the young
girl from engaging in the manly sport of fowling. Charke's response is
straightforward: "Upon this sober Lady's Hint, I was deprived of my gun . . .
and . . . resolved to revenge myself, by getting a Muscatoon that hung over
the Kitchen Mantlepiece, and use my utmost Endeavours towards shooting
down her Chimnies" (29). Tellingly, Charke responds to her mother's prohibition with defiance, not only immediately picking up a gun again but up-
ping the stakes by stealing the largest and most public weapon available—and
then turning it on the home of her outspoken neighborhood detractor. The
scene resonates with the most recent criticism of Charke, which by and large
ranges her with other early feminists and maintains that when confronted
with rigid, gender-biased institutions, she responded energetically, both in her
writing and in her daily mode of living.

Critics tend to differ more fundamentally, however, in assessing precisely *how*
Charke engaged these social strictures, and how effective she may have been
in her efforts. The anecdote of the "strait-lac'd" neighbor, after all, ends with
Charke wasting a great deal of shot and powder on the chimnies and being
"obliged to desist, and give up what I had, though wishfully, vainly attempted" (29). Sidonie Smith reaches a somewhat similar assessment of Charke's
work in an essay reprinted in this volume; for all of her efforts at transgressing patriarchal bounds, Smith argues, Charke's efforts are in vain, and she
"ends up serving rather than challenging the pleasure of the patriarchs" (Smith
122). Alternately, those critics who view Charke as an early antagonist of the
patriarchal establishment point to her offstage cross-dressing and her cohabitation with a woman calling herself "Mrs. Brown" to Charke's "Mr. Brown."
Cheryl Wanko, in a recent article, maintains that Charke's seemingly failed
"gender performance is really a triumph of a sort," because her life offers a
"rebellious assertion of a new [gender] configuration," a mode of existence
productively outside the dominant male/female duality (87).

But before discussing the more general debate concerning Charke's accomplishments and credentials as early feminist, I'll turn more briefly to another

debate, one nested inside and by rights inseparable from that larger critical argument: namely, was Charke's cross-dressing of a social or a sexual nature, or both, and why does the answer really matter?

Mr. and Mrs. Brown: Arguing the Same-Sex Relationship

In March of 1755, when Charke sent her father the infamous letter begging his pardon, she engaged the services of "a young Lady whose tender Compassion was easily moved to be the obliging Messenger. She returned, with friendly Expedition, and delivered me my own Epistle, enclosed in a Blank, from my Father. By the Alteration of my Countenance she too soon perceived the ill Success of her Negotiation, and bore a Part in my Distress" (99). This scene, the first in which Charke introduces "Mrs. Brown," is both intriguing and highly typical in several ways. First, Charke never names her companion in the *Narrative,* but resolutely refers to her as "my Friend" or "a young Lady" or by the presumably fictitious name of "Mrs. Brown." Second, Charke speaks of the "young lady" here with evident affection and gratitude, and portrays their relationship as intimate, bordering on the conjugal: her companion bears "a Part in [her] Distress." Lastly, the pattern of interaction here—Charke dictating an agenda, and the "tender" young lady being "easily moved"—represents in miniature the pattern Charke and her companion follow throughout the text of the autobiography. As Lillian Faderman describes it, "Charlotte depicts them in a classic 'butch/femme' relationship without the slightest trace of self-consciousness. 'Mrs. Brown' leaves all the decisions to her, shows her deference in all things (even when it is apparent that because of Charlotte's bad choices they will go hungry for a while)" (Faderman 58). According to Faderman, Charke uses the advantages of her family's class and her own profession—as both the wealthy and actors in general were allowed greater latitude for eccentric behavior—to shelter a public same-sex marriage.

Before leaving the letter-carrying scene, though, I should point out that it deals with an event from 1755, the narrator's present, and in this way it serves not only as an introduction to Mrs. Brown but as a statement of her continuing fidelity and centrality as a companion. It is a complex piece of narrative structure: this scene introducing Mrs. Brown comes almost exactly at the text's midway point and initiates, through a framing snippet of the present-tense relationship, the story of the couple's past years together in the provinces that occupies the second hundred pages. It is an almost novelistic touch, and much the same can be said for the story of the couple as a whole, as constructed by Charke for her reading public in 1755.

Faderman's belief that Charke represents her relationship "without a trace of self-consciousness" comes close to the mark, as I see it, but misses a certain theatrical element—more a self-conscious unselfconsciousness—present whenever Charke makes reference to Mrs. Brown. Kristina Straub, in the second of the reprinted essays in this volume, captures the effect more accurately, by observing that Charke continually invokes the "figure of the female husband" only to refuse or abandon the character almost immediately thereafter. Straub points out that the "monstrous" idea of a woman playing husband in a same-sex marriage was invariably where eighteenth-century England drew the line, legally speaking: in general women involved in same-sex relationships were overlooked by the law unless the relationship was seen as usurping the privileged place of heterosexual marriage.[21] Accordingly, Charke's presentation of the relationship can suggest the outlines of a marriage, even one patterned on time-honored heterosexual cliché, but those outlines must then be effectively blurred. For example, when Charke attempts to fit up yet another house of trade in the small town of Chepstow, she finds herself with a rented house and no money for furniture, just as Mrs. Brown had warned her. Charke's reaction is typically and theatrically that of the traditional husband: "I own it, I was secretly chagrin'd at my Exploit, but did not dare to make the least Discovery of it to Mrs. *Brown,* who had very justifiable Reasons to reproach me for an Indiscretion she had prudently taken much Pains to prevent" (180). Here Charke reiterates the clichéd representations of heterosexual marriage that dominate the plays in which she acted; she is the thoughtless and henpecked husband, and thereby connects with both reading men and women.

A better and more sustained example occurs when Mrs. Brown receives a small legacy from the will of a distant uncle. Word of the legacy reaches the couple in Pill, where they are nearly starving as pastry-cooks. Charke tells us that she, not Mrs. Brown, was "to go to receive her Legacy, which was a genteel one, and I should have left her as a Hostage 'till my Return" (185). Again, Charke simply assumes the traditional male role here; not only will she journey to collect the money, but more essentially the money will find its way into her possession, although it is her "wife's" legacy. This, too, is a staple of the heterosexual couples portrayed in Restoration and early eighteenth-century comedy, the husband who covets and squanders his wife's fortune. It is a role Charke plays to the hilt. After borrowing a hat (to replace the one she earlier pawned) she and Mrs. Brown set off to collect the legacy together, and once they have it, Charke turns profligate rake: "I returned the borrowed Hat, and went Home triumphant in my own—Paid my Landlord, and, as long as the

Money lasted, was the worthiest Gentleman in the Country; but when our stock was exhausted, and we were reduced to a second Necessity of contracting a fresh Score, I was as much disregarded as a dead Cat, without the Remembrance of a single Virtue I was Master of, while I had a remaining Guinea in my Pocket" (188–89). Like a loveless husband from Congreve, or the "fool" brewer whom Defoe's Roxana marries, Charke squanders Mrs. Brown's legacy in being a "worthy Gentleman," and in so doing she demonstrates the same abolute control over a wife's finances allowed a man under English law. In this way, Mrs. Brown becomes an absolutely passive partner, creating an oddly stylized or exaggerated portrait of the imbalance of power in the traditional heterosexual union. As the Browns' financial situation grows more grave, this dynamic becomes even more pronounced. After sinking the very last of their funds in a failed attempt to evade the Licensing Act and stage a play, Charke writes, "I was so miserably put to my Shifts, that the Morning after my Malefit, I was obliged to strip my Friend of the ownly [*sic*] decent Gown she had, and pledged it to pay the Horse-Hire for the Players, who came from *Wells* to assist me; which, to do them Justice, was a Difficulty they were entirely ignorant of" (192). Again, it is said almost nonchalantly, but not quite. Charke was so put to *her* shifts that she was "obliged to strip" her friend—there is a latent assumption here that Charke procures the couple's money, and when they are in funds Mrs. Brown can be relatively well-dressed, but when times are hard, Charke is forced to treat even Mrs. Brown's clothes as usable capital. Again, there is a clear suggestion of dominance, of prerogative in the language; Charke decides, like a good eighteenth-century husband, how lavishly her "wife" will be dressed, and when she has decided here, she "strips" her friend. And again the crisis is precipitated by Charke's desire to appear (literally) a worthy gentleman. She takes Mrs. Brown's last gown to pay for return transportation for a set of players who came to assist her; she does them "Justice" with her "Friend's" belongings, thus privileging professional contacts over domestic need. It is the sort of act one might expect to see in her father's *Apology,* in which male comradery dramatically eclipses family life and needs.

   In all, Charke seems to want to advertise the traditionally male prerogatives she enjoys in her relationship with Mrs. Brown, in spite of the negative light this casts upon herself. It is this wholehearted adoption of the role of "husband," among other factors, which has led several critics to conclude that Charke "identified, or wished to identify herself, as strongly masculine" and that one way to do so was to play out publicly or even violently her "ambivalent relationship to symbols of femininity" (Friedli 242)—here, of course, Mrs. Brown becomes just such a symbol. More bluntly, Sidonie Smith remarks, "She does not want to be woman," the implication being that Charke's cross-dressing and central relationship betray a deep psychological need to inhabit not only male prerogatives but a male body (Smith 121).

Not everyone, of course, agrees with a view of Charke's life that places her either in a same-sex relationship or a personally ambivalent sexuality. At least two critics have argued vigorously that Charke merely used male clothing as an entreé to a less dangerous and more lucrative male world. Sallie Minter Strange, in a 1976 article titled "Charlotte Charke: Transvestite or Conjuror?" initially points out that working as a man brought "better working conditions and more sociability," in addition to allowing Charke to avoid the constant physical threats and sexual proposals to which actresses of the day were subjected (56–57). To this point, Strange makes a compelling if an abbreviated case, but having demonstrated an undeniable practical advantage to cross-dressing as a male, she poses the question, "But what of [Charke's] feelings?"

In answer to her own question, Strange writes that "There is, indeed, room for conjectures as to the relationship between 'Mr. Brown' and 'Mrs. Brown,' but again evidence points to an affectionate but non-sexual relationship. Her association with others of the same and of the opposite sex and the personality of her daughter do nothing but underscore her heterosexuality" (58). It is a curious twist of argument: having asserted that the "Brown" relationship gives rise to conjecture of a same-sex love relationship, Strange then completely ignores that decade-long relationship, turning instead to much briefer interactions and to the fact that Charke's daughter Kitty "turned out to be a 'normal' woman" (58). Clearly, Strange seeks to assert Charke's heterosexuality—that she is really more conjuror, or showman, than transvestite or lesbian—and thereby save her reputation. "Fortunately for the reputations of people such as Mrs. Charke, those who study the past are not content with easy labels and sensationalism" (59). In this way, Strange's article represents the missing link between early twentieth-century critics like Fyvie, who found Charke altogether unpalatable, and more recent writers like Straub, Friedli, and Faderman, who find Charke's same-sex relationship intriguing: Strange, while she embraces Charke as a literary personality, finds only those aspects of her life suggestive of lesbianism or romantic friendship unacceptable.

Fidelis Morgan's 1988 biography of Charke represents a much more recent and more influential attempt to demonstrate that Charke's cross-dressing and life with Mrs. Brown had nothing whatever to do with sexuality. Like Strange, Morgan gives an air of clearing Charke's name from imputations of lesbianism; but unlike Strange, Morgan works from a considerable knowledge of Charke's life, and looks more carefully at the Mr. Brown/Mrs. Brown relationship. One of

Morgan's more interesting arguments is that like any autobiographer, Charke must select details of her life to develop into a coherent, developmental narrative; as she was known for playing male roles, she is more or less forced to play up those elements of her life that cast new light on her notoriety. In this sense, the relationship with Mrs. Brown (and their extended "masquerade") would only *seem* central, while in reality other important relationships had simply been excised in the telling. Under this logic, Charke becomes more clearly a player, intent on shaping her life into an analogue of the breeches-parts for which she was known. And Morgan adds to this many of Strange's more pragmatic arguments: that men's dress protected her from being arrested for debt or prostitution, it allowed her a greater range of self-employment, and so on (Morgan 196–201). Finally, however, Morgan falls into the same sort of questionable logic and ultimately homophobic desire to shield Charke's "reputation" that was evident in Strange's work: "In her own unwitting defence, Charlotte gives one tiny indication that when she was travelling with Mrs. Brown, the two women slept separately, for she 'consulted my pillow what was best to be done. And communicated my thoughts to my friend.' . . . If she had slept with her friend she needn't have wasted any time discussing the matter with the pillow first!" (Morgan 205). This brief passage has several interesting features. First, Morgan herself "gives one tiny indication" of her own politics, by framing the question of Charke's sexuality as one requiring a "defence," a juridical figure that speaks to Morgan's own tacit assumption that innocence equals heterosexuality. Second, the questionable conclusion that Charke had to be sleeping alone if she consulted her pillow and then her friend is rendered even more suspect by the fact that Morgan here quotes Charke's *Narrative* inaccurately. In Charke's text, the line actually runs, "I consulted on my Pillow what was best to be done, and communicated my Thoughts to my Friend" (185)—an admittedly small change, but one that distinctly alters the feel. Charke's line is much more ambigous, and can be taken to mean either that she consulted with Mrs. Brown while they shared a "Pillow" or that she did so the next morning. By putting a period between Charke's "Pillow" and her "Friend," Morgan enacts typographically the same sort of need to assert a heterosexual norm that she demonstrates in her approach to Charke's life as a whole.[22]

While almost all contemporary critics agree that "the answer to the amazing riddle of Charlotte Charke . . . . shall never be solved" (Peavy 3), almost all contemporary critics investigate the problem to one extent or another. Apart from simple curiosity, why the continuing emphasis on a question that arguably can never be answered? I think the answer is two-fold. First, Charke herself clearly invites such scrutiny. Despite her outward protestations that her reasons for cross-dressing must remain secret, she alludes to these secret reasons several times, each time dragging them again before the reader's awareness. And she manages to lay out just enough detail to guide speculation into the proper channels: we are told that she "was addressed by a worthy Gentleman (being then a widow) and closely pursued" until she "consented to an honourable, though very secret Alliance" (75). Unfortunately, the unnamed gentleman dies before he can marry Charke and lift her out of her grinding poverty. The name of this gentleman, and the nature of their relationship, is interwoven with the secret of her cross-dressing, for Charke claims that "the original Motive proceeded from a particular Cause; and I rather chuse to undergo the worst Imputation that can be laid on me on that Account, than unravel the Secret, which is an Appendix to one I am bound, as I before hinted, by all the Vows of Truth and Honour everlastingly to conceal" (114–15).

In hints and tidbits, Charke creates a socially acceptable explanation for her cross-dressing—she cross-dresses at the dying request of an "honourable" man she loved, and to say more would be to betray his memory. In this way, Charke's transgressive cross-dressing and cohabitation can be comfortably "framed within a heterosexual narrative," just as eighteenth-century pornographic texts treated sex between women as always "preparatory arousal" for heterosexual sex, and hence unthreatening (Straub 130). More than one Charke critic has taken the bait and run with it: "Perhaps, as a death bed promise, Charke promised her second 'husband' lasting faithfulness by assuming masculine attire to discourage the advances of male lovers. This is a romantic theory, but . . ." (Peavy 3). If the *Narrative* contains some shrewd rhetorical tactics, this explanation that is not quite an explanation is surely the shrewdest.[23] Charke incites and fosters curiosity—a curiosity that assures her an avid readership—and guides that curiosity into speculation suited to her current enterprise of public recuperation. In a roundabout way, by honoring the dead and sainted "Gentleman," Charke claims a patriarchal absolution for her "former madness." As author, she writes in a species of forgiveness for herself as prodigal, and in this way she plays the patriarch yet again.

The second reason for the continuing examination of Charke's sexuality and reasons for cross-dressing is that these questions are wrought up in considerations of Charke's value as an early feminist figure. As Faderman writes, "Transvestites were, in a sense, among the first feminists. Mute as they were, without a formulated ideology to express their convictions, they saw the role of women to be dull and limiting. They craved to expand it—and the only way to alter that role in their day was to become a man" (Faderman 61). If Charke's mode of living can be profitably seen as political resistance, then the details of that mode of living become charged with significance. It matters, then, whether she dressed as a man at the behest of a man, or whether she scripted the man to shield herself from the consequences of having dressed as a man. And of course the task of evaluating Charke's various modes of social transgression is complicated by the fact that she writes her autobiography with an eye toward hiding or refiguring "madness" as understandable, even conservative social behavior.

Morgan remarks that "Unfortunately Charlotte never attempted to give any direct explanation for her wearing of male dress, but she played right into the hands of her detractors by trying to draw a veil of mystery over the whole procedure" (202). I couldn't disagree more. Much of Charke's genius lies in an ability to diffuse her identity, and the actuality of her life experience, through a shifting multiplicity of rhetorically useful roles or selves. By sealing the secret of her cross-dressing and her sexuality, Charke ensures that all possibilities remain ultimately in play. And it is this very play, with its troublesome implications for patriarchy and gender typing, which has fascinated a range of late twentieth-century feminist critics.

"Failed" Feminist vs. "A Triumph of a Sort": Recent Feminist Debate

Anyone surveying the tradition of Charke criticism will immediately recognize the familiar effect of feminism's extremely successful inroads into the male-dominated academic and academic publishing worlds: through the 1960s and 1970s, perhaps one or two Charke articles or treatments in book-length texts appeared per year, followed in the mid-1980s and early 1990s by a small explosion (very relatively speaking) of critical coverage. In Charke's case, the "boom" in criticism has been particularly tightly defined with regard to chronology: nearly all of the in-depth work has appeared within the last eight or nine years, roughly from 1987 to 1995.[24] Given this state of affairs, a chronological overview tends to be misleading, giving the effect of a genealogy, an ordered construction of critical ideas one built atop another. In fact, much of this recent work has been accomplished simultaneously, and it is a truism of Charke criticism that until very recently every scholar felt obliged to repeat a biographical summary of her varied life, that is, to start at least partially from scratch. This is not to detract from demonstrably influential readings of the *Narrative;* certainly work by such writers as Spacks, Nussbaum, and Smith has been picked up and debated by critics writing slightly later. Still, it is interesting to consider the most recent spate of work on Charke as having occured within a single moment of the academic tradition, to consider it as a spectrum of opinion brought to visibility at more or less the same time by a more or less unified scholarly generation. All of this work concerns Charke's viability as an early feminist figure; all of it employs, to one extent or another, postmodern ideas of the decentered or "unsutured" subject to interpret and to evaluate Charke's text, composed as it is of brief, discrete parts or "Flights," to use the author's own term (37). Let me turn now to an overview of this criticism, working from selected, representative arguments as opposed to attempting an exhaustive catalog.

At one end of this spectrum, a 1991 piece by Erin Mackie argues that feminist critics have turned a blind eye to what she sees as Charke's essentially conservative politics, her "fundamental allegiance to the patriarchy" (842). Such critics err by focusing almost exclusively on Charke's autobiography— that is, ignoring her later fictions—and by adopting "certain feminist critical standards that, despite their independent ideological validity, seem to reduce and distort" the *Narrative* in order to make it "fit into the frame of a feminist program" (Mackie 841). Central to Mackie's highly credible argument is a careful reading of several of Charke's novels (if such a term can apply to what are really brief, novella-length tales)—*The History of Henry Dumont* (1756) and *The Lover's Treat* (1758).

With the possible exception of Charles Peavy's 1969 article on Charke and Kristina Straub's short reading of *Dumont*, Mackie is correct: the fictions have received almost no attention, and they do seem to betray a sensibility markedly different from that ordinarily seen to characterize the autobiography. As Mackie sees it, the novels abound with "conventional, fictive figures" who "occupy the imaginative site of an ideal patriarchy," rather than subversive creations bent on destroying it. The defining moment in this reading comes in *Henry Dumont:* Charke's hero Dumont, when propositioned by a male transvestite named Billy Loveman, orchestrates and leads a gay-bashing while another character declares that no punishment is too great for such an aberration. For Mackie, this extended punishment scene represents the author's attempt to demonstrate conservative credentials. It is the most blatant working-out of Charke's overall fictive agenda, in which she seeks to "purify the feminine and the masculine into refined ideals" (Mackie 855).

While this argument is attractive in its forthright assertions and clear distinctions, Mackie runs the risk of simply reversing the argument she seeks to overturn. To her credit, it is a risk she is obviously aware of; as a result, the article quietly develops a bifurcation in its logic, as a way of accounting for moments (in both the *Narrative* and the novels) when Charke seems directly to challenge the patriarchy. Mackie draws a distinction between "reformative" and "subversive" fictive strains, and argues that Charke creates only the former.

"Charke seeks not to liberate herself from the limitations of the partriarchy but to reinscribe the patriarchy in a way that suits her," an agenda Mackie sums up in the phrase "corrective reinscription" (844). The Charke who expresses "manifold allegiance to the patriarchy," then, is also an author actively at work "reinscribing" that ideological structure "in a way that suits her." Mackie recognizes no implicit contradiction here—she evidently means to argue that Charke is not concerned with changing the general power structure but merely with prizing it open far enough to slip in herself. Yet certainly to invoke ideas of social reinscription, correction, and reformation is to range Charke's work with early feminist writing at one level; a late twentieth-century definition of "subversive" cannot and will not hold for women writing in the mid-eighteenth century, and Mackie's absolute link between "subversive" and "feminist" seems unwieldy in this context. To say that Charke is "transgressive in her momentary effects," but "not subversive in her aims" is to insist upon a unified construction of the author—one whose "aims" are known—and to argue out of existence the competing effect, the fragmented or contradictory position with regard to the dominant ideology (Mackie 843). All of which is to say that Erin Mackie's article proves exceedingly effective with some of Charlotte Charke, but not all of her.

Not surprisingly, more than one critic has argued for a dual model of Charke's political and literary effects. Sidonie Smith, for example, parses Charke's *Narrative* into two narratives operating simultaneously:

> Charke's proleptic dedication hints at two narrative possibilities, a doubled story of doubled desires. On the one hand, it tells the modest story of the Father's daughter, the sentimental penitent who would resume her place of dependency and subordination. On the other, it tells the titillating tale of the outcast, the daughter who would vigorously, even violently, defy the Father as a "son." If through the former role she embraces conventional forms of female selfhood and tells a woman's story in the voice of the didacticist and penitent, through the latter role she defies the conventional forms of female selfhood in eighteenth-century society: She becomes the woman who adventures in the world as a man and speaks in the jaunty, self-mocking voice of the rebel. (Smith 109)

By linking her story with the world of the rogue narrative, Charke makes it both more understandable and attractive for her audience, a reading public with a distinct taste for criminal narrative in a variety of forms. Obviously these two ongoing narratives represent distinct time-lines: the sentimental daughter narrates, primarily from the present, the past adventures of the cross-dressing rogue. The time-honored conversion story—a biblically based narrative of complete spiritual change—serves implicitly to knit the two narrative lines together. It is certainly a workable duality, but Smith goes one step further in her efforts to account for Charke's radical transformations *within* the figure of the rogue: Charke's comic rogue is "an endlessly self-fabricating figure who enacts multiple roles calling for multiple identities" (Smith 112). In this way, Charke is seen to have access to a theoretically infinite set of momentary constructions of self, but most if not all of these accessible through the rogue narrative line and thus filtered out of the present tense of the autobiography. The present-tense sentimental heroine, then, serves as a stabilizing force.

Felicity Nussbaum, treating Charke in her 1989 text *The Autobiographical Subject,* comes at Charke's autobiographical work from a similar standpoint. In Nussbaum's view, Charke's text fits into a genre of "scandalous memoir," within which female memoirists announce themselves as dangerous women who "refuse to recognize themselves as permanently attached and subjected to men" (179). But such memoirs are not purely contestatory political productions: "For fallen women to acknowledge their crime publicly and to provide minute particulars of it (even while denying it) indicates a kind of implicit consent to their condemnation by the dominant powers. These works define and perpetuate sexist assumptions about women: they reproduce heterosexual difference" (181). Thus, Nussbaum winds up with an either-and scenario: Charke's *Narrative,* like many other scandalous memoirs, contributes both to conservative, sexist attempts to dominate representation of women and to rebellious attempts to open such representation. And as with Smith's ultimate expansion of the rogue-half of her own duality, Nussbaum sees Charke—when Charke's work is accomplishing its progressive rather than regressive work—as inventing "multiple and serial subjectivities that play among the available possibilities for gendered character in the period" (195). This idea of play within a field of possible subjectivities holds open the door to a reading of Charke as a "successful" early feminist, but Nussbaum holds the door only halfway open.

While neither Smith nor Nussbaum characterizes Charke so insistently in terms of failure as Mackie, both finally see her as less than completely effective.[25] For Smith, the rogue/prodigal strain of the *Narrative* fails Charke in the end—rogue literature is too intimately tied with male dominance in its traditions and didacticism. This failure contributes to an assessment of Charke as a woman unable to contest patriarchy in any lasting way, although Smith's argument would seem to parallel Mackie's in positing "momentary effects." Nussbaum is more optimistic about Charke's work: any support Charke may have consciously or unconsciously given the institutions that repressed her is "tipped or skewed" at every turn "by her protean 'changeability,' her subversive undercutting of gender distinctions" (Nussbaum 197). Her life, therefore, may be seen as a record of limited resistance to pressure aimed at strait-jacketing her otherwise wide-ranging gender personae.

Kristina Straub's *Sexual Suspects* puts together a much more solidly positive view of Charke's influence, in part because Straub focuses less exclusively on the written product of Charke's life, turning often to a consideration of the more ephemeral social effects of cross-dressing itself. Cross-dressing, in Straub's view, served to denaturalize and call into question two fundamentals of "the modern sex/gender system: (1) the subjugation of a feminine spectacle to the dominance of the male gaze and (2) the exclusive definition of feminine sexual desire in terms of its relation to masculine heterosexual desire" (128). Further, by *performing* the elements of male gender, Charke and other cross-dressers pointed out the essentially performative nature of gender itself. Gender, then, was exposed as a construct; it was shown, in effect, to be unnatural. Straub adds one important caveat—"Charke's gender-bending self-representations should not, then, be read as conscious resistance to fixed categories of gender and sexuality"—but goes on to assert that "whatever the intention behind Charke's cross-dressing, its effect . . . is to reveal possible confusions" in the otherwise increasingly naturalized opposition of male/female (Straub 141–42). These "confusions" serve Straub much as the "multiple subjectivities" and identities discussed earlier with reference to Smith and Nussbaum. By refusing to fit comfortably within the categories of male or female, Charke suggests the possibility of other categories; similarly, in her representation of her same-sex relationships, Charke plays with established categories—among these the "female husband" rendered infamous by Fielding—but ultimately rejects them, thus suggesting new ways of viewing female same-sex desire. By process of negation, she adumbrates a set of options she cannot consciously describe. "She is 'somewhere else' on the field of sexual possibility but cannot or will not specify where" (Straub 147). The only down side of all of this, as Straub makes clear, is that Charke's method of self-definition through negation, asserting only what she is not, leads her to the violent and anti-gay-male fictions I have described previously, most notably *Dumont.*

Finally, for Cheryl Wanko, writing on the most laudatory end of the spectrum, Charke's "'failed' gender performance is really a triumph of a sort" (87). Wanko stresses the layered effect of the *Narrative,* dramatic roles positioned helter-skelter among real-life gender roles played as drama, and all of this shot through with allusion to a confusing array of dramatic texts. "The *Narrative* is thus a complex interplay between roles imposed and roles assumed, contributing to a fragmented gender performance" (Wanko 86). In this way, Charke fails to provide a unified character or gender identity, of the commercial sort that Wanko sees at work in the *Life of Lavinia Beswick, alias Fenton, alias Polly Peachum.* Yet, *Fenton* "succeeds" at the expense of buying almost entirely into pre-existing and stultifying gendered narrative categories, such as the actress as whore. Charke's *Narrative,* while it overtly "fails" at creating a seamless narrative feel, actually accomplishes far more politically as a "multifurcated performance," to use Wanko's phrase (87). Drawing from both Straub and Judith Butler, Wanko concludes that Charke's fragmented gender performances—her "discontinuous acts" (81)—run counter to the stylized and consistent performance over time essential to the notion of gender as innate. And, like Straub, Wanko is unconcerned with Charke's intentions. The interrogatory effects of her writing and cross-dressing retain their force whether they are deployed consciously or unconsciously. Wanko bears out Faderman's connection between early transvestism and early feminism; one feeds into the other through a common and public attention to the performative nature of gender. Charke performed the work, quite literally speaking, of a significant early feminist.

As I hope this overview makes clear, critical work on Charke to date is neither completely in agreement nor yet complete in its investigation of her various literary productions. As noted, work on her fiction and drama remains scarce, though several of the essays in this volume seek partially to remedy this problem. But the *Narrative* of her life has certainly come into its own, aided by new theoretical language and approaches for which an autobiographical work composed in "flights" and dedicated to its own author proves challenging rather than disappointing. And—while I have perhaps obscured this fact by surveying critical work mostly directed at Charke the literary figure—the study of her life and impact is no longer limited to purely "literary" studies. Shershow's *Puppets and "Popular" Culture,* for example, treats Charke's work in the puppet theater as both serious and socially important, making the case that this theater provided a particularly detailed and fine-tuned means of representing social protest. Charke's liabilities under traditional critical poetics have become her greatest strengths for students of popular culture, for queer theorists and postmodernists, for New Historians intent on reconstructing power relations in mid-century England. She is no longer merely an oddity to be footnoted in anecdotal patent-theater-based histories of the stage. She is no longer, to put it bluntly, her father's daughter. The following essays develop from this assumption.

Notes

1. As a means of simplifying my parenthetical references, I will cite all texts except Charke's text by giving the author's last name as well as the page number. Parenthetical references using only a number will refer throughout to the Ashley edition of Charke's autobiography (1969).

2. Charke's "exile" was produced by a number of complex factors—these included the 1737 Licensing Act, which forbade dramatic performance at any but the two "patented" or royally sanctioned theaters in London, and her own headstrong nature, which had gotten her banned from those same two patented theaters. As she was bred and raised an actress, Charke naturally took to (technically) illegal strolling companies outside the city. This set of circumstances will be discussed at greater length below.

3. Cibber's text was even more successful than his daughter's: the *Apology* ran to four authorized editions in Cibber's lifetime, as well as a number of pirated editions in Ireland and elsewhere (see pp. xvi–xxi of the *Apology* for an account of its reception) and in this way helped to validate the fledgling genre of secular autobiography and to clear the way for Charke's *Narrative* fifteen years following.

4. Charke herself remembers an interval of "about six weeks" between her first and second performances (50), but Fidelis Morgan's account suggests that Charke's recollection was faulty.

5. This characterization of the competing theaters of 1735–37 as "new wave" I borrow from Fidelis Morgan (see for instance Morgan 63). It seems to me to capture the youthful and rebellious energy exemplified by the work of Charke and Fielding at this time; both were in their twenties during their moments of greatest stage success (Fielding was just thirty when he left the stage).

6. Accounts differ regarding Charke's reason for leaving Fleetwood and Drury Lane for the second time. Charke herself is characteristically cryptic: "My Motive for leaving him the second Time, proceeded from a Cause he had no Share in . . . I can only acknowledge my Error, and beg Pardon for the Folly; and, at the same Time, apologize for my Concealment of the Reason of my second Elopement, as 'twas partly a Family-Concern, though perhaps I might be condemned, were I to reveal it" (56). The language here is very similar to that Charke adopts when discussing her reasons for cross-dressing; it is safe to assume that her circuitous expressions are meant to conceal transgressions more serious to her society. In her preface to *The Art of Management,* similarly, she refers only to "private misconduct." Colley Cibber's biographers have traditionally described the incident in terms of "immoral" behavior on Charke's part, without, of course, specifying which morals were breached. See Morgan 86, as well as 202–3, for a discussion of these traditional aspersions against Charke. It is possible that by "Family-Concern" she is referring to some entanglement with her husband, Richard Charke, who had recently left for Jamaica with another woman.

7. Henry Fielding, *Pasquin,* act I, scene i.

8. Morgan believes this letter, dated only 27 March, to refer to the Fielding problem, partially because on 21 March 1737 Cibber is known to have watched a performance of *The Historical Register,* another of Fielding's jabs at him. And if the "worthless scoundrel" were Richard Charke, presumably Cibber would have counseled Charke to bear up under the insults of her husband rather than to "dissociate" herself from him. Still, the letter's context is finally uncertain.

9. See Dudden (199) for a similar assertion.

10. Chesterfield's speech was reprinted by Theophilus Cibber in *Cibber's Two Dissertations on the Theatres, With an Appendix in Three Parts.* I am working from a copy of this pamphlet in the Rare Book Room, Graduate Library of the University of Illinois, Urbana-Champaign. Lord Chesterfield's speech is printed by Cibber in his Appendix (T. Cibber 99).

11. See Liesenfeld (131–33) for a summary of the arguments for and against Fielding's authorship.

12. Conolly 21–22. In this section, Conolly makes it clear, though, that in practice the Lord Chamberlain overlooked ad-libbed or last-minute changes in the texts of plays, the amount of overlooking depending directly on his personal relationship with a given manager or author.

13. I should point out that Charke does speak out against the Act in one moment, during her summary of her *Narrative:* ". . . which, to do *most Strolling-Players* Justice, they ought not to have the Laws enforced against them on that Score, *for a very Substantial Reason*" (218). Still, as the quotation indicates, her remark is not only buried in the last pages of her text, but phrased so vaguely as not to give offense.

14. I base this assumption partially on Charke's own representation of her relationship with Theophilus: "While we were permitted to go on, my Brother and I lived together, where I passed my Time both chearfully and agreeably: And 'tis no Compliment, to own the Pleasure and Advantage I reaped from his daily Conversation, was the Foundation of that pleasing Content I enjoyed" (137).

15. Shershow agrees with this reading of Charke's grocery, calling it a "kind of miniature theater" (Shershow 155); he also makes some intriguing remarks concerning the link between consumer goods and performance, referring to the "general aura of commodification that seems inevitably to surround a theater of *objects*" (ibid).

16. I should, of course, point out that Charke has been traditionally reviled by another subsection of critics for having "fallen" from the stage to a puppet theater. Charke, damned as a cross-dresser and as someone who performed in the "popular" cultural tradition, has had the last laugh: her revival by current literary theorists is due primarily to these two features of her life.

17. Foote apparently used a low-level tactic—"offering his entertainment in the afternoon to avoid competition with the patent houses"—but that tactic proved sufficient only given "the intercession of his aristocratic friends" (Lawhon 22).

18. Thaler (252) gives the report of the Covent Garden troupe; David Thomas (257) reproduces the account book of a small strolling company in 1741, who played Malmesbury for a take of sixteen shillings.

19. In Ireland, much the same tradition held, with strolling companies often playing in a "liberty" (a space outside of a city, controlled not by city law but by a single nobleman). Peg Woffington, one of the most famous actresses of the century, played on the rule-free ground of a "liberty" outside of Dublin, and also put together shows in a "fitted-up" barn outside of London. It is a measure of the strength of anti-theatrical movements that even the best actors and actresses occasionally needed to resort to strategems and mild evasions. See Dunbar (26–27, 118) for representative examples.

20. See Thaler (263) for a summary of the reasons why players or managers might suddenly decamp. These included being "discovered" by a theatrical scout, among other less glamorous possibilities.

21. Straub 135. See 144–45 for Straub's discussion of the way in which female same-sex marriages were recuperated into heterosexual narratives except in cases of "monstrous" behavior, the usurping of the phallic role in sex or marriage.

22. Morgan in her preface indicates that she "modernized [Charke's] spelling and punctuation throughout"; this lends greater credence to the idea that the change reflects an unspoken agenda on Morgan's part, rather than an error in transcription, say, on the part of her publisher. See Morgan xvi.

23. It is not my intention to argue that Charke wholly fictionalizes the deceased "Gentleman." Rather, I would maintain that whether he existed or not is irrelevent; Charke clearly invokes the figure of the gentleman when it serves her purposes, and uses his "memory" as an excuse to proceed no further with explanations than she sees fit. In this way, whether she creates her would-be benefactor out of whole cloth or tailors a real experience to fit this rhetorical moment is of less importance than her sealing her transgressive secrets with a heterosexual blessing.

24. There are, of course, rule-proving exceptions, notably Patricia Meyers Spacks's work in the late 1970s, Lillian Faderman's brief treatments of Charke in the early 1980s, and so on.

25. Mackie overstates the positive quality of both Nussbaum and Smith's readings in an attempt to position her own "negative" reading; she writes that "in their more generous readings, Charke is a significantly successful feminist," a statement that accords perhaps with Nussbaum but clearly not with Smith. See Mackie 843.

Works Cited

Battestin, Martin. *Henry Fielding: A Life.* New York: Routledge, 1989.

Charke, Charlotte. *A Narrative of the Life of Mrs. Charlotte Charke.* 2d ed. 1755. Ed. Leonard R. N. Ashley. Gainesville: Scholars' Facsimiles & Reprints, 1969.

Cibber, Colley. *An Apology for the Life of Colley Cibber, With an Historical View of the Stage during His Own Time.* Ed. B. R. S. Fone. Ann Arbor: University of Michigan Press, 1968.

Cibber, Theophilus. *Cibber's Two Dissertations on the Theatres, With an Appendix in Three Parts.* London: Mr. Griffiths, 1756.

Conolly, L. W. *The Censorship of English Drama, 1737–1824.* San Marino: Huntington Library, 1976.

Dudden, F. Homes. *Henry Fielding: His Life, Works and Times.* Vol. 1. Oxford: Clarendon Press, 1952.

Dunbar, Janet. *Peg Woffington and Her World.* Boston: Houghton Mifflin Company, 1968.

Faderman, Lillian. *Surpassing the Love of Men: Romantic Friendship and Love between Women from the Renaissance to the Present.* New York: William Morrow and Company, 1981.

Friedli, Lynne. "'Passing Women'—A Study of Gender Boundaries in the Eighteenth Century." *Sexual Underworlds of the Enlightenment.* Ed. G. S. Rousseau and Roy Porter. Chapel Hill: University of North Carolina Press, 1988. 234–60.

Fyvie, John. *Comedy Queens of the Georgian Era.* London: Archibald Constable and Company, 1906.

Grice, Elizabeth. *Rogues and Vagabonds, or The Actors' Road to Respectability.* Suffolk: Terence Dalton Limited, 1977.

Hartnoll, Phyllis, ed. *The Oxford Companion to the Theatre.* 3d ed. London: Oxford University Press, 1967.

Lawhon, M. L., and Dane Farnsworth Smith. *Plays About the Theatre in England, 1737–1800.* Lewisburg: Bucknell University Press, 1979.

Liesenfeld, Vincent J. *The Licensing Act of 1737.* Madison: University of Wisconsin Press, 1984.

Mackie, Erin. "Desperate Measures: The Narratives of the Life of Mrs. Charlotte Charke." *ELH* 58 (1991): 841–65.

Morgan, Fidelis. *The Well-Known Troublemaker: A Life of Charlotte Charke.* London: Faber and Faber, 1988.

Nussbaum, Felicity A. *The Autobiographical Subject: Gender and Ideology in Eighteenth-Century England.* Baltimore: Johns Hopkins Univeristy Press, 1989.

Peavy, Charles D. "The Chimerical Career of Charlotte Charke." *Restoration and Eighteenth-Century Theatre Research* 8 (1969): 1–12.

Rosenfeld, Sybil. *Strolling Players and Drama in the Provinces, 1660–1765.* New York: Octagon Books, 1970.

Ryley, S. W. *The Itinerant; or, Memoirs of an Actor.* 2d ed. London: Sherwood, Neely & Jones, 1817.

Sawney and Colley, A Poetical Dialogue: Occasioned by a Late Letter from the Laureat of St. James's, to the Homer of Twickenham. London, 1742.

Shershow, Scott Cutler. *Puppets and "Popular" Culture.* Ithaca: Cornell University Press, 1995.

Smith, Sidonie. "The Transgressive Daughter and the Masquerade of Self-Representation." In Smith, *A Poetics of Women's Autobiography: Marginality and the Fictions of Self-Representation.* Bloomington: Indiana University Press, 1987. 102–22.

Speaight, George. *The History of the English Puppet Theatre.* 2d ed. Carbondale: Southern Illinois University Press, 1990.

Strange, Sallie Minter. "Charlotte Charke: Transvestite or Conjuror?" *Restoration and Eighteenth-Century Theatre Research* 15 (1976): 54–59.

Straub, Kristina. *Sexual Suspects: Eighteenth-Century Players and Sexual Ideology.* Princeton: Princeton University Press, 1992.

Thaler, Alvin. "Strolling Players and Provincial Drama after Shakespeare." *PMLA* 37 (1922): 243–80.

Thomas, Donald. *Henry Fielding.* New York: St. Martin's Press, 1990.

Thomas, David, ed. *Theatre in Europe: A Documentary History—Restoration and Georgian England, 1660–1788.* Cambridge: Cambridge University Press, 1989.

Wanko, Cheryl. "The Eighteenth-Century Actress and the Construction of Gender: Lavinia Fenton and Charlotte Charke." *Eighteenth Century Life* 18 (1994): 75–90.

PART 2

Charke, the Self, and the Cibber Family

2

Charlotte Charke and the Cibbers: Private Life as Public Spectacle

Jean Marsden

But why make my Follies publick? Why not?
—Colley Cibber, *An Apology for the Life of Mr. Colley Cibber, &c.*

"Making public," the deliberate staging of the personal, is a central component in Colley Cibber's famed, and, in his own time, controversial, autobiography. Cibber's question raises the issue that puzzled Cibber's friends and annoyed his enemies: Cibber's desire to publicize his private life. But this same question could be applied with equal force to others of the Cibber clan, most notably his only son, Theophilus Cibber, and his youngest daughter, Charlotte Charke. All three Cibbers were public, even notorious, figures, and all three chose to exploit their notoriety through the public revelation of their personal lives, writing autobiographies and inserting autobiographical references into much of their prose and even dramatic writing. Their "going public" with folly thus serves a more complex function than the nonchalant *joie d'esprit* suggested by Colley Cibber's question and response; it allows them to construct public identities through the semblance of private revelation.

With or without autobiographical revelations, all three Cibbers remained in the public eye largely through their involvement with the theater. Colley Cibber was not only poet laureate at the time his *Apology* was written, but one of England's most successful playwrights and comic actors, as well as one of the patent holders of Drury Lane Theater. The Cibber family was at the heart of London theater, a world where Colley Cibber had long been a powerful figure. His son Theophilus, although never as successful or talented as his father, nonetheless remained in the theater business all his life, acting, managing, and writing or adapting plays, thus extending the Cibber theatrical tradition into another generation. Charlotte, like her father and brother, both acted and wrote for the theater.

To the public, the Cibbers' lives were defined by theater. The strength of this association can be seen in the anonymous *Sawney and Colley, A Poetical Dialogue,* a poem that satirizes Cibber and his quarrels with Alexander Pope. The poem depicts all three Cibbers in a theatrical light, taking on the roles they play in "real life." Colley Cibber is shown writing bad drama, attended by his two most notorious children, first Theophilus, then Charlotte. Theophilus is represented in the guise of "dutious" son, a role he tried, without much success, to adopt in many of his own writings. In this family scene, however, the dutious son begs his father for money. The footnote to this passage notes sarcastically that Theophilus is "A son of *Colley's* remarkable for his extreme Sanctity of Morals, and singular Modesty of Behaviour" (*Sawney* 4), referring obliquely to Theophilus's well-known and singularly immodest activities. "Daughter *Charke*" appears next, portrayed in the male attire for which she was well known. In its depiction of the Cibbers as playing familiar familial roles, the poem blurs the line between private life and theater. It was a line that all three Cibbers were to continue to blur in their own writings.

Using theater as their medium, then, the Cibbers provide a uniquely public redefinition of their private lives, claiming that the public wants to see "behind the scenes." Colley Cibber contends, "a Man who has pass'd above Forty Year of his Life upon a Theatre, where he has never appear'd to be Himself, may have naturally excited the Curiosity of his Spectators to know what he really was, when in no body's [*sic*] Shape but his own" (*Apology* 6). These claims of authentic disclosure cannot be accepted at face value, especially when considered within the theatrical framework that constituted the Cibber family. Like his father, Theophilus justified his use of anecdotes in his *Life of Barton Booth, Esq.* by using the idea of the actor unmasked back stage, when spectators "can step behind the Scenes to take a near View of those Performers in private Life" (*Booth* 65). But the analogy does not hold true; the reader is never really allowed "behind the Curtain" to watch the actors remove their costumes. Instead, the reader encounters yet another series of scenes in which the principal actors design their own roles. The line between on-stage and off-stage, public and private, is never clear in these autobiographies, despite the rhetoric of the writers. A more accurate assessment of the relationship between writer and work can be seen in Colley Cibber's comment "that the Publick very well knows, my Life has not been a private one" (*Apology* 7).

Thus, both stage and page provide the means for the three Cibbers to construct public identities—even while claiming to reveal, unmasked, their private characters. The use of autobiography to construct a public self was certainly not original to the Cibber family, but rarely was it exploited so completely and with such dramatic flourish as with Colley, Theophilus, and Charlotte. Although Charlotte and Theophilus were frequently estranged from their father, Charlotte for much of her adult life, they follow his lead in using the form of the "candid" autobiography to create an identity specifically for a public audience. And they are explicit about the importance of this enterprise. In the "Preface" to *The Egoist*, a sequel to the *Apology*, which Cibber designs as a dialogue about his character, he claims that "*Self* is too sacred a Subject to be profan'd." Going one step further, Charlotte dedicates her *Narrative* to herself, wittily suggesting that she has not been a real friend to herself while at the same time presenting herself in two conventional roles: the flattering writer and the noble dedicatee. Where Colley uses a dramatic format and Charlotte a textual convention, the subject is still the same—self and its public presentation.

The common context for these spectacles of self-revelation is the theater, and the Cibbers create a kind of theatrical subjectivity that is at odds with studies of eighteenth-century print culture that focus on the novel and forget the stage. Jurgen Habermas's argument concerning the development of an "audience-created privacy," a notion of bourgeois subjectivity that depended on the public's desire to read about itself has privileged the novel to the virtual exclusion of drama.[1] The Cibbers, with their evocation of the public stage rather than the closet, turn Habermas's theory if not on its head, at least distinctly sideways. Their autobiographical works create a subjectivity continually undercut by its very theatricality. The Cibbers create works in which the self is constructed by means of acting rather than confessing and in which the presence of theater confounds the personal because it is inherently public rather than intimate. This tension is established not simply by the fact of the theater, as the Cibbers relied on the public's desire to know the personal behind the public, but by the incessant intrusion of the mechanics of theater into the private realm of autobiography and confession. They do not present drama as domestic, as in the so-called sentimental drama of the eighteenth century, but the domestic as drama—with all the trappings of the theater.

In this context, autobiography for the Cibbers becomes more than a creation of self; despite its use of narrative, it becomes a drama of self construction, pervaded by references to the stage. Just as Colley "begets" both plays and children ("my Muse, and my Spouse were equally prolifick; that the one was seldom the Mother of a Child, but, in the same Year, the other made me the Father of a Play"; *Apology* 146), his offspring regard him as both their literal and literary father. With autobiographies that stage family life not as private experience but as public drama, "subjectivity," for the Cibbers, becomes a function of theater.

Colley Cibber: Paterfamilias and Literary Model

Colley Cibber's *Apology* was only the first of a series of autobiographical writings that he produced in the last decade and a half of his life.[2] The *Apology* was published in April 1740, and such was the popularity of the work that a second edition was published less than six weeks later. The text chronicles the professional life of the author, tracing his career from his earliest years as a schoolboy to the moment he sells his share in the patent of Drury Lane and leaves the theater. It is a long and frequently digressive account of theater life and one that Cibber dominates. Crucially, the *Apology* assumed that the public would want to read an entire volume devoted to Cibber (something Cibber's detractors questioned loudly).[3] The title page, with its emphatic statement "written by Himself," doubly underscores the importance of self in this skillful work of literary self-fashioning. Cibber's work is often regarded today as an entertaining and useful piece of theater history; what is often forgotten is the skill with which Cibber designs his own character within the work. After a lifetime of writing roles for himself, something, he notes, for which his fellow actors distrusted him (*Apology* 24), Cibber creates his greatest role, as hero of his finest play—a hero whose most advertised traits, folly and vanity, are strikingly similar to the characteristics of his favorite theatrical roles.

In *The Egoist: Or, Colley upon Cibber* (1743), supposedly the final "strokes" to his self portrait,[4] Cibber writes explicitly not only about the sanctity of "Self," but about the difficulties associated with constructing a literary persona:

> An Author that talks of *himself,* without being called to it, in his own Defence, like a Gentleman who treads the Stage for his own Diversion, does it against Odds; he is *himself* the only good Soul, pleased with his Performance: When we meet with an Instance to the contrary, we still know he has play'd a desperate Game. Yet, methinks, if the Author could be bold enough to write fair, and honestly rally his own Errors, he might have a better Chance for our Indulgence or Favour, than these easy Egoists, whose Labours, under all their Art, carry a visible *Penchant* to their own Panegyricks. . . . To keep clear of the Imputation I lay upon others, I have, in the following Discourse, (intended as the last Sitting to my Picture) raised up an imag-

inary opponent (by way of Shade and Light) who, whenever he perceives my Vanity peeping out from under the Masque of Modesty, shall roundly rally it; yet not
without some Indulgence to it, as a Frailty inseparable from our Nature. ("Preface")

In this passage from the "Preface: Not quite Unnecessary" to *The Egoist,* Cibber outlines the elements involved in constructing a public image. The images
he chooses to explain the process of self-representation betray his claim to be
presenting himself "fair" and "honestly," relying as they do on the concept of
representation as artifice. "Talking of himself," he concedes, is a "performance"
for an audience, an audience which is not likely to view such a performance
with "indulgence" or "favour."

Cibber's second image moves into the realm of the graphic arts, describing
him as sitting for his own self-portrait. He admits that he has created an "imag-
inary opponent" to create the effect of depth within the portrait ("shade and
light"), even when that depth may not be real. Yet the theatrical lurks even
within the image of the old man sitting for his final portrait, as Cibber suggests he only wears a "masque of modesty"; even as he draws his own portrait
he plays a role. As Cibber suggests, the self he creates in his autobiographical
writings is designed for public consumption. He has designed himself as spectacle, as a public image. Appropriately, this final "portrait" is neither narrative nor descriptive but dramatic; after the "Preface," *The Egoist* consists of a
discussion of Cibber's faults (minor) and strengths (many) conducted in the
form of a dialogue.

This construction of the self as public spectacle is also used to articulate
personal experience in Cibber's extended self portrait, *An Apology for the Life
of Colley Cibber.* On its most basic level, the history of Cibber's life is a history
of the theater. The two are inextricably linked; it is impossible to discuss Cibber's life without discussing London theater. As he himself said, he was the best
person to give a history of the stage, and this intimate association with the
world of theater provided the *Apology* with much of its instant appeal. But the
work's involvement with theater goes deeper than simply subject matter. Not
only does Cibber describe his experience upon the stage and in the tiring
rooms, he couches these descriptions, even of episodes unrelated to the theater, in dramatic terms. Thus an important event becomes a "scene" ("Give
me leave therefore to open the first Scene of my Life, from the very Day I came
into it"; *Apology* 8) while the audience of *The Apology* can become a group of
"auditors" (285) rather than readers.

Cibber's use of these theatrical images is self-conscious, often appearing at
the "open" or "close" of a chapter as he reminds his readers/auditors of the

theatrical nature of his enterprise. Thus, he recounts his legal battle with Sir Richard Steele in the language of the stage: "By your Leave then, Gentlemen! let the Scene open, and, at once, discover your Comedian, at the Bar!" The language of theater allows Cibber to avoid sounding contentious as it self-consciously sets him up as comic spectacle. The scene "opens," the curtains are drawn, and Cibber is "discovered" in a new role, defendant in a legal suit.

Ultimately, Cibber's theatrical allusions couple his narrative with his acting, suggesting that in both he plays a role. Life and life-writing become fundamentally theatrical events. As a result, what might be considered interior, individual subjectivity, becomes instead a spectacle for audience consumption. Referring to the skill with which he has described events, Cibber turns to his audience: "How this Variety was executed (for by that only is its value to be rated) you who have so often been my Spectator, are the proper Judge: If you pronounce my Performance to have been defective, I am condemn'd by my own Evidence" (125). The reader is asked to judge not the man but the performance, so that the experience of reading is inverted as Cibber calls attention to the constructed nature of the self he presents. For Cibber, autobiography is neither confession nor apology but dramatic tour de force.

Theophilus Cibber: *Sequiturque Patrem*

Of Colley Cibber's twelve children, only one son lived to adulthood, and he proved to be a dubious blessing. Theophilus Cibber remains both the most aggressively public of the Cibber clan and the least successful in his attempt to construct a public image. Like his father, his sister Charlotte, and both of his wives, Theophilus worked extensively, if not always successfully, in the London theaters. Showing early promise as a competent actor and manager (he led a successful actors' revolt against the management of Drury Lane in 1733), he squandered this potential—and the good will that accompanied it—through arrogance and extravagant living. Spendthrift and profligate, Theophilus became notorious as a wastrel and as an abusive husband who forced his wife into adultery.[5] In desperate need of money as well as in an attempt to revise his tarnished public image, he published self-revelatory documents almost obsessively: his memoirs, dissertations on the theater, numerous letters detailing his complaints against various theater managers, as well as a series of documents relating to his divorce proceedings.[6]

In his autobiographical writings, as in his theatrical ventures, Theophilus strove to cash in as much as possible on his father's fame and in particular on his father's skillful combination of theater and autobiography. Immediately after the publication of Cibber's *Apology* in 1740, he issued proposals for his own memoirs, to be based on his father's model. Before he could publish, however, a work appeared purporting to be his autobiography, titled provocatively *An Apology for the Life of Mr. T— C—, Comedian, Being a Proper Sequel to the Apology for the Life of Mr. Colley Cibber, Comedian.* Claiming to be by Theophilus, the work was actually an attack on both Cibbers, mocking them for their autobiographical aspirations as well as for their political stance.[7] Using a fictitious Theophilus as the ironic mouthpiece, the author complains that Cibber's work was *not* an Apology; it contained "not a Syllable of his private Character; not a Word for excusing, palliating, or defending little foolish Acts which merely related to Religion or Morality" (99). The object is not self revelation but self protection, "to say nothing harsh against your own dear Self" (99). The mock-Theophilus states: "I can guess what may be expected from me; what Defence of particular Conduct I may make; but I shall relate only such Things as may show my Parts, my theatrical Character, and, in short, what I think proper, not what every impertinent Person may want to know" (100). Such broadsides attacked the selective use of autobiography for the public construction of an identity—as the passage observes, a specifically "theatrical character." It would be precisely those components of Cibber's *Apology* that Theophilus would replicate when he eventually wrote his own theatrical memoir.[8]

Abashed by the appropriation of his name and autobiographical intent, Theophilus waited eight years to publish his imitation of his father's work. A rambling and unchronological series of anecdotes, letters, self praise, and congratulatory prologues, *A Serio-Comic Apology for Part of the LIFE of Mr. Theophilus Cibber, Comedian. Written by Himself* (1748),[9] proved less successful than Theophilus had hoped. Unlike the mock *Apology*, which went through four printings in less than two years, the *Serio-Comic Apology* was never reprinted. Despite its title and obvious attempt to play off the popularity of the *Apology*, the *Serio-Comic Apology* contains little humor and less charm, serving mostly as a venue for Theophilus to complain about his troubles with the management of patent theaters. It is most interesting in its attempts to refigure Theophilus's character into the dual roles of good father and good son, most notably through the inclusion of material from Theophilus's adaptation of *Romeo and Juliet*, with which the *Serio-Comic Apology* was published. While Theophilus claims that "the present Publication of it [the adaptation of *Romeo and Juliet*] gives Birth to this Apology" (*Serio-Comic* 72), a more accurate description would be that his "Apology" reinterprets Shakespeare's play as a staging of Theophilus Cibber. Theophilus staged his adaptation at the Little Theater in the Haymarket, where he played the role of Romeo, and his fourteen-year

old daughter, Jenny, Juliet. While he mentions that he performed "to the satisfaction of my Auditors" (74), he consistently downplays his role as Romeo,
choosing instead to focus on his "private" role as father, a role that he obviously believed more appealing to both his theatrical and reading audience and
more beneficial to the image of himself he strove to create.

Details of the actual production are omitted—a reader could easily forget
that *Romeo and Juliet* is a tale of star-crossed lovers—but the "private" connection of father and daughter is accentuated in the prologues and epilogues
that accompanied the production—all of which are reproduced in Theophilus's *Apology.* Both prologues and epilogues stress family bonds, presenting the
new Juliet not as a lover, but as a loving daughter. The original prologue praises
"Young JANE," and carefully points out her blood connections both to Theophilus and to Colley.[10] It concludes with the modest daughter "trembling" and
begging "a Father's Fate to share" (74). By thus using Jenny to speak on his
behalf, Theophilus constructs a public version of private life, one in striking
contrast to the well-known facts of his behavior. The role of the good father,
which Theophilus assumes indirectly, in this way masks the image of Theophilus's private life provided by the sordid divorce proceeding with his second wife, proceedings discussed all too bluntly in the 1740 mock *Apology.*[11] In
this way, the daughter's proclaimed devotion to her father exonerates that father's character.

The epilogue, allegedly by Jenny and spoken at her benefit, is even more
explicit in its praise of Theophilus. Stepping out of the character of Juliet, Jenny
begs her audience not for herself, but for her father:

> For a kind Father fain I'd Pity move:
> Pardon the Fondness of my Filial Love.
> Reflect how oft' he pleas'd, oft' gain'd Renown,
> And varied shapes to entertain the Town;
> While crouded Houses Thunder'd his Applause:
> Ye bounteous Fair,—to you I plead his Cause.
> To your Protection, gen'rous *Britons,* take,
> Th' unhappy Father, for the Daughter's Sake;
> By pow'rful Envy, Cruelly distress'd,
> He struggles 'gainst Misfortunes, hard oppress'd. (87)

Once again, the daughter's popularity is used to condone her father's conduct.
By publishing her epilogue in his memoirs, Theophilus assumes the role of
good parent and victim of others' envy, a role made plausible when related by
a third party. The epilogue even gives the spectacle of daughterly devotion a

patriotic spin, as Jenny appeals to "gen'rous *Britons*" to support her father. While the inclusion of prologue and epilogue supposedly display Jenny's talents, in reality they focus on Theophilus's character. Nonetheless, what they reveal is still a role, a public spectacle of filial fondness and parental love based on a romanticized version of private life.

No less pointed are Theophilus's references to other Shakespearean plays, all of which reiterate his position as good father and honest son. His repeated references to *The Tempest,* generally as a means of complaining about the triumvirate currently ruling Drury Lane (75, 88), suggest that in contrast to Trinculo and his two compatriots, he occupies the position of Prospero, sage ruler of a (dramatic) empire and father of a beautiful and virtuous daughter. Elsewhere, Theophilus addresses the public in the character of Edgar, the good son in *King Lear,* bemoaning his loss of paternity: "—Poor Turlura! poor Tom! / That's something yet; —Edgar I am no more."[12] He goes on, reprinting a letter published several years earlier, to berate the patentees for their failure to recognize his abilities. While this posture might be seen as an implicit criticism of his father (after all, Gloucester failed to recognize the worth of his true son), Theophilus adopts the stance of good son throughout his *Apology.* (He gives a venomous account of competing productions of *King John* in 1745,[13] attacking his rival David Garrick and writing with ingratiating warmth of "Mr. Cibber, Senior's" performance.) Theophilus even appropriates, with respectful asides, his father's voice as the *Serio-Comic Apology* draws to a close. In the memoir's final pages, he quotes extensively from his father's work, sometimes for paragraphs at a time, bringing the paternal voice directly into the filial document.

Using his father's model, Theophilus attempts to control the public spectacle of his private life, a private life that he desperately constructs as conventionally domestic. His methods are explicitly dramatic and thus at odds with his message. First, he literally stages himself by means of the prologues and epilogues he includes. In addition, he situates himself, even within his own life, as a figure within a drama, using references to Shakespeare and incorporating familiar literary tropes to construct an identity with which his readers can sympathize. Ultimately, however, the private subject becomes lost in the public construction, and Theophilus's assumption of roles never quite succeeds as had his father's adoption of the mask of the genial fool. Bitter and self-aggrandizing by turns, Theophilus is unable to create a character for himself, whether as industrious but loving son or as caring father. Never the actor his father was, he cannot even play the autobiographical role he sets out for himself.

Charlotte Charke: A Genius for the Stage

More so than either her father or her brother, Charlotte Charke sought to market the "sham-private" (Habermas 160) world of the Cibber family, at the same
time striving to incorporate the histrionics that set the Cibbers apart from their
audience. Her method is not simply performative, but explicitly theatrical, as she
sets out to stage rather than reveal the self she creates. For Charke, like her father and brother, theater was a way of life from her earliest days. She began a
career as a professional actress at seventeen and spent most of her adult life on
and off the London and provincial stages. But within her autobiographical writings, theater becomes more than a career; it becomes a means of telling her life
and of creating and shaping a public identity. The extended portrait of "daughter *Charke*" in *Sawney and Colley* provides a clear image of her onstage/offstage
role-playing. Shown pleading with her father for money, she is described as:

> In Day-light breech'd a bullying Spark,
> But a mere *Female* in the Dark.
> "*G—d d—n my Liver!* cry'd She-He,
> "Down, Father, with your *Dust,* d'ye see;
> "I must have *Rhino, by the D—v—l,*
> "So, *'Sblood!* You may as well be civil." (*Sawney* 4)

Not only does the poem itself present Charke in her well-known male garb
(but reassuringly identified as "a mere *Female* in the Dark"), the accompanying footnote depicts her life as a series of similar roles, both on and off the stage,
describing her as "celebrated for her Performances in the *Hay-Market Theatre,*
where, in the Farce of *Pasquin,* the *Historical Register, &c.,* she play'd off her
Father and Brother with surprising Humour to the high Recreation of many
Audiences: And has since chose to communicate herself to the Publick by Daylight in Men's Cloaths. The *Part* she is said to excel in at present, is that of crying
Black-Puddings, Sheep's Trotters, &c." (*Sawney* 4). In its explicit connection of
the roles Charlotte played on the stage with the "*Part* she is said to excel in at
present," "acting" the butcher,[14] the satire deliberately blurs the line between
(private) life and theater. In her own writings, Charke herself leaves the line
between performance and life undrawn, creating an identity that is fundamentally performative.

Charke plays with the idea of self-representation even in her first published
work, *The Art of Management* (1735), a short satiric play attacking Charles
Fleetwood and his treatment of actors at Drury Lane. The play is literally self-
dramatization; Charke writes herself into the action as Mrs. Tragic, Fleetwood

as Brainless, and her brother as Headpiece, the hero of the play. She states forthrightly in the "Preface" that she intends to portray her dismissal from Drury Lane, and the play shows the wronged Charke ultimately redeemed as Fleetwood/Brainless loses the patent to Drury Lane while the heroic Headpiece takes over the theater to the cheers of his fellow actors. Her Mrs. Tragic is a madcap character, not unlike the figure she represents in the *Narrative*, full of tragic rant and extravagant emotions.[15] While this attempt to make (perceived) injustices public was unsuccessful, Charke would follow a similar pattern in nearly every other work she published, particularly in her most popular work, *A Narrative of the Life of Mrs. Charlotte Charke.*

Despite the work's title, the *Narrative* has more in common with drama than with narrative. While her later fictional works such as *The History of Henry Dumont* and *The Lover's Treat; or, The Unnatural Hatred* take on the form of Charke's family crises, in her "narrative" Charke relies on drama as a structuring device, not fiction. Indeed, the *Narrative* reads like a frequently chaotic series of scenes, jumbled together, from Charke's earliest appearance in the costume of her father, to her final role as the penitent daughter. Having, as she admits, "a Genius for the Stage" (55), she translates this genius into her depiction of everyday life. Events become "scenes" and her life itself becomes both "tragical narration" (127) and "ridiculous farce" (70). Most notably, Charke presents herself from childhood as an actress, always adopting a new persona to present to the world. When speaking of one of her adolescent attempts to stage new roles for herself, Charke remarks: "I thought it always proper to imitate the Actions of those Persons, whose Characters I chose to represent; and, indeed, was as changeable as *Proteus*" (40). This protean quality informs the *Narrative* as Charke juggles roles both onstage and offstage. Recalling her years with the strolling players, she recounts how, faced one evening with an audience full of "drunken Butchers" (203) and their talkative spouses, she and a fellow actress "took a Wild-goose Chase through all the dramatic Authors we could recollect, taking particular Care not to let any single Speech bear in the Answer the least Affinity; and, while I was making Love from *Jaffeir*, she tenderly approved my Passion with the soliloquy of *Cato*" (204–5). This episode provides a neat parallel to the *Narrative* itself, where Charke shifts from role to role, persona to persona, even from gender to gender, with startling speed. A repertory actress even in real life, she fills her autobiography with accounts of roles she has played, and as *Sawney and Colley* observes, the "Parts" she "communicated to the Publick" went far beyond those she enacted on the stage.

Charke's treatment of life as performance and her need to market this life to a reading public provide keys to her much debated cross-dressing. Eighteenth-

century readers were clearly fascinated by cross-dressing, and Charke deliberately calls attention to her transvestitism in order to situate her work within the
context of other popular narratives of cross-dressed women.[16] It is equally important to locate her cross-dressing within the larger context of her theatrical
career. Simple as this proposition may seem, twentieth-century readers have
been inclined to read Charke's cross-dressing as either progressively subversive
or as a capitulation to the patriarchal system represented most directly by her
father.[17] While both positions have some merit, both approach gender as an
either/or proposition, a proposition that becomes moot if we, like Charke, consider gender a performative act. Rather than trying to *be* a man, Charke is *playing* the man. For her, the sexes are defined not by physical difference but by
costume: masculinity is synonymous with periwig and breeches, femininity
with skirts and needles. While she never masters needlework, as she relates on
several occasions, she is able to change roles from female to male as opportunity presents itself, acting her father, a groom, a wife, a husband, a daughter, a
mother, and all the professional roles her various careers demand, from stage
heroes and heroines, to actual waiters and valets, a sausage maker (but not fish
seller), and ultimately an authoress. Thus, "playing the man" becomes only one
role in her repertoire, one whose prominence owes much to the contemporary
interest in female transvestitism.

If the variously gendered characters Charke creates for herself owe much to
her stage genius, her prose is itself studded with references to Restoration and
eighteenth-century drama. Over and over, she glosses events in her life with
dramatic tags, casting herself in both male and female roles to illuminate her
experiences. A flirtation with a young lady becomes a scene from Steele's *The
Funeral* (109), her quarrel with Fleetwood the dispute between Peachum and
Lockit in *The Beggar's Opera* (64). Explaining the failure of her marriage, she
cites the famous final scene in Farquhar's *Beaux' Stratagem*, "finding that we
were in the same Circumstances, in Regard to each other, that Mr. *Sullen* and
his Wife were, we agreed to part" (53). The reference clarifies the situation and,
in the process, identifies Charke as the heroine, and her husband as the brute.
As with the accounts of the "characters [she] chose to present," these references create the impression Charke is always, even in private, on stage. As in
her father's various autobiographical enterprises, we are encouraged to view
Charke as we would a dramatic scene—to picture her en tableau.

Crucially, these references are most densely scattered through those segments
of the narrative where Charke most hopes to manipulate the response of her
audience, namely when she discusses her family troubles, especially her es-

trangement from her father and her sense that her sister Catherine has widened the breach. Here, concerns that would appear intensely subjective become instead overtly theatrical. As she explains candidly, her autobiography is written in hopes that it will effect a reconciliation with her father; her sense of having been unfairly driven from her father's affections, "of being deem'd an Alien from the Family" (24), becomes a refrain to which she returns throughout the work. Near the center of the *Narrative* (pages 116–27 of the second edition), this topic breaks loose of chronology as Charke suddenly turns to "one of the most tragical Occurrences of my Life," which she remarks, happened "but last Week" (117). Throughout this lengthy account of her most recent attempt to make peace with her father, Charke uses allusions to drama in order to shape her narrative and to suggest an appropriate emotional response to her audience. References to a diverse range of drama appear on almost every page; interestingly, it is on Charke's one nondramatic allusion, to the Prodigal Son, that critics have chosen to focus.[18] Such a narrow focus ignores the complex structure of Charke's appeal not only to her father, but to her audience. While she draws on the seeming intimacy of confession in her narrative, its most emtional moments are couched in theatrical scenes with which her audience would have been familiar. In this way, drama becomes a means not simply of articulating experience, but of providing a context for her readers, establishing the narrative as spectacle rather than confession. After a pleading letter was returned to her unopened, she turns to her brother Theophilus's adaptation of *Romeo and Juliet* to express her dismay[19]—and also to engage her audience's sympathies by aligning herself with the ever-popular star-crossed lovers. Immediately after, she assumes the character of Charles in her father's own play *Love Makes a Man; or, The Fop's Fortune,* whose words Charke appropriates to exclaim melodramatically: "I'M SORRY THAT I'VE LOST A FATHER" (118).

Two pivotal references follow as Charke introduces her family troubles as tragic spectacle. First she suggests appropriate behavior for her father; rather than ignoring her, he should take on the role of Thorowgood in George Lillo's *The London Merchant:*

> The last Mr. *Lillo's* Character of *Thorowgood,* in his Tragedy of *Barnwell,* sets a beautiful Example of Forgiveness; where he reasonably reflects upon the Frailties of Mankind, in a Speech apart from the afflicted and repenting Youth—'*When we have offended Heaven, it requires no more; and shall Man, who needs himself to be forgiven, be harder to appease?*'—Then, turning to the Boy, confirms his Humanity, by saying; '*If my Pardon, or my Love be of Moment to your Peace, look up secure of both.*'
> How happy would that last Sentence have made me! (121–22)

Thorowgood's paternal relationship with his apprentice Barnwell remains affectionate despite Barnwell's crimes; clearly Charke hopes to stage exactly such a reconciliation with her father. Shifting from one popular tragedy to another, she concludes with an assessment of her family filtered through Shakespeare, describing "she who was once my eldest Sister" (125) as Goneril, Cibber's many grandchildren as "a Brace of *Cordelia's* [*sic*],"[20] and Cibber himself as the perhaps mentally unstable Lear who, despite the control exerted over him by his eldest daughter, "has yet some Power over himself; and, though deaf to me, has listened to the tender Call of Mercy, by a seasonable Protection of their Youth and Innocence" (126).

Such explicit use of dramatic parallels creates a narrative in which the publicity of autobiography represents an extension of that associated with the stage—both become public performance. While Charke's autobiography is more completely the story of her life than either her father's or her brother's, it seems she can express subjective experience only by means of theater. In Charke's public/private life, the line between life and drama is deliberately and extraordinarily blurred, a lack of distinction Charke makes explicit in an episode late in the *Narrative*. Thrown in prison during her years as a strolling player (the Keeper "insisted on our going into the Jail, only for a Shew," a show that moments later becomes real), she is urged to sing by one of her fellow actors. He insists, "as he had often seen me exhibit Captain *Macheath* in an Sham-Prison . . . that he might have the Pleasure of saying, I had once performed IN CHARACTER" (215–16). Theater becomes life and vice versa, a fluidity of medium that characterizes both Charke and her narrative.

All autobiography is a form of self-creation; where the Cibbers stand apart is in their compulsive yoking of two seemingly inimical qualities, the theatrical and the subjective: theater represents a necessarily public spectacle and demands an audience, while subjective experience, the traditional material of autobiography, in theory remains interior and private. If these works do not differentiate between life and theater, they also fail to distinguish between text and performance. In these the supposed accounts of personal experience, subjectivity itself becomes performative. Each writer demands an audience, addressing this audience directly, or, by using allusions to drama, setting the reader in the position of spectator, watching the drama unfold. Under these circumstances, subjectivity itself becomes spectacle. Where Colley Cibber retreats behind his mask, creating a persona in his *Apology* that closely mimics the roles he played for so many years on the stage, his two children choose to expose their private troubles. Using the medium of theater to render their grievances recognizable to their audience, they attempt to reinscribe their fam-

ily, a sometimes uneasy alliance that of necessity turns the personal into public spectacle. We see them not as individual subjects, but as stock figures out
of dramatic texts, texts staged within the confines of the personal narrative.

Notes

1. Habermas outlines these concepts in *The Structural Transformation of the Public
Sphere*. See in particular chapter 2, "Social Structures of the Public Sphere." Here
Habermas explains that "subjectivity, as the innermost core of the private, was always
already oriented to an audience (*Publikum*). The opposite of the intimateness whose
vehicle was the printed word was indiscretion and not publicity as such." This led to
"the authentic literary achievement of that century: the domestic novel" (49).

2. In addition to *The Apology*, Cibber published *A Letter from Mr. Cibber to Mr. Pope*
(1742); *The Egoist; or Colley upon Cibber* (1743); *A Second Letter from Mr. Cibber to Mr.
Pope* (1743); *Another Occasional Letter from Mr. Cibber to Mr. Pope* (1744).

3. As in *The Laureat* (1740) or the mock *Apology for the Life of Mr. T—. C—.* (1740),
both anonymous; the author of *The Laureat* comments that "the world would not have
been inflamed with any violent curiosity" regarding Cibber's life (15).

4. Cibber uses an epigraph from Dryden: "But one Stroke more, and That shall be
my Last."

5. Desperately in need of money, Theophilus encouraged the affections of a wealthy
young man, William Sloper, toward his second wife, Susanna. He assisted in their adultery, reportedly forcing Susanna into bed with Sloper at gunpoint.

6. The Eighteenth-Century Short Title Catalog lists the following works, some of
which, such as as the letters regarding Theophilus's adultery case, went into second or
third printings: an advertisement regarding the elopement of his wife and William
Sloper (1739); *Cibber and Sheridan: or, the Dublin Miscellany. Containing all the advertisements, letters, . . . lately publish'd, on account of the theatric squabble* (1743); an Epistle
from Mr. Theophilus Cibber, Comedian, to Mr. Thomas Sheridan (1743); an Epistle
from Mr. Theophilus Cibber, to David Garrick (1755); Four Original Letters, viz. Two
from a husband to a Gentleman: and two from a husband to a wife (1739); a Letter from
Theophilus Cibber, Comedian, to John Highmore, Esq (1733); a Lick at a Liar: or, Cal-
umny detected. Being an occasional letter to a friend from a Theophilus Cibber (1752);
Mr. Cibber's address to the publick (1746); A proper reply to a late scurrillous libel,
entitled, Mr. Sheridan's address to the town (Dublin, 1743); the Serio-Comic Apology
(1748); the tryal of a cause for criminal conversation, between Theophilus Cibber, Gent.
plaintiff, and William Sloper, Esq; defendent (1739, 1740).

7. See Goldgar 196.

8. In addition, the mock *Apology* uses direct comparisons of father and son in which
the distinctions between the two are ultimately erased: "Some future Historical may
thus write of us: . . . their private Virtues, publick Modesty, and Sentiments of Morality
were, in fact, in the one and the other the same, though their public Conduct was ex-

tremely different. —COLLEY had rather *be* immoral than be esteem'd so; THE' thought it more Glory, the more he acquir'd the Character of being so. —The Reputation of the one was only founded on private Rumour, but that of the other is on publick Record. In Short, the *Father* had few Equals, the *Son* not *one*" (143–44).

9. The full titlepage reads: *A Serio-Comic Apology for Part of the LIFE of Mr. Theophilus Cibber, Comedian. Written by Himself. In which is contained, a PROLOGUE, and EPILOGUE, and a POEM, Wrote on the Play of Romeo and Juliet being first Revived in 1744; Also some Addresses to the Publick, on different Occasions; LIKEWISE Original LETTERS that passed between the late Sir Thomas De Veil, and Mr. Theo. Cibber, (Relating to the Stage-Act) On a Stop being put to the Playing at the Hay-Market. Interspersed with Memoirs and Anecdotes concerning the STAGE-Management and Theatrical Revolutions, in the Years 1744, 1745, and 1746, &c. AND Cursory Observations on some Principal Performers; Particularly Mr. Quin, Mr. Ryan, Mr. Delane, Mrs. Woffington, Mrs. Ward, and Miss Bellamy; Mr. Garrick, Mr. Barry, Mrs. Cibber, Mrs. Clive, Mrs. Pritchard, and Others.*

10. Kindly remember from what Root she came,
    And own her just, hereditary Claim;
    Her Grandsire found a double Road to Fame,
    And to the Player join'd the Poet's Name:
    Sometimes you've smil'd upon her Sire's Endeavours,
    Who humbly hopes Continuance of your Favour (73–74).

11. See pages 62–64.

12. Theophilus quotes from a version of Nahum Tate's adaptation of *King Lear* here.

13. Colley Cibber's adaptation of *King John, Papal Tyranny in the Reign of King John* opened at Covent Garden February 15, 1745, with Cibber as Pandulph, Theophilus as the Dauphin, and Jenny Cibber as young Arthur. Five days later, Lacy staged a revival of Shakespeare's *King John* at Drury Lane with Garrick in the title role. Theophilus viewed this as unfair competition, although the Drury Lane production was evidently delayed several days so as not to run head-to-head with Cibber's adaptation.

14. See pages 138–43 in the *Narrative,* where Charke describes her experiences as a sausage maker.

15. Although entertaining, the play itself was not a success. Charke fell ill the first night, and the play closed shortly after. See Koons 140–41.

16. Works such as the accounts of Mrs. Christian Davis, published variously as *The Life and Adventures of Mrs. Christian Davies, Commonly Call'd Mother Ross* (first edition, 1740; second edition, 1742) or as *The British Heroine; or, An Abridgment of the Life and Adventures of Mrs. Christian Davis* (1742). (The works are virtually identical except that the *Life and Adventures* are first person while *The British Heroine* is reportedly by "J. Wilson., formerly a Surgeon in the Army.") Another such work was *The True History and Adventures of Catharine Vizzani,* Written by Giovanni Bianchi, Professor of Anatomy at Sienna, the Surgeon who dissected her. This text went through at least two editions (1751?, 1755).

17. Where Nussbaum has seen Charke's cross-dressing as a positive example of subversion, Smith and Mackie describe it as a capitulation to patriarchal power structures (Mackie even going so far as to describe Charke as "a cross-dressing failure," 846). Notably, the two scholars who identify Charke's cross-dressing as performative, Straub and Wanko, are the only two who discuss in depth Charke's connection with the theater.

18. See, for example, Mackie (846) and Smith (112).

19. "*Fathers have flinty Hearts! No Tears / Will move 'em!—Children must be wretched!*" (Charke 118).

20. Smith misidentifies the Cordelia figure in this passage (Smith 114). While the implication is clear that Charke is the good daughter, the text describes not a single Cordelia, but a "brace" of Cordelias—in this case Colley Cibber's grandchildren.

Works Cited

An Apology for the Life of Mr. T—. C—. 1740.

Bianchi, Giovanni. *The True History and Adventures of Catharine Vizzani.* London, 1755.

Charke, Charlotte. *The Art of Management; or, Tragedy Expell'd.* London, 1735.

———. *A Narrative of the Life of Mrs. Charlotte Charke.* 2d ed. 1755. Ed. Leonard R. N. Ashley. Gainesville: Scholars' Facsimiles & Reprints, 1969.

Cibber, Colley. *An Apology for the Life of Colley Cibber, With an Historical View of the Stage during his own Time.* Ed. B. R. S. Fone. Ann Arbor: University of Michigan Press, 1968.

———. *The Egoist: Or, Colley upon Cibber. Being His own Picture retouch'd, to so plain a Likeness, that no One, now, would have the Face to own it, but Himself.* London, 1743.

Cibber, Theophilus. *Life of Barton Booth, Esq.*

———. *Romeo and Juliet.* London, 1748.

———. *A Serio-Comic Apology for Part of the LIFE of Mr. Theophilus Cibber, Comedian.* London, 1748.

Goldgar, Bertrand A. *Walpole and the Wits: The Relation of Politics to Literature, 1722–1742.* Lincoln: University of Nebraska Press, 1976.

Habermas, Jurgen. *The Structural Transformation of the Public Sphere: An Inquiry into a Category of Bourgeois Society.* Trans. Thomas Burger. Cambridge: MIT Press, 1991.

Koons, Helene. *Colley Cibber: A Biography.* Lexington: University Press of Kentucky, 1986.

The Laureat. 1740.

The Life and Adventures of Mrs. Christian Davies, Commonly Call'd Mother Ross. 1st ed. 1740, 2d ed. 1742.

Mackie, Erin. "Desperate Measures: The Narratives of the Life of Mrs. Charlotte Charke." *ELH* 58 (1991): 841–65.

Nussbaum, Felicity A. *The Autobiographical Subject: Gender and Ideology in Eighteenth-Century England.* Baltimore: Johns Hopkins University Press, 1989.

Sawney and Colley, A Poetical Dialogue: Occasioned by a Late Letter from the Laureat of St. James's, to the Homer of Twickenham. London, 1742.

Smith, Sidonie. "*A Narrative of the Life of Mrs. Charlotte Charke:* The Transgressive Daughter and the Masquerade of Self-Representation," in *A Poetics of Women's Autobiography: Marginality and the Fictions of Self-Representation.* Bloomington: Indiana University Press, 1987. 102–22, 196–98.

Straub, Kristina. *Sexual Suspects: Eighteenth-Century Players and Sexual Ideology.* Princeton: Princeton University Press, 1992.

Tate, Nahum. *The History of King Lear.* London, 1681.

Wanko, Cheryl. "The Eighteenth-Century Actress and the Construction of Gender: Lavinia Fenton and Charlotte Charke." *Eighteenth-Century Life* 18 (May 1994): 75–90.

Wilson, J. *The British Heroine: or, An Abridgment of the Life and Adventures of Mrs. Christian Davis.* London, 1742.

3

The Transgressive Daughter and the
Masquerade of Self-Representation

Sidonie Smith

This tragic story, or this comic jest,
May make you laugh, or cry—as you like best.
—*Prologue to "The What d'Ye Call it,"* A Narrative
of the Life of Mrs. Charlotte Charke

Margaret Cavendish set upon the "open road" to announce to the world her desire for "fame in after ages." Yet she carefully sheltered herself within the carriage-like enclosure of proper feminine gentility. As a result, the fundamental ambivalence she felt about her desire for a transgressive female heroism permeates the story she tells about herself. Charlotte Charke, also a famous, or rather notorious, daughter and wife, evinced little ambivalence when she launched her own independent career almost one hundred years after Cavendish began writing. In an age when acting was the legitimate secular profession open to women, Charke strutted across the stage invigorated by the theatrical possibilities of self-dramatization. Unlike Cavendish, she embraced the transgressive life of the open road with a kind of male bravado. Yet to the extent that she did so, she lost the affection of her father and fell into a life of destitution. It is a story of transgression, prodigality, and vagabondage that Charke tells as she attempts to regain her father's love. Of course, stories of the road and the rogue fascinated the eighteenth century generally, more so than they did the less politically and socially stable seventeenth century. Nonetheless, this particular story of female vagabondage startles the reader even now.

The autobiographer prefaces *A Narrative of the Life of Mrs. Charlotte Charke* with an epistolary dedication entitled "The Author to Herself." Denouncing the excesses of flattery common to dedications, she parodies her dedicatee's eminence: "I hope I shall escape that Odium so justly thrown on poetical Petitioners, notwithstanding my Attempt to illustrate those WONDERFUL QUALIFICATIONS by which you have so EMINENTLY DISTINGUISH'D YOURSELF, and gives you a just Claim to the title of a NONPAREIL OF THE AGE."[1] In fact, she replaces excess flattery with excess mockery. Her dedicatee's distinction as a woman without peers lies in such "virtues" as "thoughtless Ease," a misguided "Fortitude of Mind," an "exquisite Taste in Building . . . magnificent airy Castles," "an indolent Sweetness of . . . Temper." She is indeed peerless, but as an "Oddity of Fame," a "curiosity," rather than as a serious eminence. Nonetheless, Charke appeals to her for assistance: "If, by your Approbation, the World may be persuaded into a tolerable Opinion of my Labours, I shall, for the Novelty-sake, venture for once to call you FRIEND,—a Name, I own, I never *as yet have known you by*" (vii–viii). Expressing hope that her patron will be struck with "reproach" so that the two of them "may ripen our Acquaintance into a perfect Knowledge of each other, that may establish a lasting and social Friendship between us," she suggests that such a rapprochement now seems both desirable and possible since "your two Friends, PRUDENCE and REFLECTION . . . have lately ventur'd to pay you a Visit; for which I heartily congratulate you, as nothing can possibly be more joyous to the Heart than the Return of absent Friends, after a long and painful Peregrination" (ix). Charke's dedicatee is, of course, herself, a self-reflexive phenomenon that makes of the dedication a particularly complex introduction. Maintaining the critical distance of cavalier self-mockery, the autobiographer creates of herself a quixotic figure, a kind of perpetual naif, who, destitute of common sense, blunders along in life. In this "unflattering" portrait she becomes overimaginative, indolent, careless, unrealistically optimistic, imprudent, unreflective. And yet, with this prefatory gesture, the autobiographer also announces at the outset a flair for dramatic posturing, an energetic preoccupation with theatrical entertainment and self-fabrication that enhances the reader's pleasure.

The "entertaining" self-parody, the dramatic bravado, and the rebellious speaking posture betray, on the one hand, the depth of Charke's isolation from community. The fact that she dedicates her autobiography to herself reveals the extent of her dissociation from respectable society. She recognizes no one of social standing as worthy of her attentions and, by implication, reveals her understanding that she may not be worthy of theirs.[2] And the self-parody speaks to her recognition that for the reader she is a truly eccentric character, one who lives outside the conventional norms of that middle-class society into which she was born. Mirroring in her self-mockery the moral stance of the

community from which she has been banished, Charke would affirm her identification with it. Through such affirmation she unmasks a sentimental longing for psychological rapprochement with and physical return to that community. On the other hand, the self-mockery and dramatic bravado betray the
fragile exuberance, defiance, and pride of the outcast: there is relish in the role
of the quixote. As Patricia Meyer Spacks suggests, "the dedication of her book
to herself, defiantly asserting her self-sufficiency, conveys her determination
to celebrate herself if no one else will celebrate her."[3] Thus, while Charke eschews flattery, she effectively enhances the portrait of herself as eccentric rebel
and, additionally, piques her reader's curiosity with the promise of unusual
revelations.

Two desires and two narrative intentions therefore emerge in Charke's opening dedication. Eager to reveal her strange story, Charke seems to flaunt her
waywardnesses before the reader, relishing even the self-deprecation. A true
actress, she entertains her audience by playing the "role" of a quixotic, even
roguish protagonist, a prodigal who strays from the family, defying convention to lead the transgressive life of the female vagabond. Such "role" playing
is doubly entertaining: the narrative of a quixote always challenges cultural
norms and teases conventional pieties; and the story of the female transgressive titillates even further the reader's desire for scandal. Moreover, the drama of ironic self-deprecation subverts the sense of self-importance and self-
aggrandizement inherent in the autobiographical project. But entangled in
those quixotic entertainments lies the story of the prodigal who desires to return "home." Through this story, Charke presents herself as the sentimental
heroine, a woman who accepts and reflects the values of the community, including its expectations of appropriate female behavior. The doubled identification of Charke as sentimental penitent and female rogue both informs and
unhinges the narrative and drama of her autobiography.

Born into a comfortable middle-class family at the beginning of the eighteenth century, Charlotte Cibber was the youngest child of a famous father.
After receiving a generous education, especially for a girl, she married too
quickly a man who exploited her for his ambition's sake: the daughter of the
famous actor and author, she was an attractive match for an aspiring musi-
cian. The marriage failed, forcing Charlotte, now Charke, to support herself
and her child. She began what seemed to be a promising career on the stage,
following in her father's and brother's footsteps. After alienating herself from
family and friends, however, she spent the rest of her life on the margins of
society, pursing a variety of "careers," as puppeteer, grocer, sausage maker,
waiter, and finally as strolling player. Imprisoned several times for debts, she

lived continually on the verge of disaster. Eventually, she tried to support herself by writing novels and the autobiography through which she sought her father's absolution for her prodigal life.

Attentiveness to the father was particularly critical for a woman of the eighteenth century, as Spacks emphasizes in her analysis of four autobiographies, Charke's among them: "Women did not expect their husbands' continued love. Emotional investment in fathers, made earlier and enduring longer, paid off more dependably, although sometimes stormily."[4] The father provided protection. Under his roof and under his authority, the daughter could be sure of survival. Writing expressly to overcome the profound estrangement from her father, therefore, Charke becomes one of those "women identifying themselves as daughters," joining others who "declared their dependency, their need, and their sense of where that need might be gratified, asserting their identities to inhere in their roles rather than their deeds."[5] Alluding explicitly to the stormy nature of her relationship with Colley Cibber in the opening pages of the autobiography proper, Charke confesses that "since my Maturity, I lost that Blessing: Which, if strongest Compunction, and uninterrupted Hours of Anguish, blended with Self-conviction and filial Love, can move his Heart to Pity and Forgiveness, I shall, with Pride and unutterable Transport, throw myself at this Feet, to implore the only Benefit I desire or expect, his BLESSING, and his PARDON" (14). Unable to speak directly with her father, who refuses to acknowledge her claims on his love, Charke turns to print as the medium through which to achieve reconciliation and to affect a reprieve from her reputation as undutiful daughter: "I hope, ere this small Treatise is finish'd, to have it in my Power to inform my Readers, my painful Separation from my once tender Father will be more than amply repaid, by a happy Interview" (15). The fact that her story is serialized over a period of eight weeks significantly enhances the very real drama of the "life."[6] Both she and her readers await the outcome of her petition for absolution, await, that is, the father's word.

To regain her reputation as the dutiful daughter and to return metaphorically the home of the father (and all patriarchal fathers), Charke must duplicate for her culture its privileged story of female selfhood. As she writes her story and awaits the father's word, therefore, she appropriates the speaking posture and story of the sentimental heroine, that dependent, vulnerable, and victimized woman struggling to do the morally right thing, struggling to please the father. When, in the early installments, her father's word is imminent, she assumes a particularly generous stance, playing the devoted daughter through the language of true filiality. In dramatic commentary and descriptive passages, she presents her father as a tender, affectionate parent whose "paternal Love omitted nothing that could improve any natural Talents Heaven had been pleased to endow me with" (16). She lavishes praise on him as she acknowledges the breadth of his parental love: "My Obligations to him in my bringing up are of so extensive a Nature, I can never sufficiently acknowledge 'em; for, notwithstanding 'tis every Parent's Duty to breed their Children with every Advantage their Fortunes will admit of, yet, in this Case, I must confess myself most transcendently indebted, having received even a Superfluity of tender Regard of that Kind" (25). If she is at all critical, as she is in discussing his role in her marriage to Mr. Charke, she mutes the criticism, delicately referring to his indulgence and tenderness as possible sources of her difficulties, only conceding that "out of pure Pity, [he] tenderly consented to a conjugal Union" between his daughter and Mr. Charke (51).

Coupled with the presentation of her father as loving and generous is her presentation of herself as "a sincere and hearty Penitent," an undeserving daughter who acknowledges the "oddity of [her] youthful Disposition" (51) and who apologizes for her pursuit of an independent career. Throughout she plays the prodigal humbled by her errancy: "I have too much Reason to know, that the Madness of my Follies have generally very severely recoil'd upon myself, but in nothing so much as in the shocking and heart-wounding Grief for my Father's Displeasure, which I shall not impudently dare deny having justly incurr'd" (23–24). Labeling her childhood escapades "strange, mad Pranks," she "beg[s] Pardon for not having put [her education] to a more grateful and generous Use, both for HIS HONOUR and MY OWN CREDIT" (25). Not only does she confess sins of filiality; she also apologizes for sins of friendship, asking pardon from those whom she has wronged in the past with former meannesses. Moreover, she promises a conversion to orthodox filiality: "I shall lay it down as a Maxim for the remaining Part of Life, to make the utmost amends by PRUDENT CONDUCT, for the MISCARRIAGES OF THE FORMER; so that, should I fail in my Hopes, I may not draw any farther Imputation on myself" (25).

While she admits that the loss of her father's affection comes "partly through my own Indiscretion," however, she qualifies her culpability by assigning greater blame to others. Imitating other sentimental heroines, she plays the destitute and deserted victim of a vicious, corrupt world, a "conventional" woman, passive and vulnerable.[7] She may have dabbled in rebelliousness; but ultimately her errancies were exploited by others who would separate her from her father: "I dare confidently affirm, MUCH PAINS has been taken to AGGRAVATE MY FAULTS, and STRENGTHEN his Anger; and, in that Case, I am certain my Enemies have not always too strictly adher'd to TRUTH, but

MEANLY had recourse to FALSEHOOD to perpetrate the Ruin of a hapless Wretch, whose real Errors were sufficient, without the Addition of MALICIOUS SLANDERS" (24). A stepmother and a sister, jealous of her place in her father's heart, intervene maliciously between father and daughter. A husband's "loose and unkind Behaviour," exploding any illusions of an acceptable marriage, "made me extravagant and wild in my Imagination" (53). "The cruel Censure of false and evil Tongues" further exacerbates her alienation from her father. Thieving strangers take her goods and her money.

Charke sanctifies the role of victimized heroine by infusing it with the virtues of Christian piety, especially charity and forgiveness. Acknowledging obligations she owes to others who have helped her, she repays their charitable deeds with "printed" thank-you's: "Tis certain, there never was known a more unfortunate Devil than I have been; but I have, in the Height of all my Sorrows, happily found a numerous Quantity of Friends, whose Commiseration shall be taken Notice of with the utmost Gratitude, before I close this Narrative" (84). Specifically she mentions her sister and the actor Garrick, both of whom she showers with appreciation. She presents herself as maintaining her commitments to others, despite her continuing destitution. Affirming the importance of sibling loyalty, she pleads for charity for a sister as destitute as she. She even goes so far as to advertise in a later installment her sister's new restaurant, hoping thereby to help her succeed financially (146). Finally, she plays the charitable Christian by forgiving those who have wronged her. Of her husband, she writes: "But peace to his *Manes!* and, I hope Heaven has forgiven him, as I do from my Soul; and wish, for both our sakes, he had been Master of more Discretion, I had then possibly been possessed of more Prudence" (79). By playing the generous Christian to the hilt, she establishes her spiritual superiority over those malicious (but comfortably positioned) people who have directed neither charity nor forgiveness toward her.

Finally, Charke plays the sentimental heroine by assuming the posture of a moralist who seeks common ground with her audience of ladies and gentlemen. Conscientiously, she maintains the decency and morality of her narrative itself, announcing in the opening paragraphs:

> I must beg Leave to inform those Ladies and Gentlemen, whose Tenderness and Compassion may excite 'em to make this little Brat of my Brain the Companion of an idle Hour, that I have paid all due Regard to Decency wherever I have introduc'd the Passion of Love; and have only suffer'd it to take its Course in its proper and necessary Time, without fulsomely inflaming the Minds of my young Readers, or shamefully offending those of riper Years; a Fault I have often condemn'd, when I was myself but a Girl, in some Female Poets. I shall not descant on their Imprudence,

only wish that their Works has been less confined to that Theme, which too often led 'em into Errors, Reason and Modesty equally forbid. (12)

Taking a high moral tone, she purposively dissociates herself from earlier women writers by denouncing their excessive preoccupation with passion and the theme of love. By doing so, she allies herself with those cultural critics during the mid-eighteenth century fiercely concerned about the very questionable morality of the literature of love, including the new novel. Such critics decried the impact that stories of romance and love would surely have on the minds and hearts of the young ladies who read them. Poetry, romance, and novels of love, they argued, were potentially as seductive of the affections and the morals, even the bodies, of women as was any nefarious man. Or, rather, imaginative seductions prepared the way for actual ones.[8] Echoing those sentiments, Charke disengages herself from the potentially subversive element of common narrative, from its immoral and indecent themes, as she asserts her text's decency, reasonableness, modesty, prudence.

And she maintains that posture toward her narrative throughout. After describing some of her early escapades, she comments: "Were I to insert one quarter Part of the strange, mad Pranks I play'd, even in Infancy, I might venture to affirm, I could swell my Account of 'em to a Folio, and perhaps my whimsical Head may compile such a Work; but I own I should be loth, upon Reflection, to publish it, lest the Contagion should spread itself, and make other young Folks as ridiculous and mischievous as myself" (23). Not only does she present her narrative itself as moral; she also, within the content of her tale, embeds moral directives. She discusses the importance of adding experience of the world to sedentary education. Telling the story of her "fortunate Escape" from a vile deception, she presents a maxim to "set others on their Guard, who may be liable to an Accident of the same Kind" (197). She describes her plan to support an impoverished sister, not "with any Regard to myself, but with the pleasing Hope of being the happy Example to others, from whom she may have an equal Claim, both from NATURE AND GRATITUDE" (68).

Affirming at once her repentence and her childlike innocence of numerous charges of errant rebelliousness, Charke devotes much of her time in the first installments of the autobiography to establishing her identity as the sentimental heroine victimized by parental dotage, family intrigue, marital exploitation and infidelity, communal viciousness, and unkind fortune. Before her reader and her father, she plays the devoted daughter who embodies the virtues of Christianity, its devotion, charity, morality, its magnanimity and forgiveness. Beyond that, she defends herself against charges that she was "a giddy, indiscreet Wife" and presents herself, in some of the most lavishly sentimental passages, as a devoted mother who tries to protect her own daughter from unwarranted suffering in the midst of poverty and humiliation. Right-minded but wrongly treated, she is "woman," more victim than agent, unjustly thrown into a cruel, inhuman world. Moreover, she speaks as sentimental heroine in a voice that is neither ironic nor self-mocking as is the voice of the transgressive Charke, but one that is dramatically sentimental, emotionally intense, lavishly devotional, humbly self-effacing. As she shares the panoply of values, visions, and voices dear to eighteenth-century sensibility and thus dear to her reader (and father), Charke seeks to exonerate her transgressive life by affirming her true membership in the class from which she herself as prodigal daughter has strayed. To the extent that she appears humbled by her errancy, blameless before the malice of others, and a true woman of her class, she vindicates herself and commands her father to reconsider his rejection of her.

As noted earlier, however, Charke's proleptic dedication hints at *two* narrative possibilities, a doubled story of doubled desires. On the one hand, it tells the modest story of the Father's daughter, the sentimental penitent who would resume her place of dependency and subordination. On the other, it tells the titillating tale of the outcast, the daughter who would vigorously, even violently, defy the Father as a "son." If through the former role she embraces conventional forms of female selfhood and tells a woman's story in the voice of the didacticist and penitent, through the latter role she defies the conventional forms of female selfhood in eighteenth-century society: she becomes the woman who adventures in the world as a man and who speaks in the jaunty, self-mocking voice of the rebel. While the sentimental heroine's story takes place in the dramatic passages where Charke addresses her reader and, through her reader, her father, the rogue's story consumes the narrative portion of the autobiography. Therefore, entangled in the story of the penitent is a competing story, the sensational, the transgressive, the exotic story of the rogue and her progress.

In the opening pages Charke identifies herself as "one who has used her utmost endeavours to entertain" the reader with a dramatically compelling "adventure" story. Even as she makes claims for the universality of her experience—"I have, I think, taken Care to make 'em so interesting, that every Person who reads my Volume may bear a Part in some Circumstance or other in the Perusal, as there is nothing inserted but what may daily happen to every Mortal breathing"—she promises "to give some Account of my UNACCOUNTABLE LIFE" (13). In fact, the irony of the preceding disclaimer is acute. After reading her narrative the reader can hardly identify with much that has happened to her. And she herself acknowledges that her readers "will own, when they know my History, if Oddity can plead my Right to Surprise and Astonishment, I may positively claim a Title to be shewn among the Wonders of Ages past, and those to come" (13). Thus she reveals an understanding that the idiosyncratic and transgressive, that is, the "criminal" nature of her experience as a female nonpareil who lives outside the bounds of convention and propriety, will "please" and "satisfy" her reader. In doing so, it will foster sales of her "life."

As soon as she begins to tell her story, Charke re-creates the transgressive lines of her life. She describes how, at the age of four, she donned her brother's waistcoat and her father's hat and wig and walked up and down a ditch waving to everyone who came along. "But, behold," she continues, "the Oddity of my Appearance soon assembled a Crowd about me; which yielded me no small Joy, as I conceived their Risibility on this Occasion to be Marks of Approbation, and walked myself into a Fever, in the happy Thought of being taken for the 'Squire" (19). The next year she mounted a small foal and rode through town followed by a procession of common people, to the great amusement and shame of her father. She describes how as an adolescent she became preoccupied with hunting and shooting, contemptuously rejecting the activities more appropriate for young girls. She assumes the role of doctor, impersonating a healer as she dispenses weird concoctions to the country people surrounding her family's home. Next she acts the part of the gardener, then stableman, then assumes the role of her mother's protector as she "saves" her from the supposed threats of the displaced stableman. Her mother, she remembers, "communicated her Fears to me, who most heroically promised to protect her Life, at the utmost Hazard of my own" (44). That occasion offered her "an Opportunity of raising my Reputation as a courageous Person, which I was extream fond of being deemed" (44–45). Moreover, she notes that she received during those years "a liberal [education], and such indeed as might have been sufficient for a Son instead of a Daughter" (17), and further that she failed in learning the fundamental of home economy, the conventional "curriculum" for girls, "in which needful Accomplishment, I have before hinted, my Mind was entirely uncultivated" (30).

The picture Charke provides of her childhood and early adolescence suggests the degree to which the young girl desired to be the central figure in an "adventure" played out in the wider world and the degree to which that world was open only to men. Dressed as her father, she enjoys the brief belief that she is taken for him, a figure of prominence in the child's and the community's eyes. She yearns for and enjoys the adulation that the crowd accords to male heroes (herself in the ditch, on the horse, before the intruder in her home). She recognizes and enjoys the power inherent in male skills (the control of the gun) and roles (the doctor's healing, the stableman's protection). As a young girl, Charke desired to be the "son" by dressing in her father's clothes and by following in his footsteps. As a son she could effectively play a public role, protecting her mother, ministering to her neighbors, guarding property. The older autobiographer labels the childhood preoccupation with impersonation "my former Madness"; but the label is more rhetorical and revelatory than convincing. Those "madnesses" unmask her early desire for public significance (and attention), for activity, adventure, meaning. They suggest also that for a woman male impersonation, with its clothes, its strutting posture, its mobility, provides access to the world of movement and meaning and promises the powers and privileges, the self-enhancements and presentments that accrue to male selfhood and autobiography. She calls them madnesses for her reader's, but most particularly for her father's, sake, in order to neutralize the transgressive desire inherent in such cross-dressing. But they are unqualifiedly the fantastic entertainments and empowerments of a female child who, desiring to press more meaning out of life than she sees in the lives of women around her, including the mother whom she erases from the text, defies conventional expectations of a young girl's proper education, disposition, values, and sense of identity.[9] Beyond that, her pranks reveal, not so subtly, the young Charke's desire to displace the father, to challenge his authority and to escape her dependence on him. They are gestures of independence and personal authority, the gestures of a son rather than of a daughter.

After reconstructing her childhood self as the girl who would be boy, it is not surprising that Charke does not go on to trace the "conventional" story of a woman's actual and autobiographical life in the eighteenth century: youth spent in preparation for marriage, young adulthood spent in pursuit of the proper marriage partner, life after marriage spent fulfilling the roles of wife and mother, and a narrative "life" devoted to cataloging the accomplishments of husbands and edifying the youth of sons. This plot would more closely mirror the plot enacted by that sentimental heroine she plays in the dramatic scenes of her autobiography. When she describes her marriage, she does so sparely: Mr. Charke quickly vanishes and dies. In fact, the event that serves as the happy conclusion of so much eighteenth-century fiction brings with it the disillusionment and economic insecurity that force Charke to venture into the world as a female vagabond. Instead of providing the stabilizing plot for Charke's female life, marriage catapults her into the destabilized plot of roguish adventures.

As Charke chronicles the "unnatural" life of a female vagabond who moves through a startling variety of worldly adventures and careers in search of economic and psychological independence, she establishes resonances with the picaresque tale. Although Charke does not tell of a life lived as a literal criminal—she does not steal, murder, violate the law—she does narrate the life of a "criminal" woman, a prodigal daughter who travels through the world entangled in a "rogue's progress" of adventures, misfortunes, betrayals, deceits. As the female prodigal, she presents herself as restlessly defiant of conventions and norms, careless of reputation, alienated from her middle-class family, reduced by poverty to make a living among the homeless and the destitute, implicated in deceits and deceptions. In that world of homelessness and mutability, impermanence and vagabondage, Charke becomes a comic rogue, an endlessly self-fabricating figure who enacts multiple roles calling for multiple identities.[10]

But Charke goes further, introducing into her story an even more subversive duplicity; for what was playacting for the child becomes critical deception for the woman. She describes how, during the long years of peregrination, she dons male clothing and male identities in order to "venture into the World." Playing "the well-bred Gentleman" Mr. Brown, she becomes "the unhappy Object of Love in a young Lady, whose Fortune was beyond all earthly Power to deprive her of, had it been possible for me to have been, what she designed me, nothing less than her Husband" (106–7).[11] For a short period she becomes a "gentleman's Gentleman." She works as a waiter in a restaurant until the woman who owns it falls in love with her. Then she goes on her nine-year adventure as a "male" strolling player, even describing the experience in the male imagery of war: "I think going a Strolling is engaging in a little, dirty Kind of War, in which I have been obliged to fight so many Battles, I have resolutely determined to throw down my Commission" (187). Sometime during this period she is put in jail where, dressed as a man, she spends the night singing the songs of Macheath from *The Beggar's Opera* (215). Charke's narrative tells the story of a girl who would play the boy, a woman who would play the man, an actress who would play male roles, a sexual transgressor. In fact, the deceit of gender is the fundamental deceit around which her life turns. Presenting herself as a prodigal "son," she entertains her reader with an illicit tale of roguish cross-dressing as Mr. Brown moves through the world with energy, duplicity, and aggressiveness.

Terry Castle cautions that it is frustratingly difficult to establish an etiology of cross-dressing in earlier centuries.[12] Certainly, Charke never self-reflexively accounts for the psychological motivation behind her continued cross-dressing or the advantages of such duplicity. Any evidence of an etiology remains implicit in the childhood pranks she catalogs. The tendency to dress as a man and to play a man's role seems always to have been part of her life and imagination. And the language with which she reconstructs those earlier scenes suggests that for her the father's, rather than the mother's, world offers possibilities for self-expression. "Symbolically embracing otherness," Charke puts on the identity of a man in order to move more easily through her world, in order to escape the limitations and the vulnerabilities of female identity and life scripts.[13] On the psychological level, her cross-dressing speaks to female desire for authority, adventure, power, and mobility, the accoutrements of male selfhood. It speaks also to female desire for freedom from the physical and psychological vulnerabilities of female dependency. Male impersonation promises empowerment.

Most important, on the narrative level the story of the cross-dressed rogue allows Charke to write an autobiography. In providing the reader with an interesting, even titillating story of rebellious duplicity and filial errancy, it allows her to tell a story that will be read by her culture. But beyond its pleasurable quality, the story of female rogue mirrors the culture's idea of "male" life scripts. Responding personally in life and narratively in text to the generic expectations of significance in life stories, Charke finds a story that resonates with privileged cultural fictions. There is adventure, mobility, action, self-assertion. There is a public career. There is the challenge to the father, with the subsequent life of economic independence. Finally, there is the suppression of the mother and the realm of the feminine that characterizes male autobiography. Assuming the adventurous masquerade of man, Charke reinscribes the myth of origins constitutive of the story of man and claims her place in the world of men, words, and public spaces.

In the very writing of the autobiography, Charke engages in a carnivalesque drama of impersonation, linking the process of writing autobiography with the dynamics of selfhood captured in the remembered moments of her life. As noted earlier, the scenes of childhood Charke includes in the early pages of her autobiography center on her impersonations, her preoccupation with acting as someone else, with assuming the postures and the lines of others. On one level, the scenes become the "substantive content of the *remembered* experience"; but on another, such moments speak to "a special order of experience in the life itself that for the autobiographer is inseparably linked to the discovery and invention of identity."[14] Assuming other people's identities, roles, lines, living the plots of fictive heroes and heroines, Charke creates herself through recourse to the lives and lines of others. In that way her embrace of "impersonation" becomes, to use Olney's phrase, a kind of "metaphor of self."[15] Moreover, if impersonation becomes early on the characteristic way of creating her identity before the public, it becomes also the characteristic way she presents her autobiographical self to the world. Through writing her life story, Charke continues the process of acting out before an audience, and "repeat[s] the psychological rhythms of identity formation" that reach far back into childhood.[16]

The product of a cultural scavanger, Charke's autobiography is the narrative of an imposter who masquerades in a variety of roles, plots, and characters, establishing throughout her autobiography resonances with fictional and dramatic heroines and heroes. She speaks through a cacophony of lines from plays, poems, and novels, borrowing the language of literature to shape her narrative in the patterns of maternal and paternal stories of selfhood. In her endlessly fictive imagination, Charke patches together the thematic motifs and the rhetorical tones of social stature, low comedy, high tragedy, sentimental fiction, picaresque adventure, and criminal biography. Charke assumes all rhetorical postures, takes on all characters, plays all scenes for the dramatic possibilities inherent in them. Her autobiographical narrative imitates those theatrical productions she describes in the text. Lines, characters, speeches, and events from a variety of disparate plays and stories are woven into one polyglot presentation.

The prevalence as well as the ambivalence and confusion of this polyglot, this storytelling selfhood—which suspends Charke between the imperatives of maternal and paternal narratives—is dramatized powerfully in the central scene of the autobiography, the moment when Charke describes how her father has returned her letter of supplication unopened. Precipitating "a full Account of, I think, one of the most tragical Occurrences of my Life, which but last Week happened to me" (117), her father, "forgetful of that TENDER NAME, and the GENTLE TIES OF NATURE, returned [the letter she sent him] in a Blank" (117). Responding to his silence, Charke assumes a variety of figurative stances. She becomes the ill-served prodigal who is not "joyfully received by the offended Father." She becomes the convicted criminal on the verge of death: "Nay, MERCY has even extended itself at the Place of Execution, notorious Malefactors; but as I have not been guilty of those Enormities incidental to the foremention'd Characters, permit me, gentle Reader, to demand what I have done so hateful! so very grievous to his Soul! so much beyond the Reach of Pardon! that nothing but MY LIFE COULD MAKE ATONEMENT? which I can bring Witness was a Hazard I was immediately thrown into" (121). She becomes Cordelia, the inherently virtuous and loving daughter, wronged by a malign Goneril "who neither does, or ever will, pay the least Regard to any Part of the Family, but herself," cast away by a misguided old father who becomes a kind of fool (122). Finally, she reaches for the moral superiority of the Christian saint by claiming her own act of forgiveness and thereby her greater Christian charity. Metamorphosing from role to role, figure to figure, Charke plays the dramatic scene to her audience with resourcefulness as well as with desperation.

The scene of painful metamorphosis functions as a scene of betrayal. Yet it is not Charke's father who has betrayed her most profoundly. Literature, storytelling itself, has betrayed her. Grasping at autobiographical "roles," she becomes their victim because the very metamorphosis from female role to male role calls attention to the fictive quality of Charke's narrative postures and because neither maternal nor paternal narratives serve her.

Certainly, the maternal story of the sentimental penitent, the story of vulnerable, dependent, and victimized woman, does not, cannot work for her. If she is a Cordelia, that epitome of dutiful daughter betrayed by a malign Goneril, she is a Cordelia whose father never realizes her virtue, never calls her back home to his heart. Or, rather, she is no true Cordelia, precisely because the narrative posture is transparent as imposture. If she is a Clarissa, struggling to maintain her purity and integrity in the face of familial betrayal, she is a Clarissa who does not "die" to preserve her virginity. Nor is she a Pamela, the serving girl whose true spirit wins her a title. Instead of climbing up the economic ladder through the preservation of her virginity, Charke has descended the economic ladder after sacrificing hers. Nor is she the true Christian saint, willing to suffer and to forgive her tormentors. The female roles cannot serve her because they do not fit the reality of her circumstances or the texture of her disposition. For, while she attempts to maintain the "dramatic" penitential stance of the victimized heroine who, finding herself unjustly alienated from family and social class, struggles mightily to remain true to conventional Christian values, this woman seems to relish more her role as good-natured transgressive "picaro." She becomes more rogue than penitent, romping through the world in search of adventure, however desperate that romp may be. She also romps through her narrative more as male impersonator than as sentimental heroine.

Donning the narrative clothes of the prodigal, she parades herself through town as a "manly" narrator. The "manliness" of the narrative style lies in Charke's anarchic energy, evidenced in the aggressiveness with which she tells her story and engages her reader (and her father) in her autobiographical challenge. It derives also from the loose, episodic chronology, the explosive bursts of events, characterizations, pronouncements. And the speaking posture of that "manly" narrator is jaunty, cavalier, brash, brusk, infused with the comic bravado of the self-styled rogue who remains immune to cuts and criticism, who creates herself self-expansively and self-mockingly. Willing to entertain her reader even at her own expense, Charke seems recklessly careless of her reputation: "I am certain, there is no one in the World MORE FIT THAN MYSELF TO BE LAUGHED AT. I confess myself an odd Mortal, and believe I need no Force of Argument, beyond what has already said, to bring the whole Globe terrestrial into that Opinion" (86). Mocking her own efforts to achieve meaning and public significance in her life, she nonetheless maintains the energy and power of the narrative transgressor. For one twentieth-century critic, "Charlotte Charke remains the same strolling player, careless, wild, irresponsible even in her quotations"; and "the effect produced by her narrative is one of undirected power, thunderous and murky, masculine."[17] Although that critic does not necessarily admire the reckless masculinity of Charke's narrative, he testifies to its active power.

The aggressiveness of Charke's narrative style disrupts and subverts the penitential anguish of the letter scene. Playing the transgressive and roguish "son," she prefaces the histrionic lamentation of the misunderstood and abused penitent with a defiant gesture of rebellion. Exacting a kind of vengeance on the father she would woo, Charke introduces into the text two anecdotal stories she labels as apocryphal. She describes how rumor has it that, dressed as a highwayman, she

> stopp'd [his] Chariot, presented a Pistol to his Breast, and used such Terms as I am ashamed to insert; threaten'd to blow his Brains out that Moment if he did not deliver. . . . Upbraiding him for his Cruelty in abandoning me to those Distresses he knew I underwent, when he had it so amply in his Power to relieve me: That since he would not use that Power, I would force him to a Compliance, and was directly going to discharge upon him; but his Tears prevented me, and, asking my Pardon for his ill Usage of me, gave me his Purse with threescore Guineas, and a Promise to restore me to his Family and Love; on which I thank'd him, and rode off. (114)

Categorically denying having accosted her father in that way, Charke effectually "accosts" him in recounting the rumor. As a "fictive" rogue she gives the scene to the deep-seated anger at her dependency on her father and at his abandonment of her and thereby reveals her desire for vengeance. Beyond that, she creates a father emasculated, even "feminized." Pitiful, helpless, humiliated, unheroic, he is reduced to tears of contrition. Finally, in this fantasy the daughter-"son" assumes the power of life and death over the father, reversing the dynamics of power in their real-life relationship. Charke may protest against the viciousness of the rumor, but, as she incorporates that story within her story, she enacts a fantasy of filial defiance. The second story has to do with her response when her father runs into his fishmongering daughter: rumor has it she slaps him in the face with a fish. Again, the introduction of the rumor, if only to deny its facticity, unmasks Charke's anger and resentment at the unnatural refusal of her father to accept his prodigal daughter's repentence. In both rumors she makes of her famous father a Colley Cibber victimized by female violence, reduced to humiliating and unmanly postures. In both stories she makes of herself a Charlotte empowered to strike back, to inflict a wound on the enemy, a hero vigilant before the forces of oppression. Ironically, while Charke desires rapprochement with the father and his world, she exacts a kind of vengeance.

The "masculine" defiance captured in the apocryphal gestures characterizes the rhetorical posture of Charke's narrative after her letter has been returned unopened. She does not cower before the rejection of her father. Having vented her distress at his rejection, she subdues the stance of penitent and continues her narrative with renewed energy and intensity. What others might be reticent to reveal, Charke, with her flair for theatrical self-presentation, reveals with a kind of abandon, apparently reveling in telling her reader about her trials and tribulations. Claiming that she tells only the truth of her experience, she focuses unabashedly on her vagabondage and destitution, re-creating vivid scenes of pathos, describing constant destitution, humiliating nights in jail, flights from bailiffs and creditors, recourse to begging at the doors of rich friends. The narrative becomes a chaotic, luxuriating romp of life lived on the margins. In the midst of her narrative she even presents her plans for future enterprises, revealing a kind of "chronic" optimism underlying her errant rebelliousness. And she lashes out more directly at father, siblings, and strangers who have betrayed her. Specifically, she continues to undermine her father's authority by questioning his generosity and by making of him a kind of unnatural father. He may be famous and well respected; but, her story reveals, there is a black, "unnatural" side to the famous and revered poet laureate. Moreover, this undutiful daughter gives the reader the story of a famous father and daughter that enhances their pleasure in the scandals of the well known. The spectacle of Colley Cibber's daughter dressed as a man, imprisoned in a country town, singing the songs of Macheath from *The Beggar's Opera*, playing, that is, in drag, would undoubtedly have created a particularly titillating scandal for those interested in the lives and idiosyncrasies of the rich and famous. In her apparent effort to rescue her father from a reputation as hardened and unaffectionate parent, Charke actually emasculates him, entertaining the reader by making a fool of her father before his public. Forced to sell the body of her text to support herself, she sells his along with it.

The very writing of her life becomes a complex effort at holding her father up for ransom in an act of filial blackmail. It affects a roguish fish slap in her father's face. She professes in the opening pages her disinterested desire to recover her father's affection; but such profession is fundamentally duplicitous. In fact, the material purposes of her "small treatise" are assuredly very real. Writing her life is her latest scheme for making money and easing her destitution. If her narrative wins her reconciliation with her father, she can count on his financial support to relieve her. Like the other schemes she chronicles throughout her narrative, however, this one proves to be just another failure: her father will not "buy" it. But her audience will; and so, when the first of her purposes fails, she continues to "sell" her life for her living, forced as she is by the economic exigencies she chronicles so effectively into an act of survival that if it fails to earn her reconciliation with her father, at least it earns her some money.

This middle-class daughter of a famous father seems, despite the very real destitution she experienced, to enjoy the writing of her autobiography, to take a perverse pleasure in recounting her romp through life as an outcast rogue, a woman defiant of all conventions, including the fundamental convention of sexual difference. The sexual cross-dressing that amplifies and thickens the pleasure of the text combines with the economic down-dressing, or cross-class dressing, to create an environment of intense disorder, social, sexual, and narrative. And yet Charke's autobiographical victory is a Pyrrhic one since the stories through which she fashions her life betray her in the end. While she provides her reader with a kind of autobiographical carnival, embedding in her story biographical fictions of her age, she does not recognize that the narrative patterns do not fit. Thus, as she cavorts with maternal and paternal narratives, they cavort with her. I noted above how the narrative of the sentimental penitent fails her. But Charke has always been more interested in paternal, rather than maternal, narratives; and it is the narratives of "masculine" selfhood that betray her most profoundly.

As Charke dons a man's story, cross-dressing narratively, she effectively unmasks her desire for a cultural life story that will bear significance, that will "speak" to her reader. In the story of the essentially good outcast who is thrown on the road to make "his" way in life, the narrative recalls that of Tom Jones. Yet, while she is like a Tom Jones thrown on the world as outcast, she is not a man, but a woman dressed as a man; and she is not a son who goes from bastardy to true filiality, but a daughter who falls from true filiality to a kind of metaphorical bastardy. Moreover, as a woman she cannot absorb the moral errancies of a Tom Jones into her tale. Tom is forgiven his healthy sexual desire. Charke must repress whatever desires she may have. There is no place for a female Tom Jones in her culture.

Nor do the stories of the prodigal and the criminal serve her any better. Playing the prodigal son, Charke informs her secular autobiography with typological references to the sacred text. Part of the "typological habits of mind" of the eighteenth century, this biblical type functioned as a popular cultural figure.[18] Yet the prodigal was a culturally valued figure of male selfhood, whose androcentric story fulfilled the culture's desire for both prodigality and reincorporation into community. In fact, rejection of the father and his authority became a sign of entry into the world of the fathers, a sign of manhood. It thereby became a figure of selfhood identified with formal autobiography. When Charke assumes the story line of the prodigal, therefore, she must wrench it to fit her story, "abstract[ing]" the biblical figure, "draw[ing it] away from the theological field of action" and embedding it in the detailed realism of a woman's sensational life story.[19] As the type is pressed through the specificities of Charke's strange story, it becomes too culturally distorted. In the end, the story of the prodigal wrapped around the story of a woman does not undermine the sanctity of the type so much as it undermines her attempt to add sanctity to her story. As a prodigal "son," she is more ridiculous than significant.

Her relationship to the story of "masculine" criminality is equally problematic. During the first half of the century especially, biographies of criminals and criminality itself captured the imagination of the English. In response to that cultural preoccupation and in turn promoting it, balladeers, pamphleteers, the new novelists (Defoe, Fielding, Smollet), prison officials—all wrote sensationalized biographies of rogues and criminals, both factual and fictional.[20] A source of great curiosity in an age enamored of the variety, eccentricities, and especially the excesses of human experience, such stories fed the culture's fascination for the narrative possibilities inherent in the lives of aberrant transgressors of social codes, laws, and relationships. Generally, however, criminal or rogue biographies of the eighteenth century served two disparate yet complementary purposes; and they told two stories. On the one hand, they spoke of grave yet exuberant transgression, ennobling the lives of figures rebellious against the laws of society and propriety. On the other, they spoke of penitence and eventual reintegration into community. After "threaten[ing] the world with disorder and with domination by the dark and often violent forces of evil," the criminal acknowledged his wrong ways and returned to the arms of social convention "so that society might be seen exercising its power to redeem the world and, in many cases, the criminal as well."[21] The structures of power within the church and the state were thereby reaffirmed, rebellion forestalled, subversiveness domesticated. Criminal biographies therefore fused titillating tales of the illicit with moralizing, sentimental tales of social rapprochement. Because they reflected both the prurient and the religious interests of the eighteenth century, criminal biographies and autobiographies "sold."[22]

Charke links her narrative explicitly to stories of criminality in the first passage of her text. She identifies herself as a female author who acknowledges the disadvantages of female authorship: "As the following History is the Product of a Female Pen, I tremble for the terrible Hazard it must run in venturing into the World, as it may very possibly suffer, in many Opinions, without perusing it" (11). Talking about the fate of female works, she alludes to the more general fate of females. For a woman (as for her work), "venturing into the World" is necessarily a "terrible Hazard" in the sense that such venturing is unconventional, improper, perhaps even illicit. Consequently, she pleads for special consideration: "I therefore humbly move for its having the common Chance of a Criminal, at least to be properly examin'd, before it is condemn'd" (11). Since Charke's grammar blurs the referent of "it," she forces an inelegant association between her "text" and a "criminal," the transgressor who, acting out of the ordinary, defies cultural codes.

Charke certainly challenges her culture's comfortable sense of its own order, revealing the fragilities of conventions and identities by providing an arena in which hierarchy is defied. Engaging in her masquerade she enters the arena of "transformation, mutability, and fluidity," where she becomes the amoral, sexually ambiguous protagonist defiant of social and sexual identities.[23] Further, her story insinuates a world of female-female relations into the text. After all, Charke describes how she traveled with a woman for many years; how they posed as man and wife; how various women fell in love with her.[24] The promise of female-female love masked by the male-female masquerade renders the life and the story even more disruptive of a social order founded on the patriarchal moralities of heterosexual relationship.

While Charke luxuriates in her "prodigal" and "criminal" masquerade, however, the story and the experience itself provide her with no illuminating moments. She is truly, as she claims in her dedication, "thoughtless" and intellectually "indolent." The masquerade in bit parts goes on and on, uninterrupted by any moment of truth before the gallows, any greater understanding of either her prodigality or her culture. The prodigal must understand the nature of prodigality, the inevitability of rebellion, and the relationship of son to father. Repentent criminals, seeing themselves for what they are, must acknowledge their crimes and seek forgiveness from society. Yet, because she plays them unself-consciously, cavalierly, neither the plot of the criminal nor that of the prodigal work for Charke. Incapable of anything more than a cavalier, unself-conscious performance, she leaves behind rhetoric with no understanding—a self-destructive bravado of language by which to declaim herself, quite entertaining but devastatingly vacuous. She becomes nothing but the polyglot of lines of stories fused together from the "orts and fragments" of her culture's stories. Narrative impersonation, the source of endless self-fabrication, becomes in Charke's life story the mechanism for self-cancellation, a dispersion of any idea of self into a series of bit parts played with rhetorical flourish.[25]

A Narrative of the Life of Mrs. Charlotte Charke offers its reader a voyeuristic romp through the disorders of male self-representation for woman. This woman who would be man leaves behind her a silence far greater than the silence signified in her father's blank page. She does not want to be woman. We see that in the repression of the mother's story, the suppression of the story of passion and sexual desire, the subversion of the story of sentimental penitent. She renders her sexual identity "impenetrable," erasing her female subjectivity from the story of man as she erases her female body in her man's clothes.[26] Yet as she becomes absorbed in male plots and masculine speaking postures, she loses her "self" precisely because she must erase the woman that she is. Self-denial is the price exacted of her in her flight toward male selfhood. Like the female figures of the nun and the queen, even the female rogue represses that which is the center of her being, her female sexuality, in pursuit of male autobiography. But she is not and cannot be man. Promising empowerment, male literary prototypes deliver only alienation, isolation, and self-delusion. Castle says of her that she is not only the victim of family, strangers, and fate, but also, and most important, a victim of literature.[27] More particularly, she is the victim of male "autobiography," in life and in her text.

A woman dressed as a man, Charke cannot place herself comfortably within the narratives of her culture. She is truly "peerless." With no self-illumination and self-reflectiveness, she cannot discover who and what she is. Charlotte Charke's autobiographical gesture is therefore a futile one. She fails in this narrative venture as she fails in venture after venture in life. She wins no emotional or financial reprieve from her father. But more significantly she wins through to no clearer understanding of her past, herself, or her sexuality. Betrayed by both maternal and paternal narratives and her own lack of reflectiveness about those narratives, she becomes only endless words strung together.

If Charlotte Charke had had more self-knowledge, less indolence and thoughtlessness, she might have pulled off a major subversion of the ideology of gender, a major disruption in the notion of autobiography. She certainly had the energy and spirit to do so. In embracing the "male" dress of narrative impersonation, however, Charke unwittingly affirms the priority of male autobiography, and thus the ordination of man over woman, of male storytelling over female storytelling. She may appear to be rebelling against a social ideology that constructs female selfhood in certain forms of dependency and passivity in her "male" fabrications; but in her flight from conventional female selfhood to male selfhood, she reaffirms the lineaments of the ideology of gender and thus serves the very fictions that confine her.

Charke's text is like the body of those prostitutes among whom she lived. Forced by fate and the waywardness of her own character to sell her self/text to make a living, she becomes to her culture the sign of misguided, fallen woman. Her "life" becomes one of those "exempla" her culture uses to secure the ideologies of gender on which it rests, to make sure that women do not aspire to empowering life scripts. To the extent that it dramatizes the fate of misguided womanhood, it confirms the patriarchal stories of her culture by dramatically showing the price woman pays for transgressing cultural conventions and patriarchal authority: the rootlessness, destitution, and eccentricity that attend the female outcast, especially the female outcast who "admitted and realized her desire to act forcefully."[28] The power of the sign is reflected in the words of the person who writes an introduction to the 1827 edition of her autobiography: her "life will serve to shew what very strange creatures may exist, and the endless diversity of habits, tastes and inclinations which may spring up spontaneously, like weeds, in the hot-bed of corrupt civilization."[29] It is reflected also in the words of the "Sequel": "The fate of this victim to an innate taste for eccentricity and vagabondism may excite surprise, but scarcely sympathy. Born in affluence, educated with care and tenderness, and possessed of at least respectable talents, the misfortunes of this extraordinary woman are altogether of her own creating."[30] Instead of challenging convention, Charke's story ends up supporting it.

The body of the unself-conscious prostitute serves the desires of others rather than the desires of the self. Or, rather, the desires of the prostitute become so confused and problematic that she cannot see herself through the role she plays. Charke titillates, but she does not discover her own source of desire. As a rebellious "son" who lacks self-reflectiveness, Charke fails to escape her dependency on the father. Instead of throwing off the father's power and assuming her own independence, she remains disempowered psychologically, financially, narrative-

ly, ideologically. As a result, she ends up serving rather than challenging the pleasure of the patriarchs or the ordination of masculine autobiography.

Notes

This essay previously appeared as "*A Narrative of the Life of Mrs. Charlotte Charke:* The
Transgressive Daughter and the Masquerade of Self-Representation," in Sidonie Smith,
A Poetics of Women's Autobiography: Marginality and the Fictions of Self-Representation
(Bloomington: Indiana University Press, 1987), 102–22, 196–98. Reprinted with minor
editorial changes by permission of the publisher.

1. *A Narrative of the Life of Mrs. Charlotte Charke (Youngest Daughter of COLLEY
CIBBER, Esq.), Written by HERSELF.* Ed. Leonard R. N. Ashley. (Gainesville: Scholars'
Facsimiles & Reprints, 1969), iii–iv. Subsequent citations appear in the text.

2. As Patricia Meyer Spacks notes in her discussion of Charke's autobiography, the
dedication is added to her story after Charke's father refuses to send his word of forgiveness in response to the early installments (Patricia Meyer Spacks, *Imagining a Self:
Autobiography and Novel in Eighteenth-Century England* [Cambridge: Harvard University Press, 1976], 82).

3. Ibid, 87.

4. Ibid, 78.

5. Ibid.

6. The autobiography was written in weekly installments over the course of eight
weeks, from about March 1 to April 19, 1755. The letter to her father is dated March 8.

7. Spacks emphasizes this story of victimization and vulnerability. As will become
clear, I place emphasis elsewhere.

8. For a discussion of the late eighteenth century's critical response to the impact
the new novel might have on women, see John Tinnon Taylor, *Early Opposition to the
English Novel: The Popular Reaction from 1760 to 1830* (New York: King's Crown Press,
1943), 87–101.

9. Spacks briefly alludes to Charke's "ceaseless efforts to make her utility equivalent
to that of a boy" (76).

10. For discussion of the rogue in eighteenth-century literature, see such works as
Frank Wadleigh Chandler, *The Literature of Roguery,* 2 vols. (New York: Burt Franklin,
1958); Richard Bjornson, *The Picaresque Hero in European Fiction* (Madison: University of Wisconsin Press, 1977); and Jerry C. Beasley, *Novels of the 1740s* (Athens: University of Georgia Press, 1982).

11. Cynthia Merrill notes that Charke's choice of the male name "Mr. Brown" serves
a double purpose (Cynthia Merrill, "Autobiography as Cross-Dressing: 'A Narrative
of Mrs. Charlotte Charke,'" paper presented at "Autobiography and Biography: Gender, Text and Context," conference, Stanford University, April 11–13, 1986 [subsequent
references are to "the Stanford conference"]). Obviously the name is masculine. But

it is also the married name of the sister who opposes her. Thus in the name is captured her desire to masquerade as a man and her desire to be reconciled as a dutiful daughter. Merrill's analysis of Charke's text, similar to my own, emphasizes the "masculine" storytelling at the expense of the "feminine" storytelling in Charke's autobiography.

12. Terry Castle served as the respondent to Merrill's paper on Charke at the Stanford conference. In a flurry of provocative comments, Castle established certain questions that remain central in considering the phenomenon of cross-dressing for women of earlier centuries.

13. See Terry Castle, "The Carnivalization of Eighteenth-Century English Narrative," *PMLA* 99 (Oct. 1984): 903–16. In her eloquent essay on the masquerade in eighteenth-century literature, Castle argues that the scene of masquerade functions subversively on three levels. While Castle specifically explores the psychological, ideological, and narrative impact of such scenes in the century's fiction, the insights she offers about fictive scenes provide interesting ways of approaching Charke's autobiographical masquerade.

14. Paul John Eakin, *Fictions in Autobiography: Studies in the Art of Self-Invention* (Princeton: Princeton University Press, 1985), 226.

15. I refer here, à la Eakin, to the title of James Olney, *Metaphors of Self: The Meaning of Autobiography* (Princeton: Princeton University Press, 1972).

16. Eakin, *Fictions*, 226.

17. Donald A. Stauffer, *The Art of Biography in Eighteenth-Century England* (Princeton: Princeton University Press, 1941), 109. Spacks also comments on Stauffer's description.

18. Avrom Fleishman, *Figures of Autobiography: The Language of Self-Writing in Victorian and Modern England* (Berkeley: University of California Press, 1983), 88.

19. Paul J. Korshin, "The Development of Abstracted Typology in England, 1650–1820," in *Literary Uses of Typology from the Late Middle Ages to the Present* (Princeton: Princeton University Press, 1977), ed. Earl Miner, 148, quoted in Fleishman, 87.

20. For a discussion of the attraction of the century to stories of criminality, see Lennard J. Davis, *Factual Fictions: The Origins of the English Novel* (New York: Columbia University Press, 1983), chapter 7.

21. Beasley, *Novels of the 1740s*, 99.

22. Davis, *Factual Fictions*, 126–31.

23. Castle, "Carnivalization," 905.

24. Interestingly, in September 1746 a certain Mary Hamilton was tried for fraud in a series of events similar to those narrated by Charke. Hamilton, dressed as a man, had proposed to and married a Mary Price in July 1746. Within two months the fraud was discovered, but not before, as court records and news accounts reveal, Hamilton had sexually violated "her" wife. The bizarre story was apparently common knowledge, for Henry Fielding wrote a pamphlet entitled "The Female Husband" based on Hamilton's story. We can only speculate about the effect that his previous story might have had on the perceived sensationalism of Charke's life story in the minds of her readers

and in her own mind. For a discussion of the Hamilton case and of Fielding's author-ship of "The Female Husband," see Sheridan Baker, "Henry Fielding's *The Female Husband:* Fact and Fiction," *PMLA* 74 (June 1959): 213–24.

25. For a discussion of the relationship of self-fashioning to self-cancellation, see Stephen Jay Greenblatt, *Renaissance Self-Fashioning: From More to Shakespeare* (Chi-cago: University of Chicago Press, 1980), esp. chapter 1.

26. In her comments at the Stanford conference, Castle asked how the literary crit-ic could "penetrate the seemingly impenetrable sexuality" of the cross-dressed sub-ject.

27. Castle, commentary at the Stanford conference.

28. Spacks, *Imagining,* 83.

29. Charlotte Charke, *A Narrative of the Life of Charlotte Charke, Youngest Daughter of Colley Cibber, Esq.* (London: Hunt and Clarke, 1827), vi–vii.

30. Ibid., 167.

4

The Guilty Pleasures of Female Theatrical Cross-Dressing and the Autobiography of Charlotte Charke

Kristina Straub

A curious shift in theatrical cross-dressing took place in late seventeenth-century England. For a variety of complex reasons still being explored by some of our most interesting critics of sexuality and gender in the theater,[1] the tradition of boys playing women's parts on the stage became at best an outmoded fashion and at worst an unacceptable breach of gender boundaries for contemporary audiences. At the same time, of course, women entered the acting profession to play female characters. A growing capacity to perceive gender ambiguity and to find it troubling did not, however, result in the prohibiting of female theatrical cross-dressing, as it did in the limitation of the masculine version to travesty. The cross-dressed actress came into a fashion that lasted, not without changes, throughout the century. Whereas obvious travesty was crucial to the acceptance of male cross-dressing on the early eighteenth-century stage (the actor must be seen as a bad parody of femininity), it seems to have become so for female cross-dressers only in the second half of the century. At midcentury, commentary on female theatrical cross-dressers suggests that the ambiguity that was then intolerable when associated with a male was in fact part of the fun of seeing women in breeches. By the end of the century, discourse about the cross-dressed actress is both more condemnatory of the practice (which was still, however, tolerated) and more insistent that female cross-dressing, like the male, was mere travesty, an obvious parody that left gender boundaries unquestioned.

The cross-dressed actress of the early to mid-eighteenth century seems to constitute a historical possibility for pleasure in sexual and gender ambiguities. This possibility calls into question the naturalness of an economy of spectatorial pleasure that works on the premise of rigid boundaries between categories of gender and sexuality—male/female, hetero/homosexual. It asks us to unpack dominant constructions of the commodified feminine spectacle as unambiguously oppositional and other to a spectatorial, consuming male gaze.[2] Pat Rogers argues that the eighteenth-century female theatrical cross-dresser was part of a specular economy that fits our present assumptions of an objectified femininity in binary opposition to a masculine gaze. While Rogers is correct up to a point, I will argue here that the commodification of the cross-dressed actress was in fact a good deal more complicated in its audience appeal and that, hence, the cross-dressed actress is less a confirmation than a challenge to modern assumptions about the gendering of spectacle.

Popular discourse about the cross-dressed actress suggests that in midcentury England the female theatrical cross-dresser did not fit the constructions of gender and sexuality that would seem to render natural two key concepts in the modern sex-gender system: (1) the subjugation of a feminine spectacle to the dominance of the male gaze, and (2) the exclusive definition of feminine sexual desire in terms of its relation to masculine heterosexual desire. The autobiographical *Narrative of the Life of Mrs. Charlotte Charke,* a notorious account of an actress who carried her masquerades in male clothes into her life off the boards, is a particularly powerful example of how the cross-dressed actress might function in a way discursively at odds with these two concepts.

The obvious reason for dressing actresses in men's clothes at the end of the seventeenth century is virtually the same as one of the reasons for putting women on the stage at all: conventionally attractive female bodies sell tickets. Judith Milhous documents the popularity of female cross-dressing on the stage during the Restoration and links it to economic competition among the licensed London theaters.[3] Sometimes competing managers did not stop with casting single roles, but rather, as James Wright's history documents, presented whole plays "all by women, as formerly all by men" (cliii). The same incentive seems to have motivated John Mossop to cast the actress Catley as Macheath during the keen competition among theaters in Dublin at midcentury (Hitchcock 2:135), and Tate Wilkinson, as a manager, clearly had receipts in mind when, in the 1795 *Wandering Patentee,* he refers to actresses who look well in the "small clothes." One might say truthfully that the cross-dressing actress was, in the last instance, economically motivated, an example of the commodification of women in emergent capitalist society. But this commodification itself cannot be reduced to the specularization of women within the structuring principle of the masculine observer and the feminine spectacle, an epistemological and psychological principle that may have been only emergent at this moment in history. The commodification of the cross-dressed actress embodied ideological contradictions about the nature of feminine identity and sexuality; contemporary discourse about this commodification yields a complex picture of what, exactly, is being marketed.

First, as long as the cross-dressed actress was "packaged" as a commodity for the pleasure of her audience, responses to her suggest that her marketability had as much to do with a playfully ambiguous sexual appeal as with the heterosexually defined attractions of her specularized feminine body. Duality is part of the sexual appeal of the cross-dressed Margaret Woffington, one of the eighteenth century's most written-about cross-dressers. Woffington's 1760 *Memoirs* record the reaction of both sexes to her first appearance as Harry Wildair in *The Constant Couple;* the men, it is said, were charmed, and the "Females were equally well pleased with her acting as the Men were, but could not persuade themselves, that it was a Woman that acted the Character" (22). Woffington's ambiguity is presented as a commodity in which the audience takes great pleasure:

> When first in Petticoats you trod the Stage,
> Our Sex with Love you fir'd, your own with Rage!
> In Breeches next, so well you play'd the Cheat,
> The pretty Fellow, and the Rake compleat—
> Each sex, were then, with different Passions mov'd,
> The Men grew envious, and the Women loved. (Victor 3:4–5)

Similarly, a 1766 *Life* of James Quinn declares that "it was a most nice point to decide between the gentlemen and the ladies, whether she [Woffington] was the finest woman, or the prettiest fellow" (67–68).

Some of the pleasure afforded by the spectacle of the cross-dressed actress arose, then, out of the doubling of sexual attraction. The actress in men's clothes appeals to both men and women—at least as a specular commodity. This double appeal, however, depends on its containment as a theatrical commodity; offstage in the "real" world, the cross-dressed actress was usually represented in the tradition of women who dressed as men for the arousal and/or gratification of heterosexual male desire (Dekker and van de Pol 54). Popular stories about the adventures of actresses who cross-dressed out of role nearly always bracket their ambiguous sexual appeal in a narrative that privileges both an exclusively heterosexual desire and the actress's function therein. *The Comforts of Matrimony* reports that Susannah Maria Cibber crossdressed off the stage in order to facilitate her amour with William Sloper (24). Susanna Centlivre's quasi-mythical affair with Anthony Hammond was allegedly carried out by her posing as his younger "Cousin Jack" and living with Hammond while he was a student at Oxford (Mottley 185–86; Dibden 2:313). Catherine Galendo draws on this tradition when she accuses Sarah Siddons of learning the role of Hamlet in order to have the excuse to take fencing lessons from, and subsequently to seduce, her husband Mr. Galendo (16).

In another story, Woffington is said to have caused her female rival for a male lover's affections to fall in love with her, but the narrative sets this "confusion" of gender roles and sexual object choice in the context of the actress's efforts to foil her lover's infidelities. These narratives effectively define the "safe" limits of the cross-dressed actress's ambiguous appeal; as a specular commodity, the gender and sexual confusion associated with the actress could be a source of pleasure as long as it did not contaminate or compromise dominant narratives of heterosexual desire.

In this sense, discourse about the cross-dressed actress takes part in the discursive construction placed upon the eighteenth-century woman lover of women. This construction offers certain pleasures—ranging, perhaps, from voyeuristic to identificatory—in the representation of sexuality between women while paradoxically (and guiltily) tending either to deny or brutally erase the possibility of "real" sexual desire between women. Lillian Faderman's historical work on "lesbianism" in the eighteenth century suggests two dominant models for female same-sex sexuality: the romantic friendship and the "pornographic" representation of sexual "toying" between women as an adjunct to, and preparatory arousal for, the "real" thing of heterosexual intercourse. In the former model, eroticism is essentially erased, while in the latter, same-sex eroticism, like the sexual ambiguities of cross-dressed actresses, is framed within a heterosexual narrative. In either instance, sexuality—at least, "real" sexuality—between women is denied. Martha Vicinus, Rudolf M. Dekker, and Lotte C. van de Pol additionally identify cross-dressing women as possible female homosexual "types," and Vicinus refers to women, such as Marie Antoinette, whose usurpation of public male roles led to their labeling as sexually, as well as politically, "unnatural." In the first case, the cross-dressing woman is typed as a danger if she usurps masculine roles by taking on the legal form of husband in marriage or using a dildo in intercourse. In the second, the sexually "deviate" woman is represented as such for having already presumed to her right to masculine privilege. As Lynne Friedli points out, same-sex sexuality is usually seen as dangerous or evil in the eighteenth century only when a male prerogative is usurped by a woman. In this usurpation lies, perhaps, a source of guilt within the pleasures afforded by such representations of the cross-dressing woman, a cause of anxiety that runs through discourse about the cross-dressing actress.

Eighteenth-century discourse about the cross-dressed actress evinces an unqualified pleasure in sexual confusion only when that confusion is "for sale" as a theatrical commodity, an obviously artificial construction. A slightly guilty pleasure in the sexual and gender confusion embodied in the cross-dressed actress is balanced against recuperations of her gender bending within dominant sexual ideologies. This recuperative discourse often reveals, however, the very anxieties that it seeks to allay. By the mid-eighteenth century, the cross-dressed actress is the focus of rules and strictures that seek to confine her pleasurable ambiguities of sex and gender to a narrowly defined phenomenon, an illusion to be bought and kept within the marketplace of the theater. This discourse of containment voices a "monstrosity" with which the sexually ambiguous actress flirts and reveals an incipient threat to heterosexual male dominance implicit within the pleasurable ambiguity of the cross-dressed actress.

Despite the pervasiveness and popularity of the custom, commentators on cross-dressing actresses express an uneasiness about this phenomenon that can be read in their desire, by midcentury, to contain it within decorous rules, to defuse the threat of this otherwise entertaining ambiguity by referring it to a "natural" standard or social "law." This discourse of containment also speaks, however, the fears that it seeks to contain. Besides framing the pleasure afforded by the cross-dressed actress within proscriptive rules, it articulates, I would argue, the sources of anxiety about that pleasure. First, it gives voice to fears about the stability and certainty of an emergent dominant definition of masculine sexuality as it is reflected (and refracted) in the cross-dressed female's image. Second, it speaks fears that femininity may itself exceed the limits of privacy and domesticity that would seem, in dominant ideologies, to define it. In short, the cross-dressed actress is seen as threatening to the construction of a stable oppositional relationship between male and female gender and sexuality.

Biographical discourse about cross-dressing actresses becomes increasingly condemnatory by the early nineteenth century. James Boaden refers unequivocally to "vile and beastly transformations" in 1825 (*Kemble* 2:334); his repulsion at female theatrical transvestism seems to reflect the emergent consciousness of a category for "deviate" female sexuality that is documented by Randolph Trumbach in "London's Sapphists." But even as early as 1761 one can read an incipient uneasiness with the ideological effects of female theatrical transvestism. Benjamin Victor, a London theater prompter and manager of one of the Dublin theaters during the age of Garrick, reveals even more clearly what is veiled in Boaden's Victorian prose on the subject: fears about the integrity and "naturalness" of feminine gender identity. His discussion of Woffington's famous role of Sir Harry Wildair candidly states the economic motive—"she always conferred a Favour upon the Managers whenever she changed her Sex, and filled their Houses"—the cross-dressed actress as pleasurable and lucrative commodity. But he sets limits on this form of commodification: "And now, ye fair ones of the Stage, it will not be foreign to the Subject, to consider whether it is proper for you . . . to perform the Characters of Men. I will venture in the Name of all sober, discreet, sensible, Spectators . . . to answer *No!* there is something required *so much beyond the Delicacy of your Sex,* to arrive at the Point of Perfection, that, if you hit it, you may be condemned as a Woman, and if you do not, you are injured as an Actress" (2:4, 5–6, my emphasis). To masquerade as a man, and to do it too well, is to enter a no-woman's-land "beyond" femininity, to exceed the limits of "delicacy."

Furthermore, this trespassing beyond the limits of femininity may lead to ambiguities in sexual object choice that Victor plainly finds disturbing as he continues to address his hypothetical "fair ones of the Stage":

> supposing you are formed in Mind, and Body . . . like the Actress in Question—for she had Beauty, Shape, Wit, and Vivacity, equal to any theatrical Female in any Time, and capable of any Undertaking in the Province of Comedy, nay of deceiving, and warming into Passion, any of her own Sex, if she had been unknown, and introduced as a young Baronet just returned from his Travels—but still, I say, admirable and admired as she was in this Part, I would not have any other Female of the Stage attempt the Character after her. (3:6)

Victor's nervousness focuses on the sexual as well as gender ambiguity of Woffington in male dress; she is clearly an object of desire, but the question of who might desire her is carefully hedged in the hypothetical—"*if* she had been unknown." Finally, however, he does not, like Boaden, condemn actresses in male dress but rather retreats from the hypothetical threat of Woffington as ambiguous sexual object to the relative safety of theatrical tradition and rule: "the wearing of Breeches merely to pass for a Man, as is the Case in many Comedies, is as far as the Metamorphosis ought to go, and indeed, more than some formal Critics will allow of; but that custom is established into a Law, and as there is great Latitude in it, it should not be in the least extended—when it is, you *o'erstep the Modesty of Nature,* and when that is done, whatever may be the Appearance within Doors, you will be injured by Remarks and Criticisms without" (3:7). Victor seems to have in mind characters, such as Rosalind, whose masquerades as men are clearly represented *as* masquerades to the audience. By designating female transvestism as a specific form of theatrical illusion, Victor limits the threat of Woffington's ambiguous attractions; but he goes beyond this designation to demand that the illusion be presented as an illusion—further distancing the threat and containing the ambiguity of the cross-dressed actress within a decorum of theatrical representation.

Later writers on the theater apparently want to exclude ambiguity altogether, not being content with containing it within rules. When ambiguity resists erasure, they often simply insist, all logic and evidence to the contrary, that it confirms the very gender definitions it would seem to problematize. William Cooke writes in 1804 that female cross-dressing should not leave room for any ambiguity. "Where a woman . . . personates a man *pro tempore* . . . the closer the imitation is made, the more we applaud the performer, but always in the knowledge that the object before us is *a woman assuming the character of a man*" (3:6). Unlike Victor, however, who allows for ambiguous sexual attraction in Woffington's impersonation, Cooke dismisses even the possibility of successful illusion in a woman's assuming a masculine position in the sexual economy:

> when this same woman totally usurps the male character, and we are left to try her merits merely as a man, without making the least allowance for the imbecilities of the other sex, we may safely pronounce, there is no woman, nor ever was a woman, who can fully supply this character. There is such a *reverse* in all the habits and modes of the two sexes, acquired from the very cradle upwards, that it is next to an impossibility for the one to resemble the other so as totally to escape detection. (126)

By 1800, theater historians and biographers tend to exclude the ambiguity that Victor barely admits within the "rules" of cross-dressing. Boaden writes of Siddons's Hamlet (which he never saw), that "the unconstrained motion would be wanting for the most part; modesty would be sometimes rather untractable in the male habit, and the conclusion at last might be, 'were she *but* man, she would exceed all that man has ever achieved in Hamlet'" (*Siddons* 1:283). Of Dorothy Jordan playing the part of William in Brooke's *Rosina*, Boaden confidently asserts that "Did the lady really look like a man, the coarse *androgynus* would be hooted from the stage" (*Jordan* 1:46) and reads Woffington's famous Wildair through his observations of Jordan:

> When Woffington took it up, she did what she was not aware of, namely, that the audience permitted the actress to *purify* the character, and enjoyed the language from

> a woman, which might have disgusted from a man speaking before women . . . I am
> convinced that no creature there supposed it [Woffington a man] for a moment: it
> was the *travesty,* seen throughout, that really constituted the charm of your perfor-
> mance, and rendered it not only gay, but innocent. And thus it was with Mrs. Jor-
> dan, who, however beautiful in her figure, stood confessed a perfect and decided
> woman; and courted, intrigued, and quarrelled, and cudgelled, in whimsical imita-
> tion of the ruder man. (*Jordan* 1:127)

Rather incredibly, Boaden writes of Woffington's trespasses into the discourse
of a rake as if they were attempts to clean up scenes in which the male character talks of sex to a woman. The cross-dressed actress is made to serve the
dominant construction of separate spheres for men and women even as she
would seem to trepass against that separation.

This erasure of sexual ambiguity is more characteristic of biographical texts
late in the century. At midcentury, attempts to contain female cross-dressing
within rules of tradition or "nature" tend more often to name what they seek
to exclude. *The Actor* (1750?) explicitly targets the sexual content of Woffington's impersonation as objectionable: "We see women sometimes act the parts
of men, and in all but love we approve them. Mrs. Woffington pleases in Sir
Harry Wildair in every part, except where she makes love; but there no one of
the audience ever saw her without disgust; it is insipid, or it is worse; it conveys no ideas at all, or very hateful ones; and either the insensibility, or the
disgust we conceive, quite break in upon the delusion" (202). The choice between "no ideas at all" and "very hateful ones" sums up the two-pronged threat
implied in female cross-dressing, a threat that is both expressed and contained
by the biographical discourse we have been examining. First, the spectacle of
women representing masculine sexuality summons the threat of a nondomi-
nant, nonauthoritative—even impotent—masculinity. Women assuming
masculine sexual prerogative are "insipid," and their lovemaking "conveys no
ideas at all"; they are, in short, failed men and, as such, would seem to offer
no threat whatsoever to masculine sexuality. But, as I will argue, the "castrated" figure of the cross-dressed actress is also capable of holding a mirror up
to masculinity that reflects back an image of castration that cannot be entirely controlled by the mechanisms of projection. When the actress puts on masculine sexuality, even as she functions as its object of desire, she opens possibilities for challenging the stability and authority of that sexuality.

Second, the actress in male dress summons up, in the very act of specular-
izing the feminine object of desire, the "hateful" idea of a feminine sexual desire
that exceeds the limits of "normal" heterosexual romantic love. The "Tommy,"
as Trumbach says, is a category for "deviate" feminine sexuality that seems to

emerge late in the eighteenth century ("London's Sapphists"). Homophobia can certainly be seen, in chillingly recognizable forms, in Cooke's denials of sexual or gender ambiguities in cross-dressed performances or in Boaden's disgust at "vile and beastly transformations." But even as early as midcentury, discourse about female theatrical cross-dressing evinces an awareness that feminine sexuality and gender identity could stray beyond the boundaries that were coming to define the sphere of feminine feeling and behavior as man's commensurate and oppositional other. The cross-dressed actress points to a feminine desire in excess of this role, and in this case that desire is explicitly sexual. The cross-dressed actress threatened the apparent naturalness and stability of what was becoming dominant gender ideology by suggesting a feminine sexuality that exceeded the heterosexual role of women.

Charlotte Charke's autobiographical *Narrative of the Life of Mrs. Charlotte Charke* incorporates many of the characteristics of the cross-dressed actress in another commodity guise: Charke, badly in need of money, gives a textual performance of her adventures in male clothes. Charke was the daughter of the actor Colley Cibber, and an unsuccessful actress of male roles who went through an exhausting number of professions in her attempts to support herself and her daughter. Charke was a self-proclaimed "Proteus" whose special talent seems to have been for acting out a complete instability of roles.

Instability also comes into play in the question of sexual object choice in her text. After her marriage and separation at a young age, Charke's romantic encounters in the *Narrative* consistently involve a smitten woman who mistakes Charke's gender. While she claims never to have taken the "male prerogative" in love, Charke's text refuses the common recuperative strategy of framing the sexually ambiguous cross-dressed woman in a heterosexual narrative. Refusing to resolve the sexual ambiguities of her textual performance by giving her audience either a heterosexually defined romantic heroine or a "monstrous" female husband, Charke fails to participate in what was becoming the dominant construction of feminine sexuality: the woman as oppositional, defining other to male sexuality. Her masquerades in male dress refuse dominant sexuality in two respects. First, they gesture toward the performative nature of male sexuality, questioning its "naturalness" through strategic mimicry. Second, they elude both the strategies of recuperation and marginalization by rhetorically evoking and refusing the most dangerous resolution of sexual ambiguity—the "monstrous" figure of the female husband.

Charke's actual as well as figurative cross-dressing in the text parodies masculinity in the specific form of her father, the infamous Cibber. Actors, as we have seen, often embodied outlaw, at best ambivalent forms of masculine sexuality in the eighteenth century, and Cibber's old-fashioned rakishness, combined with his homoerotic subservience to aristocratic male patrons, had already established him as marginal to dominant masculinities at midcentury. Charke's mimicry of what was already an increasingly marginalized version of masculinity resists the ideology of a dominant masculinity based on its authoritative opposition to the "feminine." Charke's textual cross-dressing acts out with a vengeance a threat posed by the cross-dressed actress as a reflection of "failed," ideologically inadequate masculinities. Feminist psychoanalytic theory provides a modern analogue to the implicit threat that the cross-dressed actress posed to the dominant version of masculinity. The "insipid," sexually impotent actress in rake's clothes calls attention to the conditional nature of virility in much the same way that the "castrated" woman gestures toward the instability of phallic masculinity in psychoanalytic theory.

Kaja Silverman writes that a potential for reminding men of the tenuousness of the connection between the penis and phallic control is implicit in the psychoanalytic mechanism by which men project their fears of castration onto women as "castrated" men. "It is hardly surprising," she says, "that at the heart of woman's otherness there remains something strangely familiar, something which impinges dangerously upon male subjectivity. From the very outset, the little boy is haunted by this similitude—by the fear of becoming like his sexual other. That fear . . . indicates that what is now associated with the female subject has been transferred to her from the male subject, and that the transfer is by no means irreversible" (17–18). The cross-dressed woman would seem to be a particularly poignant reminder of this reversibility. If we think of the eighteenth-century phenomenon of anxiety about the cross-dressed actress in these terms, we can see why the actress who takes on a masculine role in the representation of sexuality must be doubly surrounded by a discourse that brands her as "insipid"—or castrated. Otherwise, she hints too strongly at the reversibility of transference and the instability of the sexual roles that make that transference possible.

The function of woman as the mirror in which man glimpses his own castration is useful in thinking about an eighteenth-century cultural phenomenon that intersects with that of the cross-dressed actress. What Silverman points out about the modern psychoanalytic relation between man and his "castrated" feminine counterpart suggests that anxiety about masculinity may be implicit in such oppositional structures of gender and sexuality as were emergent in the eighteenth century. Hence, it is not surprising to see in the latter half of the eighteenth century a recurrent, almost obsessive discourse against the "masculinization" of women. The widespread critique of women who dressed and behaved in too masculine a fashion is an aspect of the emerging construction of femininity along domestic and private lines. But the insistence that women conform to an increasingly rigid definition of femininity is also, as Armstrong suggests, linked to the formation of a masculinity increasingly posed as the opposite of that definition.[4] Midcentury discourse links anxieties about the masculinization of women to worries about the feminization of men—or, to be more precise, the latter's "deviance" from dominant masculinity. The masculinized woman is, literally, a mirror image of the castrated man.

In a crucial passage written just after midcentury, George Colman writes that "in the moral system there seems at present to be going on a kind of Country-Dance between the Male and Female Follies and Vices, in which they have severally crossed over, and taken each other's places. The men are growing delicate and refined, and the women free and easy" (2:87–88). Colman follows this statement with a series of gender reversals that culminate in a sexually "deviate" masculine figure that seems to be the dark heart of reversal. Women rape men, men are kept by women, but the figure that results from this "Country-Dance" is that of the macaroni: "There is indeed a kind of animal neither male nor female, a thing of the neuter gender, lately started up amongst us. It is called a Macaroni" (2:88–91). The primary fear that emerges from this discourse of anxiety about gender reversal is summed up in the figure of the "thing" that eludes dominant structures of gender definition: the male who fails to assume his "masculine" role, in Arthur Murphy's terms, "the pretty gentlemen, who chose to unsex themselves, and make a display of delicacy that exceeded female softness" (1:118).

In this discourse of reversal, the masculinized woman is a divining rod for detecting the failure of men to live up to the demands of dominant masculinity. In Garrick's *The Male Coquette* a cross-dressed female character exposes the falseness of the "male coquette"; the moral of the play, according to Murphy, is that while "Coquetting in the fair is loss of fame; / In the male sex [it] takes a detested name, / That marks the want of manhood, virtue, sense, and shame" (1:309). Aaron Hill's earlier prologue to *Euridice,* spoken by "Miss Robinson, in boy's cloaths," specifically makes the cross-dressed actress into a rhetorical device for attacking "failed" masculinity:

> . . . farewel to *petticoats,* and *stitching;*
> And welcome dear, dear *breeches,* more bewitching!
> Henceforth, new-moulded, I'll rove, love, and wander,
> And fight, and storm, and charm, like *Periander.*
> Born, for this *dapper age,* pert, short, and clever,

If e'er I grow a *man*, 'tis now, or never.
Should I *belov'd*—gadson—how then—no matter,
I'll bow, as *you* do—and *look foolish* at her.
And so, who knows, that never meant to *prove* ye,
But I'm as *good a man,* as any of ye. (*Works* 2:334–35)

The encroachments of the cross-dressed actress upon the territory of masculine sexuality are especially threatening since they seem to imply the inability of men to hold that territory. It is not surprising, then, that Woffington's 1760 biographer is quick to deny her the power of playing the sexually aggressive character of Lothario: "yet for a Woman, in such a Character as *Lothario,* to personate that gay, perfidious Libertine, was an absurd, an inconsistent and an impotent attempt. They [Woffington's critics] evidently proved, that any Sentence, which came from the Mouth of the *supposed Lothario,* lost its Force, by being played by a Woman . . . those who were capable of judging impartially . . . agreed that she was absolutely unfit for the character, and played it with all the Impotence of mere Endeavour" (31). The cross-dressed actress must be marked as impotent lest she imply, by cultural association, the impotence of the "real thing." But, paradoxically, her impotence mirrors back the newly constructed nature of what was coming to be the age's dominant masculinity.

Charke's mimicry of Cibber plays on anxieties about masculine identity that are implicit in discourse about cross-dressed actresses. Sidonie Smith has argued that the *Narrative* reveals Charke's failure to "be a man" (110–11), to assume and use the authorial power invested in masculinity. I would suggest that Charke's "failures" at putting on masculinity are, in fact, parodic repetitions of some of her father's more infamous differences from an authoritative, heard-but-not-seen masculine subject. Charke puts on the guise of masculinity in order to put her father on, and in the process she gestures toward a performative, "unnatural" masculinity that unsettles newly dominant assumptions about gender as legitimized according to fixed and oppositional categories.

The theatrical contexts of Charke's *Narrative* were more than usually hospitable to the production and reception of mimicry. First, an autobiography by an actress who was well known for playing parodic versions of her father for Henry Fielding at the Haymarket created its own context for reading Charke's cross-dressing in relation to Cibber. Second, the practice of players mimicking other players onstage was a well-established custom in which Charke herself took an enthusiastic part. Finally, Charke simply joined something of a family tradition by mimicking her father in print. As a parody of Cibber's memoirs, Charke's *Narrative* followed Ralph and Fielding's *Apology*

for the life of her brother, Theophilus, one of many print attacks on her father. After Theophilus's fake *Apology,* no emulation of Colley Cibber could go
innocent into the world. Charke's literary cross-dressing works across the
contexts of both theatrical mimicry and feminine theatrical cross-dressing.
Both contexts frame her autobiography as an unsettling representation of a
daughter aping a father whose masculinity is already becoming questionable
within dominant gender ideology.

The *Narrative* repeats portions of Cibber's *Apology,* with Charke picking up
and putting on many of her father's most distinctive postures. Charke carries
on her father's exhibitionism, and her cheerful promise "to conceal nothing that
might raise a Laugh" (17) echoes her father's "But why make my Follies publick? Why not? I have pass'd my Time very pleasantly with them" (5). Early in
the text she literalizes these more literary imitations of her father through the
account of her cross-dressing in imitation of her father at "four Years of Age":

> Having, even then, a passionate Fondness for a Perriwig, I crawl'd out of Bed one
> Summer's Morning at *Twickenham,* where my Father had Part of a House and Gar-
> dens for the Season, and, taking it into my small Pate, that by Dint of a Wig and a
> Waistcoat, I should be the perfect Representative of my Sire, I crept softly into the
> Servants-Hall, in Order to perpetuate the happy Design I had framed for the next
> Morning's Expedition. Accordingly, I paddled down Stairs, taking with me my Shoes,
> Stockings, and little Dimity Coat which I artfully contrived to pin up, as well as I
> could, to supply the want of a Pair of Breeches. By the help of a long Broom, I took
> down a Waistcoat of my Brother's, and an enormous bushy Tie-wig of my Father's,
> which entirely enclosed my Head and Body, with the Knots of the Ties thumping
> my little Heels as I marched along, with slow and solemn Pace. The Covert of Hair
> in which I was concealed, with the Weight of a monstrous Belt and large Silver-hilt-
> ed Sword, that I could scarce drag along, was a vast Impediment in my Procession:
> And, what still added to the other Inconveniences I laboured under, was whelming
> myself under one of my Father's large Beaver-hats, laden with Lace, as thick and
> broad as a Brickbat. (17–18)

In some sense, cross-dressing in this passage is fraught with debilitating contradictions: Charke seems, literally, weighed down by her attempt to put on
her father's authority. She marches up and down in a ditch to conceal her girl's
shoes and "walked myself into a Fever, in the happy Thought of being taken
for the 'Squire" (19). The joke is on her, in that respect, but not only on her, I
would argue.

In his *Apology,* Cibber also struts his stuff in a periwig that took on the status of a trademark in his career. Cibber recounts his meeting with the young
blade Henry Brett as taking place on account of such a wig: "And though,

possibly, the Charms of our Theatrical Nymphs might have their Share, in drawing him thither; yet in my Observation, the most visible Cause of his first coming, was a sincere Passion he had conceiv'd for a fair full-bottom'd Perriwig, which I then wore in my first Play of the *Fool in Fashion,* in the Year of 1695." Cibber goes on to eroticize the wig even further by comparing Brett's "attack" on his wig to that of "young Fellows . . . upon a Lady of Pleasure" (202). Charke's choice of her father's periwig as her object of desire is hard to read as innocent of these associations, particularly since the main source of the joke on herself—the disparity between her little body and the huge wig—echoes a similar disparity between Cibber and his famous headpiece. Lord Foppington's periwig in Vanbrugh's play is spoken of as engulfing Cibber just as it engulfed his daughter; Cibber's character wears it down to his "heels," covering all, as he says, but his eyes. Pope trotted out the same wig in his notes to the 1742 *Dunciad,* quoting the passage above from the *Apology,* with the additional information that "This remarkable Periwig usually made its entrance upon the state in a sedan, brought in by two chairmen, with infinite approbation of the audience" (728).

The joke was further compounded by the popular association of the full-bottomed periwig with actors' narcissism and exhibitionism. Joe Haines is depicted in an early eighteenth-century engraving speaking his famous prologue seated upon an ass; both actor and ass sport fine examples of the flowing wig. By Charke's time, the full-bottomed periwig was considered old-fashioned, and actors who continued to wear them were considered ridiculous. Charke's "fondness" for a periwig reads in this context more like a parodic comment on her father's earlier professional pose as Lord Foppington than like a serious desire to emulate her father.

Charke's parodic restaging of Cibber's masculine masquerade makes female transvestism as much about the ambiguity of masculine sexuality as about a woman's failed attempt to put on masculine authority. Her mimicry of her father's text marks her own distance from the masculine role she puts on, but it also marks that role *as a role*, gestures toward the artificiality—and tenuousness—of the masculinity that she, in turn, puts on. Charke's cross-dressing indicates her failure to be her father, but it also throws into relief the constructed, ambiguous, and even self-parodying nature of that father's authority.

Charke evokes the powerful trope of paternal authority (and her own daughterly devotion) only to present scenarios that explode the gendered constructions of father and daughter. She tells us, for example, of a rumor in circulation ("a most villainous Lye") that she had turned highwayman and robbed her father at gunpoint, reducing him to tears and promises of reconciliation by her threat to "discharge upon him." She comments that this is "a likely Story, that my Father and his Servants were all so intimidated, had it been true, as not to have been able to withstand a single stout Highwayman, much more a Female, and his own Daughter too!" As Sidonie Smith points out, this ostensible attempt to save her father's reputation leaves Cibber "emasculated, even 'feminized'" (116). Charke's revenge on the conveyer of this story further confuses the question of what is proper daughterly behavior: "I rushed out from my Covert, and, being armed with a thick oaken Plant, knocked him down, without speaking a Word to him; and, had I not been happily prevented should, without the least Remorse, have killed him on the Spot" (114–15).

Similarly, Charke tells us another story about slapping her father in the face with a fish she was selling—to deny it, of course. All this flailing about with guns and fish contradicts her otherwise reverential tones toward her father's authority, but it is not that her performances in drag are so successful; it is rather that they call into question whether *anybody's* masculine postures are successful. If Charke fails to come across like a "real" man, Cibber also fails as a "real" father. In another imagined confrontation with her father, Charke takes his rejection of her attempts to reconcile like "the expiring *Romeo,—Fathers have flinty Hearts! No Tears, / Will move 'em!—Children must be wretched!*" (118). From there she is "empowered to say, with *Charles* in *The Fop's Fortune*, 'I'm SORRY THAT I'VE LOST A FATHER'" (118), and finally compares herself to a rejected prodigal son. In all of these cases, Charke turns to an absurd posturing in male roles that mirrors back the failed masculinity of the "real man" in her text.

Charke's denaturalization of gender roles is, we should remember, taking place in a historical context in which, as Friedli says, "standards of masculinity may not have been very high" (250); that is, when the boundaries designating gender difference may have been far more fluid than in the nineteenth and twentieth centuries. Charke's gender-bending self-representations should not, then, be read as conscious resistance to fixed categories of gender and sexuality. Rather, they demonstrate the incomplete dominance as well as the emergence of a gender system that polarized masculine against feminine. Whatever the intentions behind Charke's cross-dressing, its effect in her autobiography is to reveal possible confusions within a supposedly "natural" oppositional relation between the genders.

The story that Charke tells of her early education and life with her parents gives us a picture of someone who seems inept at both masculine and feminine pursuits and so ends up vacillating between the two. Given an education that "might have been sufficient for a Son instead of a Daughter," Charke rejects the "housewifely Part of a young Lady's Education, call'd a Needle" (17). She is attracted to masculine pursuits, such as shooting and the stable, but her awkwardness at feminine pursuits is nearly matched by her incompetence at the masculine. Typically, her masculine vocations turn out as absurdly as her cross-dressing adventures, more parody than passing. To protect her mother from a rumored burglar she puts on a veritable fireworks display by wildly firing out of windows at random intervals. Her business as an apothecary turns ridiculous when her father cuts off her supply of drugs, and she subsequently doses a patient with garden snails. In both these cases, Charke's initial attempts at masculine activities end absurdly because she overcompensates when denied access to them by adults seeking to keep her within the boundaries of good behavior for young women. Under pressure to conform to dominant concepts of femininity, she reacts characteristically by putting on masculinity with a vengeance.

This tactic can backfire, as it does when she tries out a new horse for her father's stable: "For the Creature was very young and ungovernable, and dragg'd me and the Chaise over Hills and Dales, with such Vehemence, I despaired of ever seeing *Shillington* again. However, the subtle Devil, knowing his Way Home, set up a barbarous full Gallop, and made to his Master's House with dreadful Expedition, beyond my power to restrain; and, in the Cart-rut, ran over a Child of three Years of Age, that lay sprawling there for its unfortunate Amusement" (48). The child is miraculously unhurt, but Charke's reaction to this incident is telling; initially, she is thrown "into a Kind of Melancholly," a state of being "rather stupidly dull, than justly reflecting" that "put a Period to the Fertility of my mischievous Genius" (50). Her first "wakening" sends her into the arms of Mr. Charke: "soon after being acquainted with Mr. *Charke*, who was pleased to say soft Things, and flatter me into a Belief of his being a humble Admirer, I as foolish young Girls are apt to be too credulous, believed his Passion the Result of real Love, which indeed was only Interest" (50). Shocked momentarily out of her masculine role-playing, Charke buys into an idealized notion of love, only, as we are told to expect, to be disillusioned and to launch, once again, into a new series of roles. Charke explicitly acknowledges her protean tendencies: "I thought it always proper to imitate the actions of those Persons, whose Characters I chose to represent; and, indeed, was as changeable as *Proteus*" (40).

This shape shifting allowed Charke to negotiate through mimicry an emerging body of ideology that fixed sexual differences within a heterosexuality that was growing increasingly exclusive in its terms. Female theatrical cross-dressing, particularly at midcentury, constitutes a site of cultural resistance to this narrowing of masculine and feminine down to certain opposite, prescribed roles, even as it serves as one of the grounds of its construction. In this context, Charke's mimicry of male roles unsettles the oppositional gender structure upon which the emergent form of dominant masculinity depends. Her cross-dressing exploits in the *Narrative* also effect a confusion in sexual object choice that resists the recuperation into dominant heterosexuality that is usually the fate of the cross-dressed actress's ambiguous appeal. Instead, Charke sustains her sexual ambiguity against either recuperation or marginalization as a "monstrosity." The result is a text that may irritate, frustrate, or delight for its intractability to dominant sexual ideologies.

The intractability of this text can be read in both the irritation of late eighteenth-century readers at its transgressions against their standards of feminine behavior and in more recent attempts to "discipline" it by labeling it as definitively "lesbian" or "heterosexual." At the turn of the eighteenth century, Charles Dibden called Charke a female Chevalier D'Eon and dismissed her as a social outlaw (5:94). John Mottley saw her cross-dressing as "indecent," although more for its transgressions against her father than for what it might suggest about her sexual object choice (235). Twentieth-century readers tend to polarize in relation to the question of Charke's sexuality. For Lillian Faderman, in 1981, the *Narrative* offers evidence of lesbian activity in the eighteenth century (57–58). Fidelis Morgan's 1988 biography of Charke, on the other hand, seems to go out of its way, as Terry Castle points out, to argue for Charke's heterosexual credentials.[5] If the sexual ambiguities of Charke's on- and off-stage performances in men's clothes worry her eighteenth-century readers, they both demand and resist labeling from her later readers. Whether the sexual ambiguities of Charke's cross-dressing create an undefined uneasiness or lead to the renunciation or acceptance of the word *lesbian* seems to depend on the specific historical context of its reception. These ambiguities may, in any case, be the "point" of Charke's text, the problem or conundrum to which readers gravitate.

This recalcitrant ambiguity works as rhetorical resistance to dominant, male-centered models for same-sex feminine sexuality: the female husband, and "lesbianism" as a prelude to or extension of sex with a man. The female husband, on one hand, made sex without a man both imaginable and punishable. As Faderman, Vicinus, and Friedli point out, sexuality between women was usually detected and punished only when a woman usurped the masculine role in sex and/or marriage.[6] Dekker and van de Pol argue on the basis of impressive historical evidence that, despite these dangers, many women prior to the nineteenth century posed as men in marriage because dominant sexual ideology made sex without at least the appearance of a man unimaginable (57). On the other hand, cross-dressed women, including the actress, were recuperable within heterosexual narratives. Desire between women was either constructed without a penis, in which case it was recuperable, or constructed with a "penis" (or penis substitute) and brutally suppressed as a fraud.[7] Charke plays with the perceptual field defined on one hand by the cross-dressed actress (no penis) and on the other by the dangerous identity of the female husband (substitute penis). By playing one context off against the other, Charke represents same-sex desire in terms of an ambiguity incompletely "explained" by either context. Her cross-dressing refuses definition as heterosexual adventurism, as with a Centlivre, while stopping short of the dangerous oppositionality of the female husband. This double negation in effect calls into question the ability of either context and, concurrently, the penis/no penis distinction, to define Charke's sexuality.

Fielding's *The Female Husband,* published in 1746, is a good illustration of a dominant model of sexual perception by which "lesbianism" is defined in terms of a desire to usurp the sexual privileges accorded to heterosexual masculinity. In Fielding's text, a woman's desire for a woman is most clearly culturally visible if it is seen as an imitation of a masculine sexuality that is itself defined exclusively by "straight sex," a specific deployment of the penis. Fielding's sensational fictionalization of the well-publicized case of Mary Hamilton, a woman tried and punished for the fraud of passing both publicly and privately, gives us a contemporary's notion of what, at midcentury, might have rendered female same-sex desire a perceived threat to male-dominated heterosexuality. Fielding's story begins with the seduction of an innocent Hamilton by an older female Methodist enthusiast. As Jill Campbell recently pointed out, this sexual encounter is portrayed relatively sympathetically and without mention of phallic substitutes. When her seducer deserts Hamilton for a male lover, the latter's sexual experience becomes inexplicably dependent on a penis substitute.[8] As Hamilton's sexual identity shifts from innocent seducee to hardened seducer, her sexual activity comes to depend on a dildo to render it action at all. Fielding tells us that when one of Hamilton's wives grows "amorous," the "doctor" had not "*the wherewithal* about her" and "was obliged to remain nearly passive" (39). The "nearly" seems a bit of a hedge, as if to suggest that Hamilton did something, but not something that counts as action to Henry Fielding. Hamilton cannot decisively act "like a man" without her "wherewithal." It is the discovery of "something of too vile, wicked and scandalous a nature, which was found in the Doctor's trunk" that finally renders Hamilton's "crime" socially intolerable and leads to her punishment. *The Female Husband* provides an alternative context to that of the cross-dressing actress for think-ing about the representation of same-sex desire in Charke's *Narrative*. Hamil-ton's attempt to assume the social and sexual privileges accorded to men ren-ders sexual ambiguity freakish, a source of voyeuristic pleasure tainted with horror. Fielding's female husband marks the divide at which pleasurable am-biguity becomes transgression.

But Fielding's representation of same-sex desire is not without its own play-fulness, in spite of his insistence on the decisive presence of the penis substi-tute. The "doctor's" courtship of Mary Price blurs, at times, the rigid distinc-tions between masculine and feminine upon which Fielding finally stands. Hamilton woos her lover "as well by his tongue as his hands, whispering many soft things in her ears, and squeezing as many soft things into her hands" (43). The ambiguity of "soft things," evocative of a flaccid penis or of feminine breasts or genitals, certainly does not reflect a particularly firm notion of a phallic sexuality invested in the penis. As Terry Castle observes, Mary Hamil-ton's sexual shape-shifting appeals to a theatrical Fielding in love with the pos-sibilities for transgressing boundaries even as they are condemned by the satirical Fielding who longs for a "theology of gender" ("Matters" 604). Like the society that physically punished Hamilton for her "fraud" while enthusi-astically consuming stories—such as Fielding's—about her, Fielding, as Jill Campbell argues in another context ("'When Men Women Turn'" 80–83), is fascinated by the ambiguities he condemns. Fielding's representation of female same-sex desire evinces the pleasure in ambiguity that we have seen in responses to the cross-dressing actresses while marking the point of transgression past which that ambiguity threatens the "natural" differences between the sexes.

Charke's *Narrative* incorporates elements of the female husband model for representing female same-sex desire that we see in Fielding's text. The title page identifies the *Narrative* with such a model by suggesting that its contents go beyond the heterosexual excesses of the cross-dressing actress: "Her Adven-tures in Mens Cloaths, going by the Name of Mr. *Brown,* and being belov'd by a Lady of Great Fortune, who intended to marry her." The *Narrative* sets up Charke's claim to male social and sexual privilege in the mode of the female husband, but its follow-through reaches back to the less threatening realm of performance and theatricality. Her affair with the "Lady" combines elements of the female husband's usurpation of a masculine position in romance with the theatricality of the actresses' transvestite performance. Charke's offstage "performance" as an attractive young man has "real" results. Charke "appeared as Mr. *Brown* . . . in a very genteel Manner; and, not making the least Discovery of my Sex by my Behaviour, ever endeavouring to keep up to the well-bred Gentleman, I became, as I may most properly term it, the unhappy Object of Love in a young Lady" (106).

Charke's account of the affair moves from the actress's vanity in a good performance to the material forms of power to which that performance could give her access. The lady, Charke tells us in concrete terms, is worth "forty thousand Pounds in the Bank of *England:* Besides Effects in the *Indies,* that were worth about twenty Thousand more" (107). Besides her wealth, the lady herself "was not the most Beautiful I have beheld, but quite the Agreeable; sung finely, and play'd the Harpsichord as well; understood Languages, and was a Woman of real good sense" (112). Unlike a female husband's sexual charade, Charke's performance inevitably reveals itself as performance before any "damage" is done. But even the terms of disclosure gesture back to material conditions and "real" desires, on the part of both the performer of masculinity and her deluded "victim": the young lady "conceived that I had taken a Dislike to her, from her too readily consenting to her Servant's making that Declaration of her Passion for me; and, for that Reason, she supposed I had but a light Opinion of her. I assured her of the contrary, and that I was sorry for us both, that Providence had not ordained me to be the happy Person she designed me; that I was much obliged for the Honour she conferr'd on me, and sincerely grieved it was not in my Power to make a suitable Return" (111– 12). The incident ends in an odd mixture of romance and theatricality as, "With many Sighs and Tears on her Side, we took a melancholly Leave" (112). By keeping her transvestite[9] appearance and behavior on the level of performance, Charke diffuses the threat of the female husband's usurpation of male privilege. On the other hand, by evoking the model of the female husband, Charke imbues that performance with an ambiguity more threatening than that of the cross-dressed actress. By neither claiming the penis substitute nor defining her sexuality as "castrated," Charke creates through negation an unspecified possibility for female same-sex desire.

Charke's subsequent encounter with another woman who also develops a crush on her similarly vacillates between the safely contained ambiguities of the cross-dressing actress and the more dangerous usurpation of masculine privilege evoked by the female-husband scenario. A maid advises the cross-dressed Charke, who is working as a waiter in a public house, that she "might marry her Mistress's Kinswoman, if I would pay my addresses" (162). As with her earlier adventure with the heiress, Charke's "performance" wins her an invitation to put on economic as well as sexual privilege. Perhaps the temptation is deficient on both counts, however, because Charke is not, as with the heiress, regretful at forgoing it: "had I really been a Man, [it] would have never entered in my Imagination, for she had no one Qualification to recommend her to the Regard of any Thing beyond a Porter or a Hackney-Coachman" (163). The kinswoman is apparently angered by Charke's coldness, discovers her gender, and revenges herself by attacking Charke "with insolently presuming to say she was in Love with me, which I assured her I never had the least Conception of. *No, truly; I believe,* said she, *I should hardly be 'namour'd* WITH ONE OF MY OWN *Sect:* Upon which I burst into a Laugh, and took the Liberty to ask her, if she understood what she said?" (163–64). Charke's hypothetical "had I really been a Man" lays out the potential for usurping male privilege even as she renounces claims to that privilege. This particular performance also articulates same-sex desire as a joke, distancing it from the cross-dresser herself by putting it in the mouth of her dupe. Throughout the *Narrative*, Charke attributes the desires she creates to the deceived perception of other women; while her cross-dressing provokes it, she denies responsibility for the effects of her performance.

While this process of denial and negation is surely self-protective, it also situates her encounters with other women somewhere between the commodifiable and recuperable ambiguity of the cross-dressing actress and the dangerous and marginalized transgressiveness of the female husband. Charke uses these two contexts for female same-sex desire to define herself, only to reject both as inadequate to the job. She is "somewhere else" on the field of sexual possibility but cannot or will not specify where. Charke raises the question of why she cross-dresses only to refuse to answer. She assures us that "the original Motive proceeded from a particular Cause; and I rather chuse to undergo the worst Imputation that can be laid on me on that Account, than unravel the Secret, which is an Appendix to one I am bound, as I before hinted, by all the Vows of Truth and Honour everlastingly to conceal" (139). Charke reinforces her neither/nor position by this convoluted nonexplanation; she refuses to define herself explicitly, and neither the "safe" nor the "dangerous" models of same-sex desire she alludes to will do the job.

In 1756, a year after the second edition of the *Narrative* was published, Charke published a novel, *The History of Henry Dumont,* in which she exhibits the opposite of this evasiveness in regard to sexual desire between men. *Henry Dumont* contains a viciously homophobic attack on male homosexuality that transforms the process of negation working in the *Narrative* from an implicit critique of two dominant definitions of female same-sex desire into a rather dreary confirmation of a definition of male same-sex desire as monstrosity. In *Dumont,* Charke defines herself as unequivocally on the side of homophobic exclusions of alternatives to dominant heterosexuality, at least so far as men are concerned. Charke's homophobic representation of a "molly" is less a reversal of the evasiveness of the *Narrative,* however, than a logical continuation of it. Homosexual men are the sexual other of eighteenth-century culture in a way that "lesbians," whose generic name does not yet even exist, are not. Charke's strategy of self-definition by refusing models for sexuality between women permits her to avoid taking the dangerous position of sexual other, which, in her novel, she situates at a definitive distance from herself. While her autobiography refuses sexual definitions, even marginal and ambiguous ones, the homophobia of her novel defines her negatively in the eighteenth-century context as *not* a "monster." One might think that Charke saw a need to distance her earlier sexually ambiguous performance from "the vice which cannot be named." But since such motives can only be speculated on, one can more safely conclude that *The History of Henry Dumont* marks the difference between Charke's isolated, performative evasions of dominant sexual ideology and a concerted, politically self-conscious resistance to oppression.

In Charke's novel, the handsome hero, Henry Dumont, receives a mash note from "Billy Loveman," a particularly extreme example of the type of "pretty gentlemen" who were often railed against in the mid- to late-century popular press. I would situate Charke's homophobic caricature in the context of this growing wave of homophobic discourse against effeminate men at midcentury. A 1747 pamphlet, *The Pretty Gentleman,* may well have provided Charke with a specific model for her homophobic caricature. This essay ironically praises a "Fraternity of Pretty Gentlemen," whose "grand Principle . . . is mutual Love, which, it must be confessed, they carry to the highest Pitch. In this Respect, they are not inferior to *The Sacred* Theban Band" (13). *The Pretty Gentleman* offers sample letters between characters with names such as "Lord Molly" that seem to indicate that sodomy must necessarily involve a deterioration of orthographic skills. Charke's letter from Loveman to Dumont has similar problems with getting both spelling and sexuality "right": "When you dans'd last night, you gave the fatal blo, which will be my utter ruen, unless you koindly answer my bondless luf" (38–39). The "Pretty Gentleman" of the pamphlet receives a verbal trouncing, and Billy Loveman is even more violently punished for his desires. Dumont conspires with his friends to ambush Loveman as one of "a set of unnatural wretches, who are shamefully addicted to a vice, not proper to be mentioned." He agrees to meet with Loveman, who appears in full drag: "'I come, I fly, to my adored Castalio's arms! . . .'—stopping here, with a languishing air, said, Do my angel, call me your Monimia! then with a beastly transport, kissed [Dumont] with that ardour, which might be expected from a drunken fellow to a common prostitute" (65). Dumont's response aborts his "ardour": he "knocked him down, and disciplined him with his cane; till the monster was almost immoveable." The episode ends uncritiqued as a crowd joins Dumont in beating and ducking Loveman, who is finally rescued by his effeminate valet.

The violence with which Charke enacts this punishment of Loveman reflects not only the age's general homophobia, but a widely held desire to purge the English theater of the homosexual associations attached to its player-boys in the seventeenth century and transposed into charges of effeminacy against male players well up through the 1770s. Loveman's appearance as "Monimia" (ironically, the "manly" Charles Macklin's first role as a boy in school), ties the novel's homophobia to this "housekeeping" effort to cleanse the English theater of its homosexual associations. The pamphlet *The Pretty Gentleman* also takes part in this campaign to disassociate the stage from homosexuality, ironically asking "Should not the Theatres be *absolutely demolished*?" since the "manly" entertainment of the stage was so obviously an impediment to the projects of the "Pretty Gentlemen" (31). By placing her novel within this discourse against homosexuality, Charke defines herself against the "monstrous," her culture's sexual other. The same process of negation by which Charke challenges the validity of models for female same-sex desire leads her to reinforce the construction of a homophobic model for male homosexuality.

My reading of Charke's autobiography is its own example of the difficulties and dangers—as well, I hope, of the virtues—of reading the ambiguities of past sexualities from the perspective of resistance to the social oppression that goes by the name of normative sexuality. Charke's self-definition by the process of negation allows her to resist the cultural construction of same-sex sexuality around the determining factor of the present or absent penis. On the other hand, it also leads to Charke's subscription to one of the most oppressive mechanisms of dominant heterosexuality's hegemony—homophobia against gay men. Ambiguity is slippery stuff on which to found a politically self-conscious reading practice, and yet faithfulness to the specific histories of sexuality often asks the feminist critic to assess such politically shifty materials. As Martha Vicinus notes, the dichotomizing of our present-day identity politics and past manifestations of same-sex sexuality may prevent us from understanding the "difficulties, contradictions, and triumphs of women within the larger context of their own times" (173). Perhaps this mixing of ambiguity with a clearly defined political reading is particularly pointed within the context of gay and lesbian studies. For lesbian and gay activists of the late twentieth century, "coming out" is one of the most significant models of political resistance to heterosexism and homophobia. Paradoxically, lesbian and gay critics and theorists define their politics by clearing up ambiguities—naming the "vice which cannot be named"—in the very act of investing with "resistance" the ambiguous texts of the past.

Notes

This essay previously appeared as chapter 7 in Kristina Straub, *Sexual Suspects: Eighteenth-Century Players and Sexual Ideology,* © 1992 by Princeton University Press. Reprinted with minor editorial changes by permission of Princeton University Press.

1. Much of this work goes on in Shakespeare studies. See, for instance, Greenblatt's "Fiction and Friction" in *Shakespearean Negotiations,* 66–93. Jardine also takes up questions about the reception of player-boys in Renaissance England (9–36). Orgel's "'Nobody's Perfect'" explores reasons for the endurance of the player-boys well into the seventeenth century.

2. The main body of work in which the influential concept of the female spectacle and the male gaze is developed was done by a group of feminist film theorists associated with *Screen.* See, for instance, Mulvey's "Visual Pleasure and Narrative Cinema" and Doane for classic formulations of this concept.

3. Milhous sees female cross-dressing as a competitive strategy against the more-expensive-to-stage audience draw of elaborate settings and spectacles (93).

4. See Armstrong, 3–27.

5. Castle's review in the *Times Literary Supplement* ("Trials *en travesti*") points out the excessive zeal with which Morgan argues Charke's heterosexuality.

6. See Faderman and Vicinus for information about lesbianism in the eighteenth century, and Friedli for more specific information about the nature of sanctions against cross-dressing women.

7. Friedli points out that when the female husband was punished, it was according to laws against fraud rather than the laws against sodomy, which were confined to men.

8. As Campbell astutely notes, most readers of *The Female Husband* tend to forget this early erotic interlude, rendering even this briefly visible incident of nonphallic "lesbian" sexuality invisible. See "Illicit Enthusiasms: Methodism and Lesbian Desire in Fielding's *The Female Husband.*"

9. As above, I am using this term in the specialized sense defined by Doane's work on masquerade and female spectatorship.

Works Cited

The Actor; or, A Treatise on the Art of Playing. London: R. Griffiths, [1750?].

An Apology for the Life of Mr. T____ C____ , Comedian. Being a Proper Sequel to the Apology for the Life of Mr. Colley Cibber, Comedian. London: J. Mechell, 1740.

Armstrong, Nancy. *Desire and Domestic Fiction: A Political History of the Novel*. New York: Oxford University Press, 1987.

Boaden, James. *The Life of Mrs. Jordan*. 2 vols. London: Edward Bull, 1831.

———. *Memoirs of Mrs. Siddons*. 2 vols. London: Henry Colburn, 1827.

———. *Memoirs of the Life of John Philip Kemble, Esq*. 2 vols. London: Longman, Hurst, Rees, Orme, Brown, and Green, 1825.

Campbell, Jill. "Illicit Enthusiasms: Methodism and Lesbian Desire in Fielding's *The Female Husband*." Paper presented at the meeting of the American Society for Eighteenth-Century Studies. Pittsburgh, April 11, 1991.

———. "'When Men Women Turn': Gender Reversals in Fielding's Plays." In *The New Eighteenth Century: Theory, Politics, English Literature*. Ed. Felicity Nussbaum and Laura Brown. New York: Methuen, 1987. 62–83.

Castle, Terry. "Matters Not Fit to Be Mentioned: Fielding's *The Female Husband*." *ELH* 49 (1982): 602–22.

———. "Trials *en travesti*." *Times Literary Supplement,* Feb. 17–23, 1989.

Charke, Charlotte. *The History of Henry Dumont, Esq.; and Miss Charlotte Evelyn*. London: H. Slater, H. Slater, Jun., and S. Whyte, 1756.

———. *A Narrative of the Life of Mrs. Charlotte Charke*. 2d ed. 1755. Ed. Leonard R. N. Ashley. Gainesville: Scholars' Facsimiles & Reprints, 1969.

Cibber, Colley. *An Apology for the Life of Mr. Colley Cibber*. Ed. B. R. S. Fone. Ann Arbor: University of Michigan Press, 1968.

Colman, George. *Prose on Several Occasions*. 3 vols. London: T. Cadel, 1787.

The Comforts of Matrimony; Exemplified in the Memorable Case and Trial, Lately heard Upon an Action brought by Theo_____s C_____r against _____ S_____ , Esq.; for Criminal Conversation with the Plaintiff's Wife. London: Sam. Baker, 1739.

Cooke, William. *Memoirs of Charles Macklin, Comedian*. London: James Asperne, 1804.

Dekker, Rudolf M., and Lotte C. van de Pol. *The Tradition of Female Transvestism in Early Modern Europe*. New York: St. Martin's, 1989.

Dibden, Charles. *A Complete History of the English Stage*. 5 vols. London, 1797–1800.

Doane, Mary Ann. "Film and the Masquerade: Theorizing the Female Spectator." *Screen* 23 (1982): 74–88.

Faderman, Lillian. *Surpassing the Love of Men: Romantic Friendship and Love between Women from the Renaissance to the Present*. New York: William Morrow, 1981.

Fielding, Henry. *The Female Husband; or, The Surprising History of Mrs. Mary, Alias Mr. George Hamilton*. London, 1746.

Friedli, Lynne. "'Passing Women': A Study of Gender Boundaries in the Eighteenth Century." In *Sexual Underworlds of the Enlightenment*. Ed. G. S. Rousseau and Roy Porter. Chapel Hill: University of North Carolina Press, 1988. 234–60.

Galendo, Catherine. *Mrs. Galendo's Letter to Mrs. Siddons: Being a Circumstantial Detail of Mrs. Siddon's [sic] Life for the Last Seven Years*. London, 1809.

Garrick, David. *The Male Coquette; or, Seventeen Hundred Fifty-Seven*. London: P. Vaillant, 1757.

Greenblatt, Stephen Jay. "Fiction and Friction." In *Shakespearian Negotiations: The Circulation of Social Energy in Renaissance England.* Berkeley: University of California Press, 1988. 66–93.

Hill, Aaron. *The Works.* 3 vols. London, 1754.

Hitchcock, Robert. *An Historical View of the Irish Stage.* 2 vols. Dublin: R. Marchbank, 1788.

Jardine, Lisa. *Still Harping on Daughters: Women and Drama in the Age of Shakespeare.* Sussex: Harvester Press, 1983.

The Life of Mr. James Quinn, Comedian. London: S. Bladon, 1766.

Memoirs of the Celebrated Mrs. Wiffington, Interspersed with Several Theatrical Anecdotes; The Amours of Many Persons of the First Rank; and Some Interesting Characters Drawn from Real LIFE. London, 1760.

Milhous, Judith. *Thomas Betterton and the Management of Lincoln's Inn Fields, 1695–1707.* Carbondale: Southern Illinois University Press, 1979.

Morgan, Fidelis. *The Well-Known Troublemaker: A Life of Charlotte Charke.* London: Faber & Faber, 1988.

Mottley, John. *A Complete List of all the English Dramatic Poets.* London: W. Reeve, 1747.

Mulvey, Laura. "Visual Pleasure and Narrative Cinema." *Screen* 16:3 (1975): 6–18.

Murphy, Arthur. *The Life of David Garrick, Esq.* 2 vols. London: J. Wright, J. F. Foot, 1801.

Orgel, Stephen. "'Nobody's Perfect'; or, Why Did the English Stage Take Boys for Women?" *South Atlantic Quarterly* 88:1 (1989): 7–30.

Pope, Alexander. *The Poems of Alexander Pope.* Ed. John Butt. New Haven: Yale University Press, 1977.

The Pretty Gentlemen; or, Softness of Manners Vindicated. London, 1747.

Rogers, Pat. "The Britches Part." In *Sexuality in Eighteenth-Century Britain.* Ed. Paul-Gabriel Bouce. Manchester: Manchester University Press, 1982. 244–58.

Silverman, Kaja. *The Acoustic Mirror: The Female Voice in Psychoanalysis and Cinema.* Bloomington: Indiana University Press, 1988.

Smith, Sidonie. *Poetics of Women's Autobiography: Marginality and the Fictions of Self-Representation.* Bloomington: Indiana University Press, 1987.

Trumbach, Randolph. "London's Sapphists: From Three Sexes to Four Genders in the Making of a Modern Culture." In *Body Guards: The Cultural Politics of Gender Ambiguity.* Ed. Julia Epstein and Kristina Straub. New York: Routledge, 1991. 112–41.

Vicinus, Martha. "'They Wonder to Which Sex I Belong': The Historical Roots of the Modern Lesbian Identity." In *Homosexuality, Which Homosexuality?* Proceedings, International Conference on Gay and Lesbian Studies. London: GMP Publishers, 1989. 171–98.

Victor, Benjamin. *The History of the Theatres of London and Dublin from the Year 1730 to the Present Time.* 3 vols. London: T. Davies, R. Griffiths, T. Becket, and P. A. de Hond, G. Woodfall, J. Coote, G. Kearsly, 1761.

Wilkinson, Tate. *The Wandering Patentee; or, A History of the Yorkshire Theatres, from 1770 to the Present Time.* 4 vols. York: Wilson, Spence, and Mawman, 1795.

Wright, James. *Historia Histrionica: An Historical Account of the English Stage.* London: G. Groon, for William Hawes, 1699.

PART 3

Re-contextualizing Charke:
New Approaches

5

Charlotte Charke:
Images and Afterimages

Robert Folkenflik

The representations of Charlotte Charke, in several senses of the word, are surrounded by ambiguities. In this essay I will speak only of those portrayals of her by others, focusing on graphic representations during her lifetime and not, except in passing, about her self-representation in *A Narrative of the Life of Mrs. Charlotte Charke,* which I discuss elsewhere (Folkenflik, forthcoming).[1] While I regard the primary value of this essay as clarifying and corrective (there is a great deal of misinformation on the subject of Charke), it is also explorative and to some extent necessarily tentative. This is an iconographic introduction to Charlotte Charke. In the discussion that follows, several basic points should be kept in mind. First, even the portraits of known sitters vary greatly from artist to artist among artists of the highest quality, and reproductive prints often radically change images and values. Second, in the graphic arts identifications of artists and subjects are often driven by the wishful thinking of owners, the mercenary motives of dealers, the narrativization of critics and biographers, or some combination of these reasons.

An easy-to-dismiss example of some such interest at work is an identification tipped in from a bookseller's catalog entry in the University of California at Davis's extra-illustrated copy of the first edition of the *Narrative.* The cataloger calls a double-page illustration of "Roxana in her Turkish Habit," not a role Charlotte Charke performed, a representation of her, but it is rather a representation of Daniel Defoe's heroine. Not all the tipped-in materials in this grangerized book are fully relevant to the narrative, though it is of great interest as a whole. Probably the bookseller, coming upon the print in this volume, just made the attractive assumption.

I will also largely ignore non-lifetime representations by those who could not have seen Charlotte Charke. Later representations, such as the illustration to "Colley Cibber's Youngest Daughter" in *The Table Book* (1827; 126) are rather like the nineteenth-century paintings and engravings of Samuel Johnson standing in the rain as penance at Uttoxeter or waiting for Lord Chesterfield when Colley Cibber walks out of his room. In this one Charke is depicted as preparing to sign a contract for *Henry Dumont* with an old and a young man, both well dressed (the bookseller H. Slater, Jr. and his friend Samuel Whyte, the source of the brief, mean-spirited account of Charke set in the year her autobiography was published). She sits in a chair with a bird poised on its back, a monkey beside her, a dog at her feet, a cat squatting near the fireplace, and a hard-featured, perhaps ill-fed, servant behind her. Charke's servant, though a "tall, meagre, ragged figure," is not ambiguously of "the feminine gender" as in Whyte's tale (Whyte 221–23), nor is this domestic scene set in a "wretched thatched hovel." Charke is a plainly dressed woman sitting at her bellows-desk. This early nineteenth-century depiction of a lifetime account stresses her poverty, and the eccentricity is conveyed by her menagerie and the opposition of Charke and her servant to the comfortable bourgeois men who have come to see her.

A number of portraits are claimed inaccurately or doubtfully as Charlotte Charke. The William Robbins drawing at Windsor Castle, listed by Elaine Kilmurray in her volume of the *Dictionary of British Portraiture* as Charlotte, is identified by an invoice of 1813 as Colley Cibber's "daughter," and is one of a set with portraits of Colley Cibber and her brother Theophilus. But as long ago as 1950 this drawing was convincingly argued by A. P. Oppé to be of an older Cibber daughter. While he seems to know little or nothing of the Cibber daughters, he asserts that the identification of the portrait as Charlotte on the "modern frame" is wrong because "the girl in this portrait can scarcely have been born later than 1700" (Oppé 84). He might have added that since the drawing is dated 1715 and Charlotte was born in 1713, the identification fails. Her sister Anne (b. 1699) or Elizabeth (b. 1701) are the best candidates, and even Catherine (b. 1695), though hardly a girl, is a possibility. Nevertheless it continued to be listed as a portrait of Charlotte Cibber after Oppé's book appeared.[2]

The engraving at the National Gallery Archives (London), listed as a portrait of Charke in the *Dictionary of British Portraiture* (1979), and bearing the title, *Charlotte* [*sic*] *Charke as Scrub* and no date, a degraded re-engraving of James Sayers's 1786 engraving, has been asserted rightly by Highfill, Burnim, and Langhans as not Charke but Frances Abington (fig. 1). The highly popular Abington took the role on February 10, 1786, for her benefit night, and was a fiasco. A look at Lillian Arvilla Hall's entries for Francis Abington (#47 and 48) and Charlotte Charke (#2 and 3) in her *Catalogue of Dramatic Portraits in the Theater Collection of the Harvard College Library* (1930) will suggest the identity of the images (Hall 1:8, 235), though she herself does not. In 1787 Phillipina Hill, née Burton, published *Mrs. Hill's Apology for having been induced to appear in the character of Scrub, Beaux Stratagem . . . at Brighthelmstone last year, 1786* and it would seem

Charlote Charke as "Scrub".

Figure 1. Artist unknown, after J. Sayer (1786). Courtesy of the National Portrait Gallery, London.

a striking coincidence to see two female Scrubs in close succession without the *éclat* of success to spur the imitation, but it happened. There is no reason, however, to identify this provincial Scrub with the print.

Charlotte Charke's playing of Scrub, some decades before, led in her *Narrative* to several amusing accounts of provincial audiences while she was a strolling actress.[3] First, while playing Scrub in a scene with Archer, Elizabeth Ellrington, who was playing the role of Mrs. Sullen, "unexpectedly paid us a Visit," toasted Archer, and after calling in a fiddler, danced an improvised "minuet," which led to the actors not only blowing their original lines but also inserting speeches from other plays, "taking particular Care not to let any single Speech bear in the Answer the least Affinity" (204). Soon after, having played the role of Scrub again, she was exhorted while acting in a tragedy, *The Distressed Mother,* by a member of the audience who admired her performance in Farquhar's comedy "to oblige some of his Friends, as well as himself, by mixing a few of Scrub's Speeches in the Play." This caused her to remember the previous performance and left her more fit to play comedy than tragedy, for "I thought I should never close my Mouth again in the least seriosity" (208). These memorable passages might well lead someone to think of a further twist of Sayers's satiric print by re-engraving it as if it were of Charke. Or perhaps the intention was only to cash in on Abington's plight by adapting Sayers's print to make it appear to be that of the still notorious Mrs. Charke. Although published at least three decades after her death, such an identification was easily narrativized by reference to her autobiography.

Another possible depiction of Charke, a portrait of Colley Cibber with a girl or young woman at his side by Jean Baptiste Van Loo, one of the two most talented of all the artists discussed in this essay, has long been associated with her, though treated with more caution by Highfill, Burnim, and Langhans who call this image a "little girl" and say it "may depict Charlotte" (178). Their caption to the reproduction is "Charlotte Charke (?) and Colley Cibber." Only the fine mezzotint engraving of the painting "Colley Cibber, Esq.ʳ late Poet Laureat" by Edward Fisher in 1758, clearly in commemoration of Cibber's death on December 12 the year before, is known to exist (fig. 2). The painting is of a familiar sort with the subject, pen in hand, his left hand holding what appears to be a letter, but could be a manuscript. It is most likely a poem, and one can only hope it is not a birthday ode for the king. A number of pages of empty paper are on the table on which his left arm rests with a standish at his elbow. Behind him is a half drawn curtain showing a column and a neo-classical wall. But what serves to give the picture life is the girl (or young woman) to his left, leaning over from behind him with her left hand raised and the index finger

Còlley Cibber, Esq.
Late Poet-Laureat.

Figure 2. Edward Fisher, after J. B. Van Loo. Courtesy of the National Portrait Gallery, London.

extended, her right sharing the quill pen, holding it between his hand and the plume. She is clearly his muse, and the effect is charming. The earliest the painting could have been executed was December 1737, when Van Loo first came to England (Vertue 3:82). It could have been executed no later than 1742, when Van Loo retired to Aix. He died in 1745. However, the engraving bears the highly plausible date 1740 next to the painter's name. The girl in the painting appears younger than twenty-seven, Charlotte's age at the time, but drawing inferences of this sort from portraits is notoriously difficult. Certainly, if the girl is a daughter, it would almost have to be Charlotte, the youngest by far of her sisters, but the likelihood is small. Although she had attempted to be "the perfect Representative of my Sire" (Charke 18) since dressing up in his clothes at age four, Colley is hardly likely to have had her posing as his muse in 1740 or late 1737, the date when Van Loo presumably painted Cibber. By either date she had already decamped a second time from Fleetwood's company, been deserted by her husband Richard Charke, and, probably most importantly, performed for Henry Fielding in roles that mocked Cibber himself.

Looking into a parallel problem posed by a Charles Jervas portrait of Alexander Pope containing a muse-like young woman in the background, W. K. Wimsatt Jr. assesses the possibility that she is Martha Blount, the neighbor to whom Pope was closer than any young woman in his life, following the Lady Mary Wortley Montagu debacle. Again, the identification is not certain, and Wimsatt does not express a definite opinion but notes "a shade of anonymity and allegorization" in the figure, a phrase that might be used also of the engraving of the girl in the portrait of Cibber. Wimsatt, whose work is generally characterized by intelligence and skepticism, goes on however to comment on the Van Loo *Cibber* "in which the poet is seated at a table holding in his hand a quill which is either being offered or plucked away by an impish girl at his elbow, no doubt his daughter Charlotte" (Wimsatt 23).

On the contrary, every doubt seems warranted. In the Cibber portrait the identification of the female figure as Charlotte faces a double, and I believe insuperable, challenge. Possibly after *Pasquin* (1735) but more probably following a return to Fielding's company and the performance of his play *The Historical Register for the Year 1736* on March 21, 1737, Charlotte was called to a family conclave, and by her own account the "incensed" Colley left saying he would not return until she was gone. At that point her eldest sister Catherine unceremoniously "turned me out of Doors." Charlotte says this is "the last Time I ever spoke with my Father" (124–25). Two letters, sent by Colley to Charlotte but not quoted by her, make his feelings clear. One is dated March

27, without a year, but suggestively a week after he attended Fielding's satire (Vincent 3–4):

Dear Charlotte,
I am sorry I am not in a position to assist you further. You have made your own bed, and therein you must lie. Why do you not dissociate yourself from that worthless scoundrel, and then your relatives might try and aid you. You will never be any good while you adhere to him, and you most certainly will not receive what otherwise you might from your father.

Colley Cibber

His display of amusement at the performance of Fielding's play undoubtedly belied his actual response. In his own autobiography, *An Apology for the Life of Mr. Colley Cibber, Comedian* (1740), he represents himself as unruffled by the barbs of Pope, but vituperates Fielding, who had attacked him not just as actor, playwright, and laureate, but on his home ground in the theater. Although the part Charlotte played was "Christopher Hen," a takeoff on the auctioneer Christopher Cock, Cibber was mocked as Ground-Ivy (an allusion to his position as Poet Laureate) and through references by other characters, such as Pistol, who represented Theophilus.

The second letter seems to be later and no longer holds out any hope for her (Vincent 3–4):

To Mrs. C. Charke   21 September
Madam,
The strange career which you have run for some years (a career not always unmarked by evil) debars my affording you that succour which otherwise would naturally be extended to you as my daughter. I must refuse therefore—with this advice—try Theophilus.

Yours in sorrow, Colley Cibber

Along with the break with Cibber that surely came before the portrait was painted, there were other and by this time better candidates for the female sitter. His daughter Elizabeth's daughter Anne Brett was twenty; his son Theophilus's daughter Jenny was eleven, and her sister Elizabeth, eight, and most significantly, we do not know the age of Catherine Brown's daughter Catherine, who became Colly Cibber's residual heir following the deaths of her mother and her aunt Anne. Her mother married in 1723, so she would have been unlikely to be as old as seventeen. If, as is thought, she was Catherine Brown's second child (her son Colley seems to have died in 1728), she may have been close to Jenny's age.

After the death of Colley's wife in 1734 and Catherine Brown's husband, she and her daughter lived with him. He left Theophilus's daughters £1000 apiece in his will; he left Charlotte £5. If the Van Loo portrait of Cibber represents an actual girl or woman, the likelihood is that it is a granddaughter of Colley Cibber, most probably Catherine or Jenny. There is no reason to think it Charlotte Charke.[4]

Having said this, however, there remains one troubling consideration, which will somewhat complicate the issues involved. Kerslake says "A portrait by Vanloo, mentioned by Vertue in 1737–38, is now known only from G. Van der Gucht's head and shoulders engraving lettered *Anno Aetatis 67,* published 1740 as the frontispiece to Cibber's *Apology.* The same type was used for later engravings such as Edward Fisher's mezzotint, 1758, showing the sitter with a girl, presumably his daughter." He notes that Fisher's engraving points to Van Loo as the painter, but adds "it is not known whether this implies a second sitting since no oil is now known" (Kerslake 1:54). The Van der Gucht (reproduced in Ashley, opposite 28) indeed resembles the Fisher engraving. Although Kerslake cautiously points to the possibility of another lost painting, he writes in ignorance of the so-called *Cibber* attributed to Van Loo at the Clark Library UCLA (reproduced in a cropped form as Koon's frontispiece), but this is almost certainly a portrait of William Pulteney, Marquis of Bath. Since Cibber was one of Van Loo's first two commissions in England following his December 1737 arrival (Walpole 3:448), it is possible that a second lost portrait exists. I think, however, that the van der Gucht derives from the same painting as the Fisher engraving, and though the notion of two lost paintings, one from 1737 and one from 1740, is attractive, it is more likely that there was one and that the 1740 date of the painting on Fisher's engraving is inaccurate. In either case there are insuperable difficulties for Kerslake's standard presumption that the girl is Cibber's "daughter."

The most vexed question among the representations and pseudo-representations of Charlotte Charke revolves around the likeness that appears as the frontispiece to Fidelis Morgan's biography of Charke, *The Well-Known Trouble Maker* (1988). Morgan's accompanying note claims that it is "Charlotte Charke in one of the two surviving prints made of her during her lifetime" (Morgan [iv]). The other is the F. Garden print discussed below. While she leaves the actual frontispiece to Charke's autobiography curiously unmentioned, this one (she mentions no artist) does not appear in any lifetime edition of Charke's *Narrative,* though it is tipped in as frontispiece to the second (1755) book edition of Charke's *Narrative* in the British Library. There it bears the name of both a painter, B. Dandridge ("pinx"), and an engraver, L. P. Boitard ("Sculp."). This image and a re-engraving of it appear in a number of places in the later nineteenth and the twentieth century as representations of Charlotte Charke. The engraving can be traced back to its published source, François Nivelon's *The Rudiments of Genteel Behaviour* (1737), where it appears as plate 3 of six depictions of women, which are balanced by six of men, and illustrates "Walking" (fig. 3). All of the plates are accompanied by "Descriptions of what is proper to be imitated and practised before, and in, and at the

Figure 3. "Walking." L. P. Boitard, after Bartholomew Dandridge. Courtesy of the Harold B. Lee Library, Brigham Young University.

finishing of the Dance . . ." (Nivelon, unpaginated). The text asserts following the third plate that the woman depicted is "duly drawn from the Life." Bartholomew Dandridge was born in 1691 and was still working in 1755, but no paintings from this series are known to exist. Louis Phillipe Boitard, son of François Boitard, a French engraver who worked in England for Jacob Tonson, was settled at work in England in 1734 or earlier.[5] The British Library copy of Charke's autobiography in which the plate appears provides very limited evidence. It was purchased on July 1, 1867, from the sale by Sotheby, Wilkinson, and Hodges of the library of "the late Rev. F. J. Stainforth, consisting entirely of works of British & American poetesses, and female dramatic writers."[6] Since Stainforth's collection has no other extensively extra-illustrated books, either he was particularly interested in Charke, or the book was already grangerized when he purchased the volume. This nineteenth-century provenance will prove of interest at a later point in the discussion.

It is also suggestive, though not probative, that the only engraving of the twelve by Boitard that is illustrated in the nineteenth century is the one in the Stainforth copy. If all or most of the six female images are of the same woman, why have none of the others ever been put forward as representations of Charke (cf. fig. 4 [Boitard's plate 6], "Giving both HANDS in the MINUET")? Most significantly, Boitard's engravings are very unlikely to be the nearest to the Dandridge paintings, for a series of engravings by Hubert François Burguignon, known as Gravelot (1669–1773), which represent exactly the same activities, are characterized by the elaborate backgrounds typical of oil portraits generally and the work of Dandridge in particular (reproduced in *French Taste*, fig. 3). Gravelot, dubbed "the most important French artist to work for any length of time in England," transmitted the French Roccoco style of Boucher and Watteau to English engraving and especially book illustration (Hammelmann 40). If his engravings indeed follow lost originals by Dandridge, the choice of Gravelot was highly appropriate because Dandridge, despite the usual comparisons to Highmore in his own time, was greatly influenced by French practice. C. H. Collins Baker, speaking of his *Price Family*, says "No other picture of the English school that I recall bears such witness to the transient effect of the school of Watteau, Lancret and Pater on the English conversation piece" (Baker 135). Even better is his observation that Philip Mercier, who worked in London, "may be taken as the probable source of Dandridge's intimacy with French technique" (ibid.). Hence, the lost Dandridges may in their French elegance be well represented by the work of Gravelot.

While I am unaware of any eighteenth-century document linking Charke to the putative paintings or to either set of engravings, this ignorance may just

Plate 6.

B. Dandridge Pinx.   *L. P. Boitard Sculp.*

According to Act of Parliament.

Figure 4. "Giving both HANDS in the MINUET." L. P. Boitard, after Bartholomew Dandridge. Courtesy of the Harold B. Lee Library, Brigham Young University.

indicate the limits of my knowledge. In her autobiography Charke never mentions posing as a model for a painter, nor does she claim to have been the original of a series of engravings by the famous Gravelot or that appear in a book on genteel behavior. But it could be that those days were long forgotten or not dwelt upon by one who was mentioned in a death notice when she died five years later as memorable for her "adventures and misfortunes." Certainly as a young woman she danced and sang on the stage as well as acted, and she may have been tall, slim and attractive, as the woman (if it is only one and an actual woman) of the engravings appears to be. She would have been twenty-three or twenty-four when the engravings were made. One commentator, John D. Holland, even judges her by the Boitard engraving to be five feet six inches tall, an estimate I confess myself incapable of making. Even if we doubt on the basis of the autobiography that she was ever a model of "genteel behavior," what may serve to cast doubt on the attribution is a closer consideration of the date. The Boitard engravings appeared in 1737. Even if we accept the conjecture of the catalogers of the Kenwood House exhibition *The French Taste in English Painting* that "it now appears probable that [the Gravelot engravings] form part of an unfinished set originally commissioned from Gravelot, but ultimately carried out by Boitard" (*French Taste* 32), Charke would not have been the likeliest of models at that date for some of the same reasons that apply to the Cibber portrait, with the added disqualification that someone best known for her performances as a male would not be an obvious choice as the epitome of female deportment. And if she had received a commission to model for Dandridge, we should probably have heard of him as a benefactor at this hand-to-mouth time of her life, for she mentions by name those few people who have aided her with money throughout her autobiography.

Both Gravelot, who lived in Covent Garden and had actor friends, and Nivelon, who may have been related to a family of performing Nivelons who shared a number of bills with Charlotte Charke, could have known her (and many other actresses), but we do not know with whom the idea for the series originated. While the woman is depicted in six engravings by Gravelot, there seem to be only three of the man (although why Gravelot, despite his busy schedule, was unable to complete three when he had already done nine typically highly detailed and finished engravings is not easy to say). Since Gravelot arrived in England in 1732 or 1733 and did not leave until 1745, it is possible but unlikely that he engraved the prints earlier or that Dandridge's putative portraits date from an earlier time. That would make possible the notion that the two models were Charlotte Charke and her charming though feckless husband Richard. But unless more evidence comes to light, there is no reason to believe it.

R. B. Parkes's (1830–1904) nineteenth-century re-engraving of the Boitard is reproduced in Highfill as "engraving by Boitard, after Dandridge" (Highfill et al. 172). They also claim that "a painting of Charlotte by Dandridge is in the British Museum" (178). The Print Room of the British Museum has no such painting, and I doubt they ever did. The National Portrait Gallery lists the Parkes re-engraving of Charlotte Charke as "Parkes after Gravelot," which it clearly is not. The late nineteenth-century edition by Robert W. Lowe of the autobiography of Colley Cibber (1889), in which Parkes's version appeared, claims Parkes follows "Henry Gravelot." Actually, necklace, stomacher, head-dress, and every other feature follow Boitard. Lowe's edition of Cibber was probably the basis for the pervasive belief that the Gravelot-Boitard engravings represented Charlotte Charke (Lowe 1:288), but it cannot be the source, since the Stainforth copy is earlier. Nor can the source be John Timbs, "Colley Cibber's Daughter," in his *English Eccentrics* (1866, 135–38). The engraving, clearly after Boitard, first appears in the second edition of 1875, eight years after the Stainforth copy went on the market. Those who want the attractive Gravelot-Boitard engravings to be representations of Charlotte Charke will need to put forth evidence for the connection.

So much for the wrong and questionable identifications. There are three which, though at the moment unprovable, seem very possible, a drawing and two engravings. To take the most striking first, the brown wash drawing in the collection of the Garrick Club, long lost and never to my knowledge reproduced, was still listed as lost in *Pictures in the Garrick Club: A Catalogue of the Paintings, Watercolours and Sculpture* (1997). This drawing on laid paper (10 x 7¾ inches) is a whole length of a girl or young woman of unknown provenance and by an unknown artist (fig. 5). The drawing appears to be a study for a painting because it consists of an undefined indoor scene that seems to be composed with spatial relations in mind rather than delineation. (A problem here is that almost no artists made such preparatory drawings in England during the eighteenth century.) Her clothing consists of a loose dress or drapery and plain buckled shoes. Her hair is ringleted and perhaps caught up behind with a ribbon. She holds a flower in her right hand. There is no reason for believing this to be a theatrical scene, though that is possible. The evidence for its authenticity includes two inscriptions, one on the drawing itself "M[rs] Charlote [*sic*] Charke" and another on the mount in a different hand with brown ink rather than black "M[rs] Chark daughter of C. Cibber." I take the handwriting on the drawing, which is difficult to see in reproduction but clearer in the original, as an eighteenth-century hand, and that on the mount as possibly an eighteenth-century hand. The spelling "Chark" was used during her lifetime along with the proper spelling. If the drawing was inscribed contemporaneously with the creation, it would date no earlier than 1730, the year of her wedding, but the identification may have been added at a later time. I take it, as did its first cataloguer, to be a genuine eighteenth-century artifact. To my mind the most telling facts about the drawing may be deduced from what little we do know of the provenance. The drawing was found by the cat-

Mrs Chark daughter of C. Cibber

Figure 5. "Mʳˢ Charlote Charke." Artist unknown. Courtesy of the Garrick Club (E. T. Archive).

aloguer among others in an album of prints received by the Garrick Club from different donors before 1850. There was relatively little interest in Charke before mid-century, and her *Narrative* was only reprinted once in the nineteenth century, in 1827. The attempt to associate Charke with the reengravings of Sayers in 1786 was understandable because it capitalized on her notoriety as a cross dresser, but there is nothing scandalous about this young woman and no gain to be had in making such an identification. In other words, none of the main reasons for a false identification exists. If it is genuine, it is probably the best likeness of her extant.

The next two possible representations certainly have more immediate claims to authenticity, since they issue from her milieu, two stages that she trod, and both are satiric renderings of the scenes they exhibit. The first is John Laguerre's *The Stage Mutiny* (June 1733), which illustrates—one might even say re-theatricalizes—the secession of the Drury Lane actors, led by Theophilus Cibber, who, attired as Shakespeare's Ancient Pistol, the role with which he was identified, strikes the pose well known from an engraving of him in the role (fig. 6). Next to him to his right is unquestionably John Harper, dressed for the role of Falstaff, which he was to play the night that John Highmore had him arrested as a vagrant (to which strolling actors were subject). But Harper was a householder. Highmore, the callow young man who bought his way into unsuccessful acting roles and then purchased Colley Cibber's share of Drury Lane's patent to become a manager of the theater, precipitated the rebellion, which included locking out the mutinous actors as well as trying to have them arrested. Mary Heron is said to be standing to Theophilus's left with a banner "Liberty & Property," an election motto. Colley Cibber himself, the retired manager, sits laughing in the right corner, pointing to the egregious Highmore who holds a piece of paper that says "it cost £6000," a reference to what now seemed to be his worthless share. A monkey on a pole supporting the sign of a rose holds a banner proclaiming, "I am a gentleman," one of Highmore's constant claims. To Highmore's right, stick in hand, is John Ellys, another buyer of a share in the patent, who backed Highmore. Fidelis Morgan suggests that the two women on the managerial side are the widows of Robert Wilks and Barton Booth, Mary Wilks and Hester Booth, or possibly Wilks's widow and daughter (Morgan 222). Ronald Paulson identifies some other actors: Benjamin Griffin, Joe Miller, Benjamin Johnson, and the actor in the "'Roman shape,'" William Mills.[7] The whole action is taking place on a stage with draped curtains, though the scene is set, as Paulson points out, before the Rose Tavern in Covent Garden (Paulson 88). To this point Paulson and Morgan agree in their assessments, and with what I have outlined above, with one exception, that

THE STAGE MUTINY.

Figure 6. "The Stage Mutiny." John Laguerre. Courtesy of the Harvard Theatre Collection, Houghton Library, Harvard University.

plumed Roman whose head appears over Mary Heron's shoulder is identified as Charlotte Charke by Morgan (223): "She was one of the leaders of the stage mutiny, and apart from this would have been a suitable candidate for inclusion in Laguerre's . . . print if only because she was a Cibber. (The Mutiny was notorious because it split not only a theatre company, but also the Cibber Family.)" Actually there are two figures in Roman headdress "lurking behind Mrs. Heron and Theophilus," but at least one contemporary document suggests that the woman was not Heron but Charke. In Edward Phillips's *The Stage Mutineers* (1733), first performed in August, two months after Laguerre's engraving of the same name, Mrs. Haughty was modeled on Charlotte Charke's role in the theater rebellion:

> Truncheon: Enough, enough, my *Amazonian,* My Female Patriot,
>   who wildly talk'st of Liberty and Freedom.
> Haugh: Wildly I talk because I am a Woman,
>   But tho' a Woman I'm inspir'd with Liberty,
>   And in her Cause have boldly plac'd my Standard,
>   Under which Banner, Sir, I hope you'll list. (19)

The "Banner" with "Liberty" on it cannot but suggest to anyone aware of Laguerre's print the woman in the foreground. This would place Charke next to her brother in the van of the mutineers.

The question is most worth examining in the context of a related and more striking identification, again by Fidelis Morgan. William Hogarth's *Southwark Fair,* dated 1733 but actually published after January 1, 1734, new style, is well known and considered fully and intelligently by Paulson, so this account will be brief and focused largely on the question of Charlotte Charke (fig. 7). In the upper left hand corner of that busy engraving is a reversed image of *The Stage Mutiny* hanging as a banner for the "booth" of Theophilus Cibber, which he shared with Adam Hallam, Bullock, and Griffin at Bartholomew Fair, and appears as "*Cibber and Bullock*" here. Paulson says Cibber did not go to Southwark in 1733, and notes that Hogarth originally intended to use the generic title *The Fair* for his engraving (Paulson 87). Morgan without reference to Paulson's work comments that the two fairs "featured much the same programme" (Morgan 222). The play performed was Nicholas Rowe's *Tamerlane* (1702). Though not properly the subtitle, the advertisements billed the play as including "the Fall of BAJAZET, Emperor of the Turks," and, as Paulson observes, the scene is full of visual "falls," including the collapse of Cibber's stage. Paulson mentions that Cibber, playing Bajazet, is the "figure in the plumed Roman helmet," on stage. He does not identify the drummer girl or the figure in the

Figure 7. "Southwark Fair." William Hogarth. Courtesy of Gerald and Suzanne Labiner.

"Roman shape" in the center foreground, though he does mention Samuel Ireland's biographical anecdote that Hogarth saved a handsome drummer-girl from mistreatment at a fair (Paulson 89).

At stake for this inquiry is that Morgan, who usefully identifies the woman drummer as Mary Heron (she did not appear in *Tamerlane*), suggests that the plumed Roman being grabbed by the throat is "a caricature of Charlotte Charke." What Morgan says of the Laguerre is also asserted of the Hogarth. She notes rightly that Charke played a male role in *Tamerlane,* the Eunuch Haly. While her arguments that "the costume seems exaggerated . . . and would certainly appear to include enough of the necessary theatricality of a woman playing a man's role" and that "the helmet, too, is a little overfeathered," may be arguable, she is certainly right that "the poor gentleman is undergoing the public humiliation of being caught by the bailiffs, something Charlotte was to spend the whole of her life trying to avoid" (Morgan 223). Although it is not clear just when the public awareness of Charlotte as indigent and a dodger of bailiffs took place, an early satire of her refers to both her cross-dressing and her calling upon her father for "Dust" and "Rhino" (*Sawney* 4), cant terms for money. In her autobiography, she reminisces humorously about actors on stage stalked by bailiffs in the audience: ". . . those Assailants of Liberty, who constantly attend every Play-Night there, to the inexpressible Terror of many a Potentate, who has quiveringly tremored out the Hero, lest the sad Castrophe should rather end in a Spunging-House, than a Bowl of Poison or a timely Dagger" (103–4).

The context is her fear when backstage of her voice being recognized by bailiffs. While Paulson is probably correct about the plumed Roman in the foreground of *The Stage Mutiny* being Mills—a newspaper article of 1733 lists "Mr. Mills and Company at the Hay-market Play-house" as the target of the prosecution of Highmore and Rich—Mills did not appear in *Tamerlane,* and as Haly, Charke would have been offstage at times when Theophilus was on, if we need to take Hogarth's representation literally. The barely visible second Roman in Laguerre's engraving may be Charlotte, or more likely she is the woman in the foreground, but Hogarth's plumed figure is probably the only lifetime representation of Charlotte Charke cross-dressed for a male role.

There are two engravings of Charke that appear to be authorized. The first of which we find mention, which was possibly though not probably the first published, is an appropriately odd one by F. Garden, which was advertised by Edward Ward on the Tolzey, Bristol, in the March 22, 1755 issue of his *Bristol Weekly Intelligencer* as "a curious copperplate of Mrs. Charlotte Charke," which would be presented free of charge along with a "general title" to subscribers at the conclusion of her eight numbers at threepence a piece (fig. 8). Since the autobiography appeared serially in eight installments (none is known to be extant) on successive Saturdays between March 8 and April 19, we know from this advertisement that Charke had at least some general ideas of where the autobiography was going before the third installment was published. At the same time, from the text we can surmise that it is unlikely she knew fully the way the drama of begging her father's forgiveness would play out during the course of her serial publication (unless of course the present tense informing her audience that she is sending him a letter that she hopes to be able to inform us was successful when her next installment appears on the following

An exact Representation of M.rs Charke walking in the Ditch at four Years of Age, as described by herself in the first Number of the Narrative of her own Life, lately published.

F. Garden. Sculpt.   *Published according to Act of Parliament Sep.r 9.th 1755.*

Figure 8. "Charlotte Charke at Four." F. Garden. Courtesy of the Department of Prints and Drawings, British Museum. Copyright © British Museum.

Saturday is a fiction). She may have learned the effectiveness of the unusual ploy of serial publication of her autobiography from Con Phillips's *An Apology for the Conduct of Teresia Constantia Phillips* (1748).

F. Garden's amusing engraving is described on the plate itself as "An exact Representation of Mrs. Charke walking in the Ditch at four Years of Age, as described by herself in the first Number of the Narrative of her own Life, lately published." A few observations are worth making here. First, the engraving, which Garden presumably both designed and engraved ("sculp[si]t.") is, of course, not an "exact Representation," but an imaginative reconstruction of Charke's autobiography. It would be interesting to know if any scenes from earlier autobiographies in English had been illustrated. This is the first autobiography of an English actress, and its theatricality, as in this scene, makes it highly dependent on an implied pictorialness. In the foreground Charke stands in a ditch (she is not walking) with the ground behind her providing a backdrop. To the left behind her are five figures (probably farmers or gardeners, given the shovels and pitchforks, though one with his pack on a stick is heading towards the gate to the extreme left), displaying varying degrees of consternation or amusement. To the right is her surprised father, Colley Cibber, standing before what we take to be his house in Twickenham. It seems to be located on the Thames. At least it is clearly on water, though in appearance more like a lake than a river. One might compare this house with the white house to the right in P. A. Rysback's engraving of "Mr. Pope's house at Twickenham" (1735). Garden may be provincial but he is not contemptible. Little Charlotte in the enormous wig, tricorn hat, and greatcoat (her text speaks of her brother's waistcoat), set in the rural landscape of an imagined Twickenham with her father and assorted extras in the background is an arresting image.

If the date is accurate, this version of a scene from the autobiography was not given to subscribers upon completion of the autobiography in April, but appeared on September 9 of that year. The artist was probably that Francis Garden born in London who lived and worked at some point around Boston (England). He never exhibited at the Royal Academy of Art.

The only representation of Charlotte Charke that she unquestionably authorized appears as frontispiece to the successive editions of the autobiography and may have also appeared that way in the original serial edition, though since the book is published by three London publishers and the serial edition was probably published in Bristol, that is not certain (fig. 9). In any case it is unlikely that Garden was responsible for this unsigned engraving, for he was more competent than the artist who produced this one. Charke appears tall and plain in a plain room. Her long right arm has a short heavy forearm; her

Mrs. Charlotte Charke

Figure 9. "Mrs. Charlotte Charke." Artist unknown. Frontispiece to *A Narrative of the Life of Mrs. Charlotte Charke* (1755). Courtesy of the Honnold Library, Claremont College.

left hand appears to be a claw. She wears her own hair, and the eyes and upper part of the face appear most successful. The mouth, awkward and inexpressive, destroys the effect of the face. She is dressed simply with a necklace and fan (there the resemblance to the Boitard ends), and buckled shoes visible under the gown. The shadowing on the right is highly schematic. The wall is bare with only a hall table attached to the right hand wall holding a mirror. While this print seems anything but highly fashionable, the long oval face is the English ideal in this period (Ribeiro 56). It is possible that this print is meant to represent Charlotte playing a role, but the suggestion that she is performing in Joseph Dorman's *The Female Rake* seems unprovable. She is only known to have played Tim in this play and took that role in 1736. Although her image has been linked to such artists as Dandridge, Boitard, Gravelot, Van Loo, and Hogarth, Charlotte Charke, who in other circumstances might have shared a canvas with her successful father, was reduced to being depicted by provincial artists, and the only certain portrait of her is by an unknown and dubious hand. Yet in *A Narrative of the Life of Mrs. Charlotte Charke* she has portrayed herself vividly and memorably, and on that achievement this volume appropriately focuses.

Notes

This essay is related to an edition of Charlotte Charke's *A Narrative of the Life of Mrs. Charlotte Charke,* which I am currently completing. I am grateful to Jonathan Barry of the University of Exeter, who shared information on Edward Ward from his dissertation on the cultural life of Bristol, 1660–1775, Catherine Gordon and Neil Grindley of the Witt Computer Index, Cathy Cherbosque, Curator of Prints and Ephemera at the Huntington Library, Suzanne Tatian at the William Andrews Clark Memorial Library, Cathy Power, Assistant Curator of Kenwood House, M. A. Goff, John Goldfinch and Mike Crump of the British Library, Paul Goldman, Assistant Keeper at the Department of Prints and Drawings of the British Museum, John Skarstad, Head, Special Collections at the University of California, Davis, Joan H. Sussler, Curator of Prints, The Lewis Walpole Library, Annette Fern, Research and Reference Librarian at the Harvard Theater Collection, Houghton Library, Scott Duval, the Harold B. Lee Library, Brigham Young University, the Witt Library of the Courtauld Institute, and, as usual, Pamela LaZarr and her staff at Interlibrary Loans, University of California, Irvine.

   1. I intend to treat Charke's reputation (another ambiguous term) and her roles as an actress and textual role-playing separately. I have briefly discussed her dedication of her autobiography to herself in "The Self as Other" (Folkenflik, *Culture of Autobiography,* 221). The only representation of Richard Charke of which I am aware appears

on the broadside ballad, "The Batchelor's Wife Sung by Mr Charke Set for the German Flute" (Charke, Davis copy).

2. Oppé adds that "the identification of the personages may be merely a guess of the vendor." But his account gives little confidence that he is familiar with portraits of Colley and Theophilus, let alone Charlotte. The most recent work on Charke that pays significant attention to the iconography, Sue Churchill's "'I Then Was What I Had Made Myself': Representation and Charlotte Charke," *Biography* 20 (1997): 72–94, repeats a number of refutable claims, makes some new errors, and publishes as the "Frontispiece to the 1755 first edition" of Charke's autobiography R. B. Parkes's nineteenth-century re-engraving of Boitard.

3. I discuss these anecdotes in the context of the formal relation of her autobiography to farce in "Gender, Genre and Theatricality."

4. Koon (147 and plate facing 148 [a reproduction of Fisher's engraving]) speculates that the girl in the background is Jenny, mentioning age as her criterion and not canvassing the candidates. She refers inaccurately to the portrait of Van Loo as in the National Portrait Gallery. Elizabeth (Betty), daughter of Theophilus, was later described as "weak in her intellects."

5. Hammelmann (18), to whom I am indebted for details of Boitard's life, does not notice this example of the work of L. P. Boitard.

6. This information comes from correspondence with Mike Crump of the British Library.

7. Much of this information can be found in Frederick George Stephens, *Catalogue of Political and Personal Satires Preserved in the Department of Prints and Drawings in the British Museum* (London: British Museum Publications, 1978), 2:799.

Works Cited

Aston, Geoffrey, Kalman A. Burnim, and Andrew Wilton, eds. *Pictures in the Garrick Club: A Catalogue of the Paintings, Watercolours and Sculpture.* London: Garrick Club, 1997.

Baker, C. H. Collins. "*The Price Family* by Bartholomew Dandridge," *Burlington Magazine* 72 (March 1938): 132–37.

Charke, Charlotte. *A Narrative of the Life of Mrs. Charlotte Charke, Written by Herself.* London, 1755. 1st ed. (extra-illustrated), University of California, Davis. 2d ed. (extra-illustrated), British Library (the Stainforth copy). Facsimile of 2d edition, ed. Leonard R. N. Ashley. Gainesville: Scholars' Facsimiles & Reprints, 1969. Includes extra reproductions of prints. All references to Charke's text, unless otherwise mentioned, are to this facsimile edition.

Cibber, Colley. *An Apology for the Life.* London, 1740.

The French Taste in English Painting during the First Half of the 18th Century. London: Greater London Council, 1968.

Folkenflik, Robert. "Gender, Genre and Theatricality in the Autobiography of Charlotte Charke," in *Lifewriting in the Age of Reason,* ed. Patrick Coleman, Jill Kowalik, and Jayne Lewis. Cambridge: Cambridge University Press, forthcoming.

————, ed. *The Culture of Autobiography: Constructions of Self-Representation.* Stanford: Stanford University Press, 1993.

Hall, Lillian Arvilla. *Catalogue of Dramatic Portraits in the Theatre Collection of the Harvard College Library.* 4 vols. Cambridge, Mass.: Harvard University Press, 1930.

Hammelmann, Hanns, ed. and completed, T. S. R. Boase. *Book Illustrations in Eighteenth-Century England.* New Haven: Yale University Press, 1975.

Highfill, Philip H. Jr., Kalman A. Burnim, and Edward A. Langhans. *A Biographical Dictionary of Actors, Actresses, Musicians, Dancers, Managers, and Other Stage Personnel in London, 1660–1800.* Carbondale: Southern Illinois University Press, 1973.

Hogarth, William, in Paulson.

Holland, John D. *My Name Was in Capitals: Charlotte Charke (1713–60).* Unpub. Ms. in Theatre Museum, London. PN2598.C28.

Kerslake, John. *Early Georgian Portraits.* 2 vols. London: Her Majesty's Stationery Office, 1977.

Kilmurray, Elaine, comp. *Later Georgians and Early Victorians.* Vol. 2 of *Dictionary of British Portraiture.* Ed. Richard Ormond and Malcolm Rogers. 4 vols.

Koon, Helen. *Colley Cibber: A Biography.* Lexington: University Press of Kentucky, 1986.

Lowe, Robert W., ed. *An Apology for the Life of Mr. Colley Cibber, Written by Himself.* London: J. C. Nimmo, 1889.

Morgan, Fidelis. *The Well-Known Trouble Maker: A Life of Charlotte Charke.* London: Faber and Faber, 1988.

Nivelon, F[rançois]. *The Rudiments of Genteel Behaviour.* London, 1737.

Oppé, A. P. *English Drawings at Windsor Castle.* London: Phaidon Press, 1950.

Paulson, Ronald. *Hogarth's Graphic Works.* 3d., rev. ed. London: The Print Room.

Phillips, Edward. *The Stage Mutiny.* London, 1733.

Ribeiro, Aileen. *The Art of Dress: Fashion in England and France, 1750–1820.* New Haven: Yale University Press, 1995.

Sawney and Colley, A Poetical Dialogue. London, 1742.

The Table Book. London, 1827.

Timbs, John. *English Eccentrics and Eccentricities.* London: Chatto and Windus, 1856.

Vertue, George. *Notebooks.* 6 vols. Ed. The Earl of Ilchester. Oxford: Walpole Society, 1934–55.

Vincent, Howard P. "Two Letters of Colley Cibber." *Notes and Queries* 168 (1935): 3–4.

Walpole, Horace. *Anecdotes of Painting* (1762), in *Works of Horatio Walpole, Earl of Orford.* London, 1798.

Whyte, Samuel. Reprt. in David Erskine Baker, Isaac Reed, and Stephen Jones. "Charke, Charlotte" *Biographia Dramatica.* London, 1812. 1 (pt. 1): 106–7.

Wimsatt, W. K., Jr. *The Portraits of Alexander Pope.* New Haven : Yale University Press, 1965.

6

Teaching Charlotte Charke: Feminism, Pedagogy, and the Construction of the Self

Madeleine Kahn

When we read *The Narrative of the Life of Charlotte Charke* together, my students invariably direct class discussion at some point to the issue of whether or not Charke can function as a role model for them. I teach at Mills College, a small liberal arts college for women, and most of my students—whether they think of themselves as feminists or not—read texts by or about women in search of examples of strong and successful women on whom they can model their aspirations.

What they know of Charke before they start reading makes them think that her autobiography will be a gold mine of images of a powerful, uncowed woman. They have heard the story (which she claims is untrue, even as she repeats it in her autobiography) of her masquerading as a highwayman to rob her father's coach.[1] They know that she dressed and lived as a man for many years, calling herself Mr. Brown to her companion's Mrs. Brown. And they know that she wrote a scandalous autobiography, which has survived well enough to this day to be assigned to them in a course on eighteenth-century English literature.

What they find when they start reading, however, is a curious text that seems to advertise its own failure on every page. They learn right away that the *Narrative* has failed in its author's stated purpose, which was to secure her father's forgiveness—and largesse—for his "Repentant Child" (Charke 15). More disturbing to my students' efforts to see Charke as a powerful woman than this external failure, however, are both the self-mocking tone and the discouraging content of the memoir itself. For Charke's *Narrative* is a litany of failed enter-prises, with the narrator herself drawing our attention to the doomed nature of every one of her attempts to find both a role and a livelihood for herself.

Charke ridicules her own efforts to project herself into some profession or other, as if each one were a role on the stage and the necessary players and props (such as skills and money) would appear as they were required. For example, when she's recounting one of her many desperate attempts to find a way to earn a living she says, "I took it into my Head to dive into TRADE" (70). As she relates her progress from profession to profession, Charke the narrator hardly gives us a chance to empathize with the frantic efforts of Charke the entrepreneur to obtain a livelihood. Although Charke's narrative also conveys her own past enthusiasm, we readers are hardly given room to hope any of her endeavors will succeed. The content of her story as well as her manner of nar-rating it reinforce our fatalistic sense that she is doomed to failure, for her adventures are distressingly like one another. Each one begins with some new enthusiasm of Charke's, and ends with the inevitable consequences of her knowing nothing of substance about the profession she is imitating, and with some tale of her being imposed upon by her customers or neighbors or land-lords. As with her self-mockery, Charke herself draws the reader's attention to this discouraging pattern. For example, toward the end of her *Narrative* she addresses our weary hopes that this new adventure will have a different out-come: "Perhaps the Reader may think, that the repeated Rebuffs of Fortune might have brought me to some Degree of Reflection, which might have reg-ulated the Actions of my Life; but . . . I determined to turn Pastry-Cook and Farmer; and, without a Shilling in the Universe, or really a positive Knowledge where to get one, . . . hire[d] the House" (223).

Ultimately the lack of "some Degree of Reflection" is depressing. For all the brio with which Charke relates her tales against herself, for all that she self-consciously adopts a clownish persona and "paint[s her] own ridiculous Fol-lies in their most glaring Lights, [rather] than debarr the Reader the Pleasure of laughing at me" (263), these repetitive stories of energetic pratfalls and pre-carious survival are puzzling and often painful to read. For the reader, the "Pleasure of laughing" at Charke's follies often coexists with our acute aware-ness of the real danger and squalor of her life.

Initially, then, my students are balked in their efforts to turn Charke—as she represents herself in her *Narrative*—into an inspiring role model for their own lives. To my surprise, however, they don't usually give up. They continue look-ing for ways to make her a heroine. I have been puzzled by their efforts to iden-tify with Charke, who was, according to her own *Narrative,* more notorious and

ridiculous than powerful. By her own account, Charke's life is one of running
from creditors, scrounging for food and lodging, failing publicly at many endeavors, fighting with potential mentors and well-wishers, and feeling abandoned
by and estranged from her family. In my more cynical moments I've suspected
that my students identify with Charlotte Charke because she can so easily be
turned into a victim of the sort one might see today on a talk show. She had a
cold, perhaps abusive father; she had an ineffectual mother; she was subject to
gender disphoria. I have worried that such victims reassure them that their own
sense of being oppressed is not merely a sign of their own weakness. I tend to
mistrust such a valorization of victimhood as defeatist, and when I saw some of
my students claiming solidarity with Charke as an oppressed and abused woman I hoped that other students would point out how endlessly energetic she is,
how inventive, and how captivating her autobiography is, even today. But I had
underestimated my classes. They did not polarize around separate images of
Charke as victim or victorious rebel, with each group exercising selective blind-
ness about the contradictory evidence. Rather, they managed together to make
Charke a positive role model without ignoring her miseries and failures.

On the whole my students admire Charke for making the erratic progress
of her life public, and for forging ahead in the face of daunting obstacles. Most
of all, they applaud Charke for what they see as her defiant resistance to social
pressure to retreat to the private sphere. They value her attempts to achieve
both respect and an income in the most public venues. Such a response to
Charke's *Narrative* is both empathetic and resistant: it is empathetic to
Charke's chaotic quest for a public identity; it is resistant to easy categoriza-
tion. Most obviously such a reading resists labeling Charke's life (as depicted
in her *Narrative*) either a success or a failure, but it also resists confining Charke
to other categories such as subversive or conservative, lesbian or heterosexual, proto-feminist or unreconstructed supporter of the patriarchy. It is hard
to maintain a reading such as this, which pays consistent attention to what the
Narrative achieves and refuses to resolve the tensions within it. It is particularly hard in a classroom full of young women for whom questions of female
identity carry great urgency. Yet my students consistently arrive at such sophisticated readings, and they seem to do so because of their passionate investment
in the text, not despite it.

I have wondered what makes Charke so compelling a figure for my students
that they want to rescue her *Narrative* from the simpler, more confining judg-
ments that the *Narrative* itself almost dares its readers to make. None of them
has ever expressed this directly, but I have come to believe that they see in her
life the same struggle in which they are currently engaged: they see Charke as

trying to create a forceful public voice for herself. She wants to be heard, they believe, just as they want to be heard in society at large. Moreover, they want to be heard when they are speaking *as women*, whatever that might turn out to mean. They feel that Charke wants the same thing, and that this is what motivates her refusal to confine herself to one role, whether that role is as a mother, as Colley Cibber's daughter, as a simple shopkeeper, or indeed simply as a woman adhering to society's restrictive gender codes. That Charke's efforts to, as my students see it, live a public life not confined by a narrowly defined woman's role involve great cost to herself, makes her more valuable to them as a role model, rather than less valuable. It makes her example more useful to them, for she has grappled with the same obstacles that they feel they face. Like them she has confronted failure.

Clearly my students are identifying with Charke in an anachronistic way. They are attributing to her their late twentieth-century self-consciousness about the formation of identity, along with their own sort of complex feminism. They assume that this figure from another time and another culture nevertheless shares their own motives and aspirations. All of this could easily lead them into serious misreadings of Charke's *Narrative*. I have become convinced, however, that it doesn't. Rather their identification with Charke has led them to a sophisticated reading that pays close attention to the material of the text, demonstrating that such anachronistic identification may allow students to pursue their own passionate concerns while honoring what the text has to offer on its own terms.

Each time I have taught Charke's *Narrative*, my students have arrived at three major observations about the text: that Charke leads a resolutely public life, that she is attempting to create a multifaceted role for herself as a woman, and that she has consciously chosen both of these tasks, as demonstrated by her use of narrative technique. These observations have led them to a rereading of that aspect of the *Narrative* that has received the most critical attention—Charke's relationship to her father. They have led me to reconsider how much I stress the essentially alien nature of eighteenth-century texts when I teach them, and similarly to reconsider my suspicion of my students' desire to find in any text we read a conduct book for the broader public lives to which they aspire. I used to believe that if I allowed my students to follow their natural inclinations to read everything as if it had been written just for them, then they would ignore anything in the text that wasn't immediately familiar to them. I also feared that they would come to wishful interpretations that could not be anchored in close readings of either the content or the method of a given text. However, my experience of teaching Charke has led me to believe that such a personally involved, empathetic approach may instead lead students to be more receptive, and less anxious to close down the process of interpretation and define a single meaning for a text. In fact my classes arrive at readings of the *Narrative* that, although heavily influenced by their identification with Charke, are nevertheless consistently borne out by the evidence of the text.

Charke's *Narrative* amply demonstrates my students' first observation that she lived her life almost entirely in the public realm. She was born into the public realm because her father, a successful actor and playwright, and poet laureate, was a famous enough figure that even his private life had a public function. (This, of course, is one of the reasons Charke found a reading public for her autobiography.) Her father's kind of fame attracted her all her life. As she details in her *Narrative,* even before Charke herself found success on the stage she was playing out roles and seeking public attention. She reports all of this in her *Narrative,* but she is curiously silent on the subject of any private life. Reading her autobiography we barely learn of the existence of her daughter; we know nothing about "Mrs. Brown," with whom she lives for many years; and Charke's only explanation for one of the more striking details of her daily existence—that for some time she dressed as a man in public—is that it was "for some substantial Reasons" (90). Moreover, most of her entrepreneurial efforts involve highly public careers: on the stage, with puppets, as the proprietor of a store, and so on. In all of these ways Charke makes it clear that for her real life takes place in the public arena.

This much is clear to anyone reading the *Narrative.* What my students' identification with Charke brings to the surface is that Charke chose to live in the public arena; her life might have been otherwise. Because many of my students are themselves single mothers, they see significance in the fact that for much of her life Charke was a single mother attempting to support herself and her daughter in an inhospitable environment. Identifying with Charke leads these students to assume that, just as it would be easier for them to lower their aspirations than to be trying to raise children while getting a college education, so it would have made Charke's life as a mother easier if she had faded into obscurity. Perhaps, they suggest, her father would have been more generous if she'd led a more private life. Perhaps she could have quietly supported herself at some less flamboyant job, or some job more typical for a woman. Or perhaps she could have found someone to support her (perhaps the heiress who falls in love with "Mr. Brown?" [106–13]) if she had been more willing to be silent, and to confine herself to one role in life.

Whatever the plausibility of these scenarios, my students have amply made the point that Charke seems to be exercising some choice when she pursues such a public life. Similarly, she careers from role to role both onstage and off not because new personae are thrust upon her by circumstance, but because she seeks them out. She glories in each new occasion to exhibit her prodigious talent for improvisation, and she clings tenaciously to the notion that she can inhabit more than one role in life. Once again I believe that my students' own concerns have made them particularly sensitive to the way Charke's text works. Charke tells us that each persona that she takes on proves to be too confining. She equates this confinement with her failure in each role: she is not really a physician or she knows nothing about making pies. But my students, who want so desperately not to have to choose among mutually exclusive social roles themselves, see that it is rather Charke's initial success in each of her roles that prompts her to move on. They believe Charke feels the way they do: that she doesn't want to give up the other possibilities that success in one role would necessitate; for these students are also trying out roles—as student, as intellectual, as adult, as mother, as political or sexual radical, and so on. When they see Charke fling herself so wholeheartedly into each role they are prepared for her to run headlong into its limitations, just as they do. They are convinced that like them Charke finds some part of herself silenced by the demands of maintaining any one persona. This leads them to notice that she is in fact remarkably successful in each of her attempts. Even in the case of what she calls her "passionate Fondness for a Perriwig" (17), she gathers an approving crowd about her, even though she is in a "Grotesque Pigmy-State" (19) and is clearly not the Squire. No one role is ever adequate to contain her. She wants to be an actress and a playwright, a person of leisure and an entrepreneur, a daughter and an outlaw.

Charke has chosen her frenzied, chameleon-like existence, then, as a way of resisting being confined to the one-dimensional social roles that are available to conventional women. Rather she is trying to combine several roles to create a more capacious social arena for herself. When she draws our attention to how unsuitable any given role is she is not—as it seems—only mocking her own brash failures, but also mocking the idea that she could be defined or contained by any of these personae she tries on. Both Sidonie Smith and Kristina Straub, in essays reprinted in this volume, suggest that Charke's subjectivity is fluid or unstable. This observation leads them to very different conclusions about what Charke's *Narrative* can tell us about (for Smith) the creation of a self in autobiography and (for Straub) the essentially performative nature of gender roles. My students also recognize that Charke's identity is unstable, but for them this observation brings with it an urgent need to frame or comprehend that fluid identity. This urgency comes of their identification with Charke. Thus when my students make the observation that Charke keeps adding new roles to her persona because no single one allows her a public existence, they are scouring Charke's *Narrative* for her solution to their shared problem of creating a female identity. They desperately want Charke to model a solution for them. For these students the crucial questions are not, What does Charke's text reveal about an eighteenth-century concept of self or gender? or even, What was Charke's intent in writing the *Narrative?* but rather, What can I learn from this text that will help me create a strong public identity for myself? They have a passionate interest, then, in understanding how Charke moves from role to role.

They find some enlightenment in the structure of the *Narrative* itself. For in telling her tale, Charke has also chosen a role for herself, that of penitent daughter. But this role too proves to be inadequate for autobiography. Accordingly, she slips out of even that role in the course of her *Narrative* at various times: to express the glee with which she launched many of her adventures and, later, to express her disappointment and anger when her father refuses the role of forgiving patriarch. Charke also slips out of the role of dutiful penitent when she presents us with the double perspective through which she recounts most of her adventures. Her use of this double perspective reinforces the notion that she finds any single role too confining, as well as the notion that she is trying to create a more capacious or multifaceted identity for herself. It also demonstrates considerable authorial self-consciousness, implying that Charke knows what risks she is taking. This self-consciousness is crucial to my students' use of Charke as a role model, and their observations about her narrative technique arise from their search for evidence that she is like them. They want to believe that Charke continues to risk ridicule and poverty because she knows her very survival is at stake in her attempts to create a forceful, public, female identity. Their identification with Charke thus leads these students to collaborate with her in her attempts to juggle several roles at once and makes them receptive to the two roles she plays within the autobiography itself: the protagonist of her story (a character from the past), and the knowing interpreter of it (a character from the narrative present).

This narrative doubleness is part of what makes Charke's *Narrative* so compelling for my students: when Charke recreates the optimistic glee with which she embarked on each new role, she offers something to my students' hopes; when she highlights the depressingly familiar demise of each new scheme she addresses their fears. Sustaining both these narrative roles requires the same improvisational skill as an author that she has amply demonstrated as an actress and entrepreneur and allows my students to admire Charke's skill. It also results in a text that offers them fertile ground for constructing their own multiple roles. Charke's juggling of roles on so many levels means that her *Narrative* contains many voices and so is available for continual reinterpretation. As such it becomes a useful environment for my students' own experiments with voices and personae. Their exploration of Charke's narrative roles allows them to try out her various relationships to her audience.

For example, Charke's story of her adventure with her father's periwig (which I will treat in detail later) contains both the passionate and amazingly oblivious belief she felt in her role at the time, ("I walked myself into a Fever, in the happy Thought of being taken for the 'Squire" [19]) and the ironic self-awareness that she acquired in retrospect ("I conceived their Risibility . . . to be Marks of Approbation" [19]). When she writes about her "dive into TRADE" (70), which I have already mentioned, she conveys both that the scene was "ridiculous" and that she and some part of her audience believed in it absolutely. And when she relates her stint as a physician she draws two different conclusions from within those different perspectives. From her belief in herself at the time, and from her temporary success, she concludes that believing in a role makes it real: "That Success, which Travelling-Physicians frequently meet with . . . is rather founded on the Faith of the Patient, than any real Merit in the Doctor or his Prescriptions" (39). But from her ultimate and by then familiar failure, she draws the ironic conclusion that: "I thought it always proper to imitate the Actions of those Persons, whose Characters I chose to represent; and, indeed, was as changeable as Proteus" (40).

Charke moves, then, from the conviction that any role can be genuine if it is well enough acted (something my students want most fervently to be true), to the conviction that, for her at least, there is no such thing as a single genuine persona (something they desperately fear is true for them as well). She veers between these two perspectives in her accounts of adventure after adventure, pointing out to us both her temporary success in every role and its ultimate failure. She conveys both the excitement of her optimism in the historical present and the disappointment of her hindsight in the narrative present.

Charke displays the same two perspectives on her autobiography itself. When she looks ahead to the reception of her not-yet-finished text, which she does frequently within her story, Charke displays both the perspective of the time in which she lived these events and the perspective she has as she writes. She thus makes her stint as an author yet another role that she has taken on and the writing and publishing of her autobiography yet another adventure. This role is not more definitive than her stage roles or her time as a pastry maker. Nor is its success any more assured. That she employs the same device for the frame of her *Narrative* as she does for the stories she tells within it demonstrates that Charke is self-conscious about the effects of this double perspective on her audience. As she does with her other adventures, Charke uses the insecurity and instability of her role as an author to engage us in the narrative. She also attempts to script our responses to her tales. She engages us by imagining many possibilities for the fate of her *Narrative.* At one point she shares her fears that this performance on paper will "instead of being honour'd with the last Row of a Library, undergo the Indignancy of preserving the Syrup of many a choice Tart; which, when purchas'd, even the hasty Child will soon give an Instance of its Contempt of my Muse, by committing to the Flames" (12). Here she is the powerless author, offering up her creation to the judgment of an anonymous public. Elsewhere, however, she affects great confidence in her story's power to move her readers—and one reader in particular—to compassion: "And I hope, ere this small Treatise is finish'd, to have it in my Power to inform my Readers, my painful Separation from my once tender Father will be more than amply repaid, by a happy Interview; as I am certain neither my present or future Conduct, shall ever give him Cause to blush at what I should esteem a justifiable and necessary Reconciliation, as 'tis the absolute Ordination of the Supreme that we should forgive, when the Offender becomes a sincere and hearty Penitent" (15). Here she uses a kind of prolepsis to project both her father's response to her tale, and her public readers' responses to her father's response. She also uses a Richardsonian "writing to the moment" to engage her readers in the present drama of her exile from and hoped-for return to her father's graces. Finally, she calls on a power even higher than her father to attest to the justness of her cause.

All of these narrative devices underscore Charke's self-consciousness about the role she plays in relation to her father, and also about the role she is scripting for him to play with her. When she chooses to move from one narrative perspective to another in her current role as author she similarly emphasizes the choices she made each time she abandoned one of her earlier roles for a new one. In the case of her father, she is to be the reformed prodigal whose "present or future conduct shall never give him cause to blush." He is to be again the "tender Father" she paints in anecdotes from her childhood. With her use of prolepsis Charke thus bases at least one aspect of her *Narrative*'s success on her father's response to it. For her role as penitent prodigal her father is her first audience, just as he has been for so many of her roles. In her *Narrative* she tries to recreate him as that "tender Father" whose fondness and admiration for her liveliness, she believed, made him indulgent.

My students pay particularly close attention to the varied ways Charke tries to connect to and to imitate her father in the *Narrative,* for it is clearly within her relationship to her father, and to her image of her father, that Charke tries to work out how to create an effective public female identity. If they are to use Charke as an exemplar they need to see clearly to what uses she puts her own exemplary figure, her father. Fortunately this is Charke's explicit task as well and she provides us with an account of her early relationship to her father while also engaging us in the present drama of his reception of the *Narrative.*

Early in her autobiography Charke provides a model of the kind of event she is going to relate, and the form in which she will relate it. This model is the episode in which she masquerades as her father by parading around in his wig. Charke refers back to this episode often, clearly establishing it as a template for her continuing attempts to make a place for herself in the public sphere. It also serves as a template for our experience as readers, for it exhibits both Charke's double narrative perspective and the uses to which she puts that double narrative. She plays up the perspective of the madcap adventurer when she wants to charm us with her daring and her skill; she plays up the perspective of the reformed author of the *Narrative* when she wants to instruct her audiences in the proper response to her story.

Even at the age of four Charke was seeking public consequence, and even then she was adept at throwing herself into any role that seemed to offer it. Characteristically she first conveys what now looks most ridiculous about her efforts to take over her father's role with the aid of his "enormous bushy Tie-wig" (18). Yet, even while she is conveying how ridiculous she looked in retrospect and how powerless she turned out to be, Charke still conveys the delight and the success her four-year-old self snatched from the moments before her family discovered her: "But, behold, the Oddity of my Appearance soon assembled a Croud about me; which yielded me no small Joy, as I conceived their Risibility on this Occasion to be Marks of Approbation, and walked myself into a Fever, in the happy Thought of being taken for the 'Squire" (19). This dual perspective gives Charke the narrative maneuverability she needs to try to position her audience to be responsive and receptive in just the ways she desires. For example, she introduces and concludes her account of her masquerade in her father's wig with directions about how we are to receive her tale. The introduction tells us that we are to be amused and a bit awestruck at what Charke calls her "former Madness" (17): "As I have promised to conceal nothing that might raise a Laugh, I shall begin with a small Specimen of my former Madness, when I was but four Years of Age" (17). The conclusion tells us that we are to empathize with her delusions of grandeur rather than being affronted by her arrogance, and to find her as loveable as her parents once did, or as she liked to believe they did: "The Drollery of my Figure rendered it impossible, assisted by the Fondness of both Father and Mother, to be angry with me" (19).

As my students emphasize, however, more is at stake in Charke's efforts to school her readers into being the audience she needs us to be than whether or not we find her escapades as a four year old more appalling than charming. For the continued existence and success of her public self, the self on which she has staked her entire identity, depends on whether or not we are the receptive and empathetic audience she requires. This gamble with public identity is, I think, what my students are responding to, and what makes them so identify with Charke despite the obvious differences in their situations. For many of my students are experimenting as urgently and as inventively with the creation of a public voice and a public identity as is Charke. They have chosen a women's college in the hope of finding an environment that won't force them into one narrowly defined role or another. What they hope to forge in this environment is an identity strong and flexible enough to allow them at least two functional selves: a powerful and authoritative public self, and a more permeable, more receptive private self. Moreover, they want these selves to inform each other. They want to bring the insights of the private self to bear on their public roles; they want the power they exercise in public to protect their more vulnerable private selves. They see Charke as grappling with this same struggle to forge an identity capacious enough to contain disparate aspects of herself, and they read the urgent, headlong tone of the narrative as evidence that Charke, like themselves, feels that her very survival is at risk in the attempt.

Charke herself is quite explicit about what's at stake for her in this *Narrative* of her life. The threat of an unheeding audience is ever present, most immediately in her father's silence, and then in our own possible indifference. As her *Narrative* repeatedly demonstrates, she needs others to believe in her roles if she is to have an enduring and powerful public identity. She reveals as much when she relates the emblematic story of trying to inhabit her father's public self by parading about in his wig, for this was clearly an early and undisguised attempt to appropriate the powerful public identity she knew. She further advertises her awareness of how much she depends on her audience's receptivity when she tries to control it. We have already seen this in her hopeful reconstruction of her father's fond tolerance. It is also present in the *Narrative* when Charke turns to us, her public readers.

Even as she tries to teach us to respond as she wishes, Charke prepares for the possibility that her readers will be hostile. On occasion she interrupts her stories of her attempts to win fame and fortune to fend off what she imagines to be the unreceptive reader's response to her story. After claiming that "there is none in the World MORE FIT THAN MYSELF TO BE LAUGH'D AT" (86), she preemptively attacks those readers who might dare to mock her current role as an author:

> It has been hinted . . . that I should never have Patience to go through the Process of my Life. I . . . am sorry for their Want of Humanity, as this Work is at present the Staff of my Life; and such an Insinuation must naturally deter many from taking it in, if they suppose me capable of such an Inconsistency: So far from it, that were I by Miracle, capable of riding in my own Coach, I would still pursue my Scheme, 'till I had brought it to a Conclusion; for, a happy Change of Circumstances makes "Misfortunes past prove Stories of Delight;" And what is now my SUPPORT, would then be my AMUSEMENT. (87)

It is worth taking a close look at this appeal to the not-yet-hostile reader of her *Narrative*. Most obviously, Charke is appealing to our humanity (as opposed to the "want of Humanity" in those who would spread such a tale and, eventually, in her father) to make us sympathetic readers of this work that, while it is designed for our mere amusement, is her sole support. Indeed, she tells us that "this Work is at present the Staff of my Life," which an empathetic reading such as my students' reveals to be a reference not only to her hopes to earn some money by its publication, but also to her attempts to create an enduring and relatively consistent self on the page where she has repeatedly failed to do so in life.

Charke's dedication to herself at the beginning of her *Narrative* makes explicit what is implicit in this passage: that writing the *Narrative* is—like wearing her father's wig, or playing him on the stage, or writing plays, or adopting male dress and male professions—an attempt to create a public persona that is generous enough to contain multiple aspects of herself. The self that she addresses in that dedication is the perfect, empathetic reader for her tale. That true friend whom she addresses is the identity Charke hopes to create in her *Narrative*. There is one significant difference in the description of that public persona she offers in her dedication, however. Her dedication is to herself as a woman. The true friend and empathetic reader she describes there is not appropriating male power to be heard in public; she is an empathetic female reader of a woman's autobiography:

If, by your Approbation, the World may be perswaded into a tolerable Opinion of my Labours, I shall, for the Novelty-sake, venture for once to call you, FRIEND; a Name, I own, I never as yet have known you by.

I hope, dear Madam, . . . that you and I may ripen our Acquaintance into a perfect Knowledge of each other, that may establish a lasting and social Friendship between us. (vii–viii)

This role of true friend and generous reader is the role my students want to fill for Charke and for themselves. They want to achieve a kind of solidarity with Charke as women attempting to be each other's own best audience in a society that they believe devalues (both now and then) collaboration among women. They want, moreover, to achieve a kind of solidarity with themselves of the kind that Charke playfully attests to in her dedication. That is, if Charke the author of the *Narrative* and Charke the dedicatee of the *Narrative* achieve "a lasting and social Friendship," then they stand a better chance of persuading "the World . . . into a tolerable Opinion of [their] Labours" than either did alone. In Charke's dedication to herself my students see evidence that she finally achieves what they so fervently hope she will achieve: a powerful public voice as a woman. She does not dedicate her *Narrative* to her father, they point out, even though so much of it is taken up with appeals to him and imitations of him. Rather she addresses the self that her *Narrative* creates. Here she acknowledges what her story amply demonstrates: that she has not often been her own friend, just as she has lost track of her other "two Friends, PRUDENCE and REFLECTION" (ix). Perhaps, my students suggest, the process of becoming her own friend, which we witness in the *Narrative,* is the process of giving up her imitations of her father and learning to create a female identity for herself.

My students' reading of Charke's *Narrative* as a story of a woman who achieves feminist enlightenment and so abandons her attempts to be an honorary man is clearly a wishful reading. As such it is at times difficult for them to maintain in the face of Charke's energetic pursuit of what her society defines as male prerogatives and power. Erin Mackie asserts that "emulation of the father is the origin and end of Charke's self-representation" (Mackie 847) and much of the *Narrative* bears out this assertion. As our class discussion begins to focus on what happens in Charke's relationship to her father as she portrays it in the *Narrative,* the class often splits temporarily into two factions. One faction holds tenaciously to the image of Charke they find in her dedication, which is sufficiently subversive to be of use to them. The other points to the stories that make up the bulk of the *Narrative* to assert that the only way Charke sees to create a powerful public voice is by appropriating male dress and male roles, most specifically her father's wig, his roles in the theater, his place as an author of an autobiography, and so on.[2]

In our classroom discussions the perspectives of both of these factions are brought to bear on our investigation of Charke's relationship with her father in the *Narrative*. Clearly Charke starts out fully invested in the idea that her father will bestow some of his wealth and power on her if she behaves properly. Thus she confidently writes with the full expectation that he will see her as she sees herself. When Charke imagines Cibber responding to her efforts to "throw myself at his Feet, to implore the only Benefit I desire or expect, his BLESSING, and his PARDON" (14), she imagines that he is the benign father welcoming home the repentant, prodigal daughter, and the father who is too fond and too amused by "the Drollery of my Figure . . . to be angry with me" (19).

Thus in the early parts of Charke's *Narrative* she assumes that Cibber's response will mirror her own, but with one significant difference: Cibber has power in the real world, which Charke covets. Charke clearly hopes that one outcome of the "happy Interview" she imagines would be rescue from the poverty that has prompted her to write the *Narrative*. But even in the beginning it is also clear that the *Narrative* serves other purposes for her as well. Even as she tries to negotiate for some of her father's power, Charke is already exploring the possibility of creating a public persona without him. She does this most obviously by writing the *Narrative,* which exists as a proleptic product of its own success. That is, if she writes it and we read it, she has created a public voice for herself. And that public voice does not depend on her father's approval, or on an appropriation or imitation of his power. In fact, as those students who see Charke as ultimately subversive point out, the *Narrative* can succeed as autobiography only if it fails to elicit her father's forgiveness. Only when she stops addressing her father can Charke create an authoritative voice of her own.

A reading of Charke's *Narrative* that emphasizes process and change eventually emerges out of this debate in the classroom between those who see Charke as trying to imitate a male public voice and those who see her creating a new kind of female public voice. This reading owes something to my students' own desires, and it owes something to the classroom process. They want to believe that it is possible for Charke—and by extension for themselves—to turn away from her attempts to be "by Dint of a Wig and a Waistcoat . . . the perfect Representative of [her] Sire" (18) toward the creation of what they would regard as a more feminine and therefore more authentic self. Even those students who fear that she can only try, and largely fail, to imitate her father would rather believe that there is another path to creating a public female voice. Therefore both factions eventually work together to find in Charke's *Narrative* a creative process and a change in her goals, one that culminates in the consciousness they see in her dedication.

Significantly, my students come to this reading together as a group. As a group they tend to work toward consensus. In general my classes resist resolving difficult issues through conflict; they really don't want one point of view to vanquish the others. Instead they work to be inclusive of difference; they negotiate connections between seemingly disparate or contradictory longings. This combines with their desire to find useful knowledge and good advice in everything they read to make them particularly receptive to Charke's request for an empathetic reader who might be a better friend to her than she has been to herself. My students are as fervently interested as Charke is herself in finding in the *Narrative* a model for the creation of female identity that can allow for multiple roles and multiple goals. They follow closely what they see as Charke's evolution, for they feel equally engaged in the same process. They are searching in Charke's *Narrative* for the answers to the questions that preoccupy them: Do they have to be as much like men as possible to have power in the public realm? Or might they achieve a powerful public role without abandoning the parts of themselves that they feel are unrecognized or undervalued by the men with public power?

Their self-interested reading leads my students to see a change in Charke's relationship to her father in the course of the *Narrative.* Originally Charke punctuates her lively accounts of her adventures with attempts to convince her father that she is now a different sort of creature who is wiser, calmer, and more like him. In this vein she pleads early on in her *Narrative* to "throw [her]self at his Feet" (14). But we hear the most about Charke's humble desire to prostrate herself before her Sire much later, after her father has refused to respond to her plea. She reprints the letter she sent to her father upon the publication of the first installment of her *Narrative* only when she can use it to emphasize his cruelty. For my students this is evidence that she is beginning to break away from him and from the hopes she had of being welcomed into his wealth and his power. She moves from an attempt to be like her father so she can speak with his voice to a direct address to us, her other readers, in which she is critical of her father and his abuse of his position. In her original letter to him she claims her position as her father's offspring and asks: "if I may be admitted to throw myself at your Feet; and, with sincere and filial Transport, endeavor to convince you that I am, / HONOUR'D SIR, / Your truly penitent / And dutiful Daughter, / CHARLOTTE CHARKE" (119). But when she reports that her messenger returns "and delivered me my own Epistle, enclosed in a Blank, from my Father" (120), she deftly shifts her direct appeal from her father to her public readers, just as she has previously switched from tradesperson to pastry maker: "The Prodigal, according to Holy Writ, was joyfully received by the offended Father: Nay, MERCY has even extended itself at the Place of Execution, to notorious Malefactors; but as I have not been guilty of those Enormities incidental to the foremention'd Characters, permit me, gentle Reader, to demand what I have done so hateful! . . . so much beyond the Reach of Pardon!" (120–21).

In my students' reading, this is a crucial moment, in which Charke turns her father's rejection into an opportunity to forge an inclusive female identity, rather than an ersatz male one. When she turns away from her father to us, her public, perhaps more receptive readers, she begins to construct the voice that has made the *Narrative* endure. Eager for her to succeed in this endeavor, my students gladly respond to her appeal, championing Charke over her father and finding in the enduring liveliness of her *Narrative* proof that she succeeds in creating a public voice without him. They thus resolve the contradictions that have prompted other critics to debate whether Charke does or "does not want to be a woman" (Smith 121) by positing that Charke grows and changes in the process of writing the *Narrative*. Here again their view of literature as a source of possible solutions to their own problems has led them to an anachronistic and yet revealing approach.

Their own hopes and fears about creating public voices for themselves make my students particularly receptive to the variability of Charke's narrative persona. They see her resisting binary categories and this gives them hope that they too might be able to negotiate for some subjective space between the urge to be as like a man as possible and the urge to forge an identity without regard to what they see as male standards and strictures. Thus, rather than posit that the strategy of Charke's *Narrative* is finally either imitation of her father or rejection of conventional gender roles, they suggest that in the course of her tale Charke moves away from the first toward the second, but never wholly settles in either role.

With this reading my students accomplish two things of paramount importance to them: they preserve Charke's voice from silence, and they enact in the classroom the very model for the creation of a public identity that they have found in Charke's text. They offer their empathetic "Approbation," as Charke requests in her dedication, so that "the World may be perswaded into a tolerable Opinion of [her] Labours." With their idea that Charke moves away from imitating her father toward addressing her female audience, including herself, they provide a container for her disparate narrative endeavors. They arrive at this idea in the classroom by finding a way to contain the disparate responses of various students to Charke's *Narrative*. What they come up with is a model that does not require exclusion. When they say that Charke progresses toward the goal of including more aspects of herself than imitation of her father can encompass, they have found a way to accommodate their own varied responses both to Charke's dilemmas and to her solutions to those dilemmas.

My own participation in this classroom process has led me to see greater coherence in Charke's text than I had before. It now seems to me less like a collage of painful failures than like a brave attempt to express an identity that is not easily contained in traditional gender roles. The experience has also led me to change the way I teach eighteenth-century texts. I now invite my students' identification with characters in the text. I encourage their anachronistic and wishful readings, because I know that if we pursue the implications of those readings we will learn something not only about my students' hopes and fears, but also about the different models of unity their identification might lead them to uncover in those texts.

Notes

1. She refers to the story as "a most villainous Lye," but then goes on to relate the story in some detail (Charke 114). Except where indicated, all future citations are from this text.

2. Critics are also divided along these lines, with some asserting that Charke's *Narrative* is finally feminist and subversive, and others that it is ultimately conservative and that Charke has no desire to undermine the patriarchy. See especially Friedli, Nussbaum, Smith, and Straub.

Works Cited

Charke, Charlotte. *A Narrative of the Life of Mrs. Charlotte Charke*. 2d ed. 1755. Ed. Leonard R. N. Ashley. Gainesville: Scholars' Facsimiles & Reprints, 1969.

Friedli, Lynn. "'Passing women': A study of gender boundaries in the eighteenth century." *Sexual Underworlds of the Enlightenment*. Ed. G. S. Rousseau and Roy Porter. Chapel Hill: University of North Carolina Press, 1988. 234–69.

Mackie, Erin. "Desperate Measures: The Narratives of the Life of Mrs. Charlotte Charke." *ELH* 58:4 (Winter 1991): 841–65.

Nussbaum, Felicity A. "Eighteenth-Century Women's Autobiographical Commonplaces." *The Private Self: Theory and Practice of Women's Autobiographical Writings*. Ed. Shari Benstock. Chapel Hill: University of North Carolina Press, 1988. 147–71.

Smith, Sidonie. *A Poetics of Women's Autobiography: Marginality and the Fictions of Self-Representation*. Bloomington: Indiana University Press, 1987.

Straub, Kristina. "The Guilty Pleasures of Female Theatrical Cross-Dressing and the Autobiography of Charlotte Charke." *Body Guards: The Cultural Politics of Gender Ambiguity*. Ed. Julia Epstein and Kristina Straub. New York: Routledge, 1991. 142–66.

7

"A Masculine Turn of Mind": Charlotte Charke and the Periodical Press

Hans Turley

Scant attention has been paid to the influence of the periodical press on the historical milieu of mid-eighteenth-century England.[1] The enormous success of such monthly publications as *The Gentleman's Magazine* and *The London Journal* suggests the effect these periodicals had on shaping the taste for readers of the period. This essay argues that *The Gentleman's Magazine*—the most prominent periodical of the 1750s—attempts to reconcile Charlotte Charke's racy *Narrative of the Life of Mrs. Charlotte Charke* with conventional notions of feminine propriety, and make sense of the life of a woman whom Leonard R. N. Ashley calls "somewhat frighteningly indomitable."[2] Kristina Straub is correct when she contends that Charke's autobiography "is a text that may irritate, frustrate, or delight for its intractibility to dominant sexual ideologies."[3] In the October, November, and December 1755 numbers of *The Gentleman's Magazine*[4] Charke's autobiography was rewritten completely by taking her first-person narrative and turning it into a third-person redaction. Extraordinary space—over ten thousand words or fifteen tightly packed two-column pages—was devoted to a detailed summary of Charke's book.[5]

Even from a cursory browse, the space the *Magazine* accorded to Charke's *Life* is striking if compared to the space accorded to essays and to other books that it reviewed in 1755, and, in fact, essays and reviews from the entire decade. For example, in February the *Magazine* gave its readers a biography of "The Life of William Cavendish, the Great Duke of NEWCASTLE" in three pages (*GM* 52–55). Johnson's *Dictionary*—a work that created great excitement in England—was given six pages in the April number (*GM* 146–51). Voltaire's *General History and State of Europe* in March of that year was given two pages (*GM* 99–100). With the exception of *Philosophical Transactions,* published the same year as Charke's *Life* and epitomized in overlapping issues with her autobiography, no other book review in 1755 was treated over more than two numbers. In fact, *Philosophical Transactions* was accorded just four pages over its three numbers; only Charke's *Life* was given so much attention by the *Magazine.*[6]

Obviously, Charke is with heady company. In the preface to the 1755 volume of the *Magazine,* a "contributor" writes: "Your account of books, whether in your catalogue, or a separate article, is a very valuable, and to me a very entertaining part of your collection. We that live at a distance are guarded against the fallacy of specious titles, and directed what books to purchase and what to neglect: Thus you at once assist the student, reward the genius, and discourage the dunce" (*GM* A3v). Why does the *Magazine* place so much emphasis on Charke's *Life,* a book that could scarcely be called respectable by its readership, and, in fact, could be construed as one of the "specious titles" that the readers should "neglect"? One reason could be that Charke's book is such an outrageous narrative. With it, the *Magazine* found the perfect subject to demonstrate what happens if a woman does not conform to notions of conventional propriety: poverty, debtor's prison, and illness.

Charke's *Life* certainly "entertains" and the *Magazine*'s redaction does, as we shall see, "discourage the dunce" from following in Charke's footsteps. But the *Magazine*'s prose erases Charke's authorial voice that shapes the character of "Charlotte Charke." The *Magazine* focuses on those aspects of Charke's life that represent gender transgression and travesty. Paradoxically, the *Magazine* "rewards" the self-proclaimed "genius" or "Charlotte Charke" (25) precisely because it chooses to tell *her* story along with the more serious articles it offers its readers. In a sense, then, the *Magazine* does "assist the student," in this case Charlotte Charke. But the Charlotte Charke "assisted" by the *Magazine* is one of its own construction, based on the parts of Charke's *Life* it uses for its own agenda. Many modern critics see Charke's *Life* as a celebration of homoerotic desire.[7] The *Magazine,* on the other hand, through its selective retelling of the events of her life, contains her authorial voice that violates female propriety. By comparing Charke's *Life* and the *Magazine*'s redaction, we can see why Charke's *Life* still arouses such fascination for contemporary queer readings. Moreover, I hope that this reading of the two texts will show the control that Charke held over the telling of her life story: a woman who wrote about her "self" with few regrets and a self-conscious exultation that she "was playing *Bo-peep with the World*" (274).

The Gentleman's Magazine represented a new kind of periodical for the English reading public. Started by Edward Cave in 1731, the *Magazine* became a way to disseminate information that—as the preface to the 1755 volume announces—wants "to represent Experience" (*GM* A2v). Through its reprinting of essays that appeared in the daily and weekly newspapers, the *Magazine* is, in a sense, canonizing the taste of its readers. By a close look at its selections, one could argue that the *Magazine* is constructing a world view. On the other hand, in the only book-length study of *The Gentleman's Magazine,* C. Lennart Carlson argues that the *Magazine* reflects its readership: "We sense the development of popular taste, we feel the surge of popular opinion. In a sense, the history of the development of the magazine is a significant chapter in the account of the liberation of middle-class England."[8] Whether the *Magazine* reflected its readership or, instead, constructed its readership's taste is, of course, open to debate, and impossible to determine in any case. What's more, "the liberation of middle-class England" is a transparently reductive and whiggish argument. If the *Magazine* is "middle-class" it is only in the broadest sense. For the purposes of this essay, more significant is how the *Magazine* seems to show a certain way of thinking about gender and sexuality through its inclusion and choices of events from Charke's *Life* within the context of all the other kinds of articles it offers.

Several factors determine a theory of the *Magazine's* influence on popular culture and who its readership might be. The *Magazine* stands apart from other newspapers and periodicals—daily, weekly, or monthly—because of its high cost. After 1725, newspapers of one or two sheets cost 2 d. In contrast, the *Magazine* was long—each number ran around forty-five pages. At 6 d. an issue, a subscription to the *Magazine* was a costly commitment. In the preface to the 1746 volume, Cave claimed a circulation of three thousand. However, the *Magazine's* circulation is hard to gauge in real numbers because its actual readership cannot be calculated. We know that its availability in coffee houses in London and—this is important—throughout England itself means that many more people besides those who bought a subscription had the opportunity to read the *Magazine.* Further, its readership included those who could afford its high cost, and had the leisure time to sit, read, and socialize. This does not mean that the readers were exclusively male, of course. But given the kinds of essays printed—scientific, philosophic, and political articles—certainly men, and men with an "interest" in new ideas about science, history, and philosophy were the targeted audience for the periodical. For the purposes of this essay, then, the audience for the *Magazine* will be those who had time, money, and interest to subscribe to a periodical that digested and epitomized newsworthy information from all around Britain. Middle-class in the broadest sense of the word, the *Magazine* formed at least some of its readers' opinions through reprinting certain kinds of articles. As we shall see, these articles appealed to a desire for variety, "enlightenment," and experience.

Before I directly compare and contrast Charke's *Life* with the *Magazine*'s redaction, I would like to discuss the *Magazine* in more general terms, and to show the place of Charke's *Life* within an issue's contents. By 1755, the year that Charke's *Life* was published, the *Magazine* had settled into a structure that varied little from month to month. Printed in quarto, each number was broken into three parts. The first section consisted of essays extracted and epitomized from other newspapers and periodicals from all over England and Scotland as well as original essays and reviews of recently published books. Poetry from all kinds of contributors took up the next section. The final section consisted of "history" or news from around Britain and the world; death, marriage, and birth notices; stock-market quotes; and a list of recent books.[9]

Charke's *Life* first appeared in the October number in the essay section. As we can see from October's table of contents, her book is notably dissimilar from the kinds of essays included in the same issue:

—View of the *French* incroachments in *America* 435
—Reflexions of a *French* writer on the ambitious views of the *English* 438
—Weather and diseases for *Sep* & *Oct.* 439
—Fire issues from the bowels of a beast 439
—Monumental plate explained 440
—Story of *Rosetta* & *Chamont* 441
—Account of *Biddeford* 445
—A genuine letter from *Muley Ishmael,* late emperor of *Morocco,* to *Q. Anne* 448
—Account of *English* poisonous plants 450
—Ancient inscription explained 451
—Letter from Mr. *Porter,* the *English* ambassador at *Constantinople,* on the practice of inoculation in that country 452
—Epitome of the last part of the *Philos. Trans.* continued 453
—Life of *Charlotte Charke* 455
—*British* settlements in *N. America,* their history, continued 458
—A fiery meteor seen in *Holland* on in the *Thames* described 462
—Curious account of the epidemic disease at *Rouen* in 1753 462
—Cures for distemper of horned cattle 464
—Eclipses of *Jupiter's* satellites till *April* 1753 465
—Description of six curious shells 465
—New bill for relief of debtors proposed 465

Charke's *Life* will be extended over the following two numbers. Her story is told in greater length than any other essay in the entire volume, with the exception of "British settlements," a history of Britain's presence in the Americas from the Massachusetts settlement through 1755. Begun in May and continued through November, "British settlements" covers about twenty pages.[10] The "Epitome of the last part of the *Philos. Trans.*" ran in September, October, and November, but only covered four pages in total (*GM* 397, 453–54, 489). Given the serious, scientific, political, and philosophical nature of many of the pieces shown here, Charke's *Life*—so obviously different from the other articles and essays published—stands out as an anomaly. Something about Charke's *Life* fascinated "Sylvanus Urban," "editor" of the *Magazine,* and a decision was made to retell her story for the *Magazine*'s readership.

In fact, as issues from the whole decade demonstrate, Charke's *Life* is an anomaly within the empirical interests shown by the *Magazine*'s redactions. Female propriety occasioned a few essays and reprints. For example, in June 1751 the *Magazine* reprinted the "Delicate education and misfortune of a young Lady: from the *Rambler*" and in September 1751 the *Magazine* offered "Directions for young ladies in reading."[11] March 1753—in an essay that reads remarkably like Pamela's list of the correct duties for a wife—saw the publication of "The duty of a woman, as to elegance, employment, and education."[12] All of these essays either emphasize that the appropriate "education" of a woman enhances her potential suitably as a wife and mother or signify that her domestic responsibilities define her relationships to men. These articles are the exceptions; on the whole the *Magazine* focuses its attentions on empirical issues. The other exception to these preoccupations—and closest in content to Charke's *Life*—is a biography in the May 1752 issue entitled "Memoirs of Mrs *Ellen Gwynn.*"[13] This biography—unlike the redaction of Charke's *Life*—is prefaced by the editor with a justification for its inclusion: "It is with great pleasure that we communicate to our readers the following account, which shews the writer to have read and conversed much about theatrical affairs, and to be zealous that they should be faithfully related. We shall be glad to receive communications of the same kind from other hands" (*GM* 199). Heavily footnoted by the author, these "Memoirs" relate Nell Gwynn's life as both a series of sexual adventures and an implicit admiration of Gwynn's ability to rise above the scandal of being Charles II's "Protestant whore." The short preface assures the readers that they are getting a "faithfully related" true account of Gwynn's life. Unlike Charke, however, Gwynn is first and foremost a woman who under different circumstances would have settled down into domestic propriety: "'Tis highly probable that Madam *Ellen* might have made a more decent figure in life, had her birth been more fortunate, and her education good" (*GM* 200). Nell Gwynn—unlike Charke—had been dead for half a century. Gwynn's sexual transgressions are acceptable—indeed foregone conclusions—precisely because she was an actress. Her "Memoirs" have historical and anecdotal interest that can be explicitly justified by the *Magazine* as a part of history. Charke—also an actress—was very much alive when the *Magazine* redacted her *Life.* Charke's life in the theater is of much less interest to the *Magazine* than the sensational non-theatrical events in her biography. Charke's birth was "fortunate," of course, since she was the daughter of one of the most famous men in England. As we shall see, the *Magazine* does not regard Charke's education as "good." One wonders why the *Magazine* chose her racy narrative for inclusion among so many explicitly educational articles?

Charke begins her *Life* with an extraordinarily brazen gesture. She dedicates the book "TO HERSELF." A direct comparison between the *Life* and the *Magazine*'s version shows the disjunction between the two works. What the *Magazine* leaves out undermines Charke's own presentation of a "self": a self-conscious construction of character and authority. The *Magazine* begins its version with Charke's birth (*GM* 455). It explicitly ignores her audacious dedication; it also omits the introductory remarks that open the autobiography. It is precisely the "noise" of Charke's self-portrayal—in this case her confident display of authorial voice—that the *Magazine* tries to silence. By contrast, in her dedication Charke-the-author addresses herself—Charke-the-"patron"—in the book's first paragraph: "THO' Flattery is universally known to be the Spring from which Dedications frequently flow, I hope I shall escape that Odium so justly thrown on poetical Petitioners, notwithstanding my Attempt to illustrate those WONDERFUL QUALIFICATIONS by which you have so EMINENTLY DISTINGUISH'D YOURSELF, and gives you a just Claim to the Title of NONPAREIL OF THE AGE" (A1r-ii). Charke's irony is evident for several reasons. First is the obvious parody of the traditional dedication. And Charke gives clear signals about how she will construct her subject in the book itself. The capital letters that scream at the reader and the characterization of her "patron" as having "WONDERFUL QUALIFICATIONS" and "the Title of NONPAREIL OF THE AGE" acknowledge the hyperbole and hypocrisy of traditional dedications. She makes "herself" the subject of the overdetermined "Flattery"—which she tells "herself" is *not* to be taken as flattery in any case. The over-the-top rhetorical strategy has the effect of excluding the reader directly. Paradoxically, this strategy indirectly allows the perceptive reader to be in on the joke, to hear her brazen voice, to unpack all the different "selves" who are the subjects of her book.

Then Charke suggests to "herself" how she should take the veracity of her stories. When her "patron" reads and thinks about the book's anecdotes, Charke asks that she "tenderly overlook *their Errors,* and, to the utmost of your Power, endeavour *to magnify their Merits*" (vii). Again, Charke asks her "patron"—and by extension, "herself" *and* those readers who get her point—to make allowances for straying from the truth of her autobiography. This suggests that exaggeration—implicit fiction?—will play a role in her autobiography. The total effect is a narrator in command of her subject, in this case an outrageous woman who refused to play her assigned feminine role. The readers are forced either to play along with the narrator and enjoy the performance, or be left behind to take her autobiography literally. They are confronted with at least three different Charkes: the author, the subject—"herself"—to whom the book is dedicated, and, as we shall see, the main character of her story.

By conflating the narrator and the subject of Charke's *Life,* the *Magazine* reduces Charke's "character" to the catalyst for a series of travesties that display Charke's transgression from female propriety. Perhaps confounded by Charke's grasp of authority, the *Magazine* ignores the dedication. Sidonie Smith argues that in the preface Charke "announces at the outset a flair for dramatic posturing, an energetic preoccupation with theatrical entertainment and self-fabrication that enhances the reader's pleasure."[14] The *Magazine*'s deletion of the dedication takes *away* any "pleasure" for the reader in its version. This has the effect of—again—containing Charke and shutting out the very loud noise she makes as the author. I would argue that the *Magazine* has three choices in rewriting Charke. It can quote Charke and comment on her dedication, thus confronting Charke the author directly and admitting her authority. It can castigate her for her self-importance or be amused by her audacity. Again, this is an admittance of a writer in control of her subject, what she calls "the little Brat of my Brain" (12). Or, finally—and this is the *Magazine*'s choice—it can ignore the dedication altogether and thus overlook the complexity of Charke's rhetorical strategy. It rewrites completely her *Life* by taking a first-person narrative and turning it into a third-person redaction.

In general, the plain style of *The Gentleman's Magazine* is in direct contrast to Charke's own extravagant language. To a reader familiar with the spirited way Charke starts her *Life,* the *Magazine*'s opening is abrupt indeed. "Charlotte, the youngest daughter of Mr *Colley Cibber,*" the *Magazine* begins, "was born when her mother was five and forty years of age, long after it was thought she would have no more children. As she was an unexpected guest, she was received with unusual pleasure, and began from her birth to suffer the peculiar misfortunes of favourites; for tho' she was taught *French* as soon as she could speak, she was never taught the use of her needle at all" (*GM* 455). The rhetorical strategy here is to suggest an impartial narrator. On the contrary, to rewrite a work like Charke's *Life*—to put her prose into its own words (and ten thousand words over three separate numbers is a lot of text)—is a labor-intensive act. This daunting task shows not only fascination but an effort to tame or domesticate a singular woman. As other essays in this volume point out, Charke's desires—what constitutes her real "self"—are difficult, if not impossible, to pin down. However, the *Magazine,* through its redaction, remakes Charke and recasts her life as a series of anecdotes that focus on her bad luck, her debt, ill health, and what it calls "her masculine turn of mind" (*GM* 456).

In the opening paragraph, the *Magazine* erases Charke's own comments on her birth: that she was the cause for jealousy from her sisters and that what the *Magazine* terms "the peculiar misfortunes of favourites" were in her words "a tender care of [her] Education" (16). Probably to the *Magazine*'s dismay, Charke celebrates what she sees as her deserved status as favorite: "a genius" for whom "all Advantages from Nature are the favourable Gifts of the Power Divine" (16). What will the reader of the *Magazine* take away from Charke's life that differs from the reader of her autobiography? A character, indeed a fabulous creation of self *constructed* by Charke, is rewritten to conform to the possible morality of the *Magazine*'s audience. In effect, the *Magazine* wrests control of Charke's *Life* from the narrator. It novelizes but *appears* to tell only the "facts" or events in her life—which Charke in her dedication has already suggested is at least in part fictive. These "facts" are, in fact, a selection that leaves out Charke's strong voice. The *Magazine*'s selective recounting of her story becomes, then, a didactic warning against female transgression couched within the impartial tone of its prose.

Charke makes another clever rhetorical gesture ignored by the *Magazine.* In the dedication, she implies the fictive nature of her work. She moves from a panegyric about her own "WONDERFUL QUALIFICATIONS" to a quote by Delarivier Manley: "I hope, dear Madam, as MANLY says in *The Provok'd Husband,* that 'LAST REPROACH HAS STRUCK YOU'', and that you and I may ripen our Acquaintance into a perfect Knowledge of each other, that may establish a lasting and social Friendship between us" (viii). Here Charke links the division between narrator and subject—which constitutes her grasp of writerly authority. Manley was a highly successful novelist and the author of one of the most amusing and self-serving autobiographies of the eighteenth century. Manley's *The Adventures of Rivella*[15] is a justification of her notorious life. She wrote *Rivella* in the first-person guise of a male admirer to explain and vindicate the life of perhaps the most popular early eighteenth-century novelist. In Charke's context, Manley's quote is provocative. Charke recognizes the low critical esteem in which Manley was held. She also recognizes her own position as author of a scandalous autobiography, one relating a transgressive life. Charke writes with the self-conscious awareness of her female forebears who have disrupted the masculinist status quo through their writing. The act of writing her own life story becomes a source of power through the way she uses her pen to justify her actions to her readers.

As Charke's *Life* opens, we see her following a tradition of female authority that can be found in such novels as *Oroonoko* by Aphra Behn and Manley's scandal fiction.[16] Behn, for example, consistently confronts the masculinist notion that her status as a woman writer might undercut her narrative's authority. She uses this approach, though, to privilege her position as an eyewitness to the events she describes and thus to authenticate the political agenda of her novel. The historical "truth" of Oroonoko told by an eyewitness compensates for Behn's lesser reliability as a woman writer. Likewise, Charke deprecates her own abilities as a woman writer in order to anticipate objections, and thus assert her own authority. "As the following History is the Product of a Female Pen," she tells her readers, "I tremble for the terrible Hazard it must run in venturing into the World, and it may very possibly suffer, in many Opinions, without perusing it; I therefore humbly move for its having the common Chance of a Criminal, at least to be properly examin'd, before it is ·condemn'd" (11–12). Charke follows the footsteps of Manley with the audacious but ironic dedication to her autobiography, and follows Behn in her deprecation of the "female pen." It might be construed as disingenuous of Charke to "tremble" at the publication of her autobiography. Charke knows, of course, full well what she is doing. Her combination of bravado—exemplified by the dedication—and modesty—asking for the "Chance of a Criminal"—seems to me to be the consummate actress accepting kudos for her role. This time her role is that of an author and the product is performance-as-author, that "little Brat of my Brain," the creation of the character "Charlotte Charke."

Much of the discomfort that *The Gentleman's Magazine* shows in its rewriting of Charke's *Life* stems from a refusal by Charke to pin "Charlotte Charke" into a fixed character. "Character"—whether a role performed by an actress or the values embodied by men and women within a particular society or, as I am arguing here, the written presentation of a particular life—was of great concern to eighteenth-century moralists. Nussbaum argues that such authors and works as "Pope, Fielding, Johnson, and the anonymous tracts on character attempt to fix gendered identity when traditional notions were disintegrating."[17] The different ways that Charke and the *Magazine* portray her education is a blueprint for the disintegration of "fixed gendered identity." The *Magazine* tells the reader: "At eight years of age she was sent to Mrs. *Draper's* boarding school in *Parkstreet, Westminster,* where she began to learn *Latin, Italian, geography, music,* and *dancing,* and after continuing there two years, she was taken home and attended by proper masters, to finish her education" (*GM* 456). Charke's own characterization of her stay at Mrs. Draper's school shows how the *Magazine's* revision of the *Life* reduces a much more complex construction of her "character." Mrs. Draper, Charke writes, "employ'd a Gentleman, call'd Monsieur *Flahaut,* an excellent Master of Languages, to instruct her boarders; . . . and as he discovered in me a tolerable Genius, and an earnest Desire of Improvement, he advised my Mother . . . to let him teach me *Latin* and *Italian,* which she, proud of hearing me capable of receiving, readily consented to" (25–26). The "proper masters" alluded to at the end of the *Magazine's* redaction could mean that Charke had tutors just as qualified as Monsieur Flahaut to teach her at home. However, the paragraph that immediately follows the *Magazine's* description above contains an ironic tone: "When this great work was thought to be accomplished, she was taken to *Hillingdon* near *Uxbridge* by her mother" (*GM* 456). This tone—seen from the diction "great work"—suggests that it was *improper* for young Charlotte to be taught such "masculine" pursuits as foreign languages or geography. The "peculiarities of sex and character" (*GM* 537) that fascinate the *Magazine* come from Charke's unsuitable education. But the *Magazine* also erases Charke's self-description as "a tolerable Genius" and her mother's pride at that "Genius." Charke's self-characterization—perhaps exaggerated—is reduced to conform to the *Magazine's* notions of what constitutes proper education for a young woman: "she did not even learn how to provide an elegant table" (*GM* 456). Whether Charke is a "genius" or not is unimportant; her lack of female accomplishments determines the parameters for her later transgressions.

After her introductory remarks, Charke says "my Education consisted chiefly in Studies of various Kinds, and gave me a different Turn of Mind than what I might have had, if my Time had been employ'd in ornamenting a piece of Canvas with Beasts, Birds, and the Alphabet" (17). "A different Turn of Mind" is ambiguous and provocative, but only implicitly gender-based. The phrase does indeed suggest that Charke had slight interest in the appropriate pursuits of little girls, but there is nothing that explicitly denotes transgressive gendered or sexualized behavior. But the *Magazine* erases ambiguity in a couple of ways. First, the *Magazine* tells us that Charke's "masculine turn of mind" (*GM* 456) soon directed her to the amusements of shooting, in which she became greatly proficient. By replacing "different" with "masculine," the *Magazine* transforms Charke's meaning from uncertainty for the reader to decided female transgression. Second, the *Magazine* moves the reworked phrase itself from right before Charke's description of her first cross-dressing episode as a little girl to *after* her relations of the episode and *after* her description of her formal education. Charke's "masculine turn of mind" is linked directly to her education and indirectly to her "early fondness" to dress in drag. Even though the *Magazine* seems to tell her story impartially, it is actually constructing Charke's "character" as transgressive both through a "natural" inclination to cross-dress as well as an an unsuitable education for a girl.

Thus, our first glimpse of Charke's "character" in the *Magazine* is a travesty in which the young Charlotte puts on her father's clothing. I am not arguing, I want to emphasize, that Charke's "different Turn of Mind" cannot be suggestive of homoerotic desire. I do believe, however, that the terms that establish Charke in the twentieth century as an emblem that celebrates homoerotic desire can be traced to the *Magazine*'s characterization of Charke as "masculine" instead of "different." In this case, of course, the *Magazine* is not celebrating Charke's "masculinity." Instead, her "masculine turn of mind" enables the eighteenth-century reader to understand why Charke led such a disreputable life. Charke's behavior can be explained away as "peculiar" masculinity caused by "an unsuitable education," whereas Charke's own self-characterization as "different" is far more enigmatic.

The *Magazine* further erases ambiguity: it ignores the self-consciously comical effect of Charke's first adventure in drag through its straightforward narrative. The complexity and pleasure the eighteenth-century reader takes from the *Life* is expunged by the *Magazine*'s version. "She relates several incredible stories of her early fondness to appear in a man's habit," the *Magazine* tells us:

> particularly that at four years old she put on a tye-wig and beaver of her father's, with his large silver hilted sword, a waistcoat of her brother's, and pinned up a dimity coat of her own to serve for breeches, and being thus equipped, marched into the fields . . . and was found some hours afterwards patrolling along the bottom of a dry ditch . . . in the midst of a crowd of people that had gathered about her. That another time she got astride on an ass, and was ushered into the town by a boy fiddling before her. But these are evidently either wholly fictitious, or so greatly exaggerated as totally to disguise the truth. (*GM* 455–56)

The first of these two anecdotes is, in fact, the only instance Charke offers of what she herself terms her "early Fondness" (17) to cross-dress. The *Magazine* does exactly what it accuses Charke of doing: it exaggerates Charke's own narrative. It does so by its method of retelling Charke's text through an impartial narrator in conjunction with an editorial aside: this is one of "several incredible storys," and a revealing direct quote: her "early fondness" to wear men's clothing. The *Magazine* downplays the performative effect of Charke's playful tone, and instead emphasizes her "early fondness" to cross-dress. Charke's complex analysis of this episode is reduced by the *Magazine* to an amusing anecdote, just as her education is reduced to giving her "a masculine turn of mind."

Charke's own version of her initial forays into transvestism pokes fun at her "escapade" and is an early recounting of her delight in disguise and exhibition, of costume and performance. Her version also shows how the *Magazine* attempts to contain Charke's construction of a self. Charke begins by undercutting the provocative effect of her cross-dressing: "As I have promised to conceal nothing that might raise a Laugh, I shall begin with a small Specimen of my former Madness, when I was but four Years of Age" (17). There is, however, an interesting tension between what she offers for "a Laugh" and her taste for men's clothing: "Having, even then, a Fondness for a Perriwig. . . . I took down a Waistcoat of my brother's" she writes, "and an enormous busy Tie-wig of my Father's, which entirely enclos'd my Head and Body, with the Knots of the Ties thumping my little Heels as I marched along, with slow and solemn pace" (18). The narrator's staging of this scene is so comically exaggerated it is hard to reconcile young Charlotte's appearance with later images of Charke as "Mr. Brown."

The impact of Charke's description relies on careful delineation of the scene as well as the tension between her desire to entertain her reader—an anecdote told for "a Laugh"—and the fascination she has for a periwig. More significantly, I would argue, Charke reveals an actor's sensitivity to place and costume, as well as the effect of her performance on an audience, in this case both her performance as a child and her performance as a writer. She shows how she prepared for her part, and is responsive to how she was perceived by her onlookers: "and, in this Grotesque Pigmy-State, [I] walked up and down the Ditch bowing to all who came by me" (19). The ironic self-awareness of an actress's role and her reception by her audience is entirely lacking in the *Magazine*'s straightforward description. "The Croud about me," she tells the reader, "yielded me no small Joy, as I conceived their Risibility on this occasion to be Marks of Approbation, and walked myself into a Fever, in the happy Thought of being taken for the 'Squire" (19).

To young Charlotte, this was a successful performance; to the author of the autobiography, this is but one story that constructs not only Charlotte Charke the actress—real-life daughter of Colley Cibber—but the character she pre-sents to her readers as well. By acknowledging the "Risibility" of her perfor-mance's effect, she shows herself fully aware of the effect of *all* her stories. She gives her readers a self-critical review of one of her own performances. The whole family, she says, came out "to be Witness of my State and Dignity" (19). Her mother and father retrieved her from her stage—the ditch—and, she writes, to her "Shame and Disgrace" she was "forc'd into [her] proper Habil-ment" (19–20). The effect of this anecdote is curious. Her "Shame and Dis-grace" are not due to what the *Magazine* terms "her early fondness to appear in a man's habit" but instead the disapproval shown by her most important critic: her father. Her own self-characterized "early Fondness for a Perriwig" is less important to Charke the narrator than her early desire to trod the boards, to perform for an audience.

The narrative technique of the *Magazine*'s version, on the other hand, al-lows no difference between Charke's narrative voice and the character of "Charlotte Charke" who enjoys spectacle. The *Magazine* dismisses both her performance in the ditch and her riding an ass as "either wholly fictitious, or so greatly exaggerated as totally to disguise the truth" (*GM* 456). On the one hand, it does relate her story, thus giving one *version* of Charke's self-charac-terization. On the other hand, it can accuse Charke of being a liar with some-thing ambiguous to hide. Charke has, of course, anticipated charges of exag-geration in the opening pages of her book. She tells the reader that shortly after her first performance in a periwig, she rode an ass "triumphantly into Town astride, with numerous Retinue" (22). The *Magazine*'s dismissal of these an-ecdotes as "fictitious" or "exaggerated" makes one wonder what "truth" the *Magazine* believes is being concealed? Is Charke's "early fondness" for men's clothes the foundation for the outrageous presentation of her later self? Or is the *Magazine* confounded by Charke's assertion of a woman's personality that even from an early age delights in, as Straub says, "intractability"? Charke's own love for disguise and display become something almost sinister by the *Magazine*'s representation of these stories as an exaggeration "to disguise" some unnamed "truth."

Charke's recollection of her father's response to the triumphant ride is tell-ing: "I perfectly remember, young as I was then, the strong Mixture of Sur-prize, Pleasure, Pain and Shame in his Countenance, on his viewing me seat-ed on my infantical *Rosinante;* which, tho' I had not then Sense enough to distinguish, my Memory has since afforded me the Power to describe, and also to repeat his very Words, at his looking out of Window, *God demme! An Ass upon an Ass!*" (22). Her audience—or at least the critic who counted—was her father. His reaction confirms the effect of both of these anecdotes: less-than-successful performances in inappropriate venues. Her father, of course, plays an essential role in Charke's *Life,* and to a certain extent, she is writing this book *for* her father, in a very public forum. Cibber's role in the *Magazine*'s redaction is nearly nonexistent. For Charke, then, these anecdotes are addressed both to her father and to her readers. The "Memory" of her father's response to this episode is a rhetorical strategy in which cross-dressing in only one part of the anecdote's total effect of Charke's self-characterization. It is not so much that she is in drag that upsets Cibber; he does after all take some "pleasure" in what he witnesses. Rather she is not behaving with the propriety of a little girl, but makes a spectacle of herself—"*An Ass upon an Ass!*"—in an inappropriate venue. Charke's retelling—fictive or not—is in fact given credence by the strong memory of her father's response to the performance. The *Magazine* dimisses the story as "fictitious" or "exaggerated," thus erasing the careful delineation of character set up by Charke's account.

At the end of the anecdote, Charke introduces a quote in the text: "'*O! Fall of Honour!*' 'Tis not to be conceived, the violent Indignation and Contempt my Disgrace rais'd in my Infant Breast; nor did I forgive my Mother, tho' I was oblig'd to ask Pardon in a few Moments of her, at the Time, who, at that Time, I conceiv'd to be most in fault" (22). Like the many other digressions in Charke's *Life,* the *Magazine* ignores this one, perhaps because these asides work to complicate Charke's many-faceted "character." Moreover, the uncertain connotation of this aside is particularly intriguing.

By the time that Charke wrote her autobiography, "honor" for women no longer signified a class-based defintion of female sexual identity. Eighteenth-century novelists from Manley to Richardson redefined honor in a paradigmatic shift from a woman's literal virture or chastity—her economic value as a sexual object—to a woman's own sense of self. "In place of the intricate status system that had long dominated British thinking," writes Nancy Armstrong, "these authors began to represent an individual's values in terms of his, but more often in terms of *her,* essential qualities of mind."[18] Nussbaum offers a partial answer to why Charke includes an aside on honor within an anecdote of childhood playacting: "Character," Nussbaum argues, is not a fixed generic paradigm. Further, Charke challenges the *Magainze*'s attempts to fix character within the confines of its editorial choices. That the *Magazine* is so fascinated with Charke's *Life* demonstrates precisely how, as Nussbaum contends, eighteenth-century female character started to "exceed the limits of privacy and domesticity that would seem, in dominant ideologies, to define it."[19]

Honor—in the context of Charke's *Life*—connotes so many meanings that Charke's ride on an ass simply cannot be reduced to an "incredible" story without the deletion of this aside. How a reader understands Charke's "Honour" is dependent on her father's and her mother's reaction, and the multiple meanings honor has for her readers: a recognition of Charke's own embarrassment at a performance ill-received, the impropriety of a girl who dresses like a boy, as well as a recognition that Charke embarrassed her parents and was misunderstood by everyone who watched her performance. Charke's "Fall of Honour," in effect, complicates her "character" for the reader even more than her analysis of her escapade. The multiple interpretations implied by her anecdote have, in turn, been simplified by the *Magazine*'s matter-of-fact relating.

The multiple interpretations that can be gleaned from Charke's text are further simplified by the *Magazine* by its emphasis on Charke's adventures in drag. For example, it relates in great detail the episode in which Charke became the object of desire for a "young lady of great fortune" (*GM* 496). Charke's stint as "*Gentleman to a noble Lord*" (*GM* 497) is given much attention, as well as her experience as "a waiter at Mrs. *Dorr's* . . . to whom she was represented as a young man reduced by misfortunes from better circumstances" (*GM* 499) and with whose daughter Charke has a flirtation. These are, of course, the most sensational of Charke's stories, and she acknowledges this. Significantly, though, she refuses to tell the "original Motivation" behind her cross dressing (139). The first time she mentions being dressed in men's clothes as an adult, transvestism is explicitly a way for her to escape creditors. After she marries for the second time, her husband dies and leaves her with no money and massive debts. Charke is arrested, and this arrest is a direct result of her unusual appearance "effected by Dint of a very handsome lac'd Hat I had on, being then, for some substantial reasons, EN CAVALIER" (90). What does Charke mean by "substantial reasons"? I would argue that on one level, the "substantial reasons" are nothing more than an effort to keep herself out of debtor's prison. But the *Magazine* does not read Charke this way.

The narrator explicates and assigns explicit meaning to Charke's drag. "Substantial reasons" could, of course, signal a transgressive desire to dress up as a man. This is how the *Magazine* translates Charke's "reasons." In the *Magazine*'s revision, "substantial reasons" become a way of life: Charke "usually appeared for some time before, in man's habit" (*GM* 458). Unnamed but implicitly economic "substantial reasons" in the autobiography are made deviant precisely *because* the *Magazine* changes the diction from "substantial reasons" to "usually appeared." The *Magazine* subtly undercuts Charke's ambivalence and foregrounds her transgressions from female propriety. It emphasizes

Charke's cross dressing and thus conflates her "masculine turn of mind" with an "early fondness" for drag. The resulting character of "Charlotte Charke" in the *Magazine*'s redaction is a transgressive sexualized subject.

All of Charke's self-reflective moments are excised from the *Magazine*'s redaction. By the end of its version, the *Magazine* condenses the last thirty pages of Charke's *Life* into one short paragraph:

> From *Bath* [Charke] wandered thro' several towns, subsisting from place to place by playing with the companies she found in her way, and at least once more set her foot on *London* streets, with only a single penny in her pocket. Her next expedient was to write the narrative of which this is an epitome, which she sold in numbers, and she was soon after engaged with her brother at the new theatre in the *Haymarket*, where she continued till his license was withdrawn, and proposes to make another attempt as an author, by writing the history of Mr. *Dumont*. (*GM* 539)

Left out of this rather breathless summary is everything that happened between her return to "*London* streets" and writing "the narrative of which this is an epitome." Charke's complaints about her daughter's "unsuitable" marriage are ignored, as are her flattering of her colleagues in the theater, her pleading to her father, and the unfair way she was treated by her sister.

It is precisely Charke's chameleon character and love of disguise—both literal and narrative—that prove so impenetrable for the *Magazine*'s redaction of her *Life*. From the moment young Charlotte puts on her father's periwig, disguise and performance play a dominant role in the way Charke relates her *Life*. Charke leaves unclear throughout the book when she is in drag and when she is dressed as a woman unless it directly affects either her economic security or provides the basis for a predicament she finds herself in. "My being in Breeches was alleged to me as a very great Error," she tells the reader in another digression, "but the original Motive proceeded from a particular Cause; and I rather chuse to undergo the worst Imputation that can be laid on me on that Account, than unravel the Secret, which is an Appendix to one I am bound, as before hinted, by all the Vows of Truth and Honour everlastingly to conceal" (139). This seems to me to be an enormously important and suggestive passage. Whatever that "particular Cause" signifies, Charke leaves unspoken. It is up to the reader to deduce what the "original Motive" and "particular Cause" may be. Further, each time she explicitly talks of transvestism, she is describing a role for herself, a disguise for her "self." For *The Gentleman's Magazine* her drag is emphasized throughout as a way to explain her outrageous, distinctly nonconforming female behavior, what it calls her lack of "diffidence and timidity" (*GM* 457), her "unaccountable follies" (*GM* 456), or her "masculine turn of mind." By disguising her self, Charke keeps the reader of her *Life* off guard. Her insistence on keeping the "Motive" a "Secret" serves to complicate a reading of her *Life* that separates transvestism and homoerotic desire.

In an early passage the *Magazine* tells us that Charke "took to gardening; and this too she affected rather to follow in the character of a clown, as a profession, than in her own, as an amusement" (*GM* 456). The *Magazine* hits the nail on the head. Charke may in fact feel "natural" about her love for gardening—for digging in the ground and dirtying her hands—as much as it seems to indicate to a twentieth-century reader that her cross dressing combined with her ambiguous relationship with "Mrs. Brown" signal homoerotic desire. But throughout the *Life* Charke gives the impression of acting a role, of assuming a character. On a certain level, the *Magazine* is reading Charke as Charke wants her readers to understand her story. She does, after all, refuse to give the motivation for her cross dressing. However, the *Magazine*'s version of the *Life* indicates its disapproval for Charke's self-characterization. By calling her a "clown" the *Magazine* shows its discomfort with Charke's "character," her self-conscious attempts to remake herself in ways that do not reflect the proper role for a young woman. As I have noted, Charke explicitly does not tell her readers why she chose to masquerade as a man. Dekker and van de Pol suggest a number of reasons that women in the eighteenth century cross dressed: "the pressures which led to the decision of cross-dressing could be both material, such as poverty, or emotional, such as patriotic fervour, or a combination of these."[20] For Dekker and van de Pol, transvestism and homoerotic desire do not necessarily go hand in hand. The *Magazine* conflates Charke's love of drag and disguise with her "masculine turn of mind." It demonstrates how sexuality becomes—as Armstrong and others have noted—a way to think about and define notions of self and subjectivity. Charke herself writes of this period, "I was entirely lost in a Forgetfulness of my real Self" (42). Her "real Self" is exactly the basis for an understanding—and a misunderstanding—of the *Life*.

The Gentleman's Magazine's epitome shows that it is not possible to understand completely Charke's "real Self" as she presents it. Her life is a series of anecdotes with tantalizing hints of homoeroticism through her cross dressing, her friendship with "Mrs. Brown," and her romances with young women who mistake Charke for a man.[21] The *Magazine*, in the end, foregrounds the events of her life and erases Charke's reflections on her "mad-Cap Self" (33) or "former Madness" that complicate her self-described "different Turn of Mind." The *Magazine* essentializes Charke's identity through its emphasis on her cross-dressing episodes and love of "masculine" pursuits. The impartial tone of the *Magazine*'s revision reveals the unease it feels toward this woman who refuses to see herself in any normative female role. The result of the editor's emphasis on Charke's "masculinity" and transgressive, distinctly unfeminine behavior anticipates the twentieth-century criticism of Charke's *Life,* a result crucial for an understanding of the impact of her book. To read the *Magazine*'s redaction now—in conjunction with Charke's *Life*—demonstrates the dangers of a too-narrow analysis of Charke. The character that Charke presents in her book certainly exhibits traits of homoerotic desire. But the *Magazine* leaves out the self-conscious narrative voice that constructs the larger "character" of "Charlotte Charke." Her explicitly individual voice is tranquilized and her book is reduced to a cautionary tale. By pushing the "mad-cap" escapades and focusing on Charke's transgressive female behavior, the *Magazine* undermines the authority Charke seizes with her pen.

Sexuality in the eighteenth century—as writers such as Trumbach, Epstein and Straub, Foucault, and Armstrong have shown—is an unstable notion.[22] A comparison of Charke's *Life* to *The Gentleman's Magazine* shows why Charlotte Charke still holds such fascination for twentieth-century feminist and queer readers. Nussbaum is absolutely correct when she writes that "Charke . . . remains uncertain about the way to assign gender to the subjectivity produced by culture."[23] *A Narrative of the Life of Mrs. Charlotte Charke* celebrates *all* of her transgressions: as a woman, an actress, a mother, a transvestite, and—at times—a failure. *The Gentleman's Magazine* tries to contain and explain Charke through its revisions. Further, the *Magazine* shows how "transgression" is determined by rules of its and Charke's culture. We cannot reconstruct Charke's own sexual persona. On the other hand, we can begin to understand how she was perceived by the normative culture she so gleefully and transgressively inhabited.

Notes

1. Aside from J. A. Downie and Thomas N. Cors, eds., *Telling People What to Think: Early Eighteenth-Century Periodicals from the Review to the Rambler* (London: F. Cass, 1993), based on a special issue of *Prose Studies* 16:1 (April 1993); most of the attention paid to the periodicals of the period has been in the context of politics, and not cultural history. I believe that closer study of such periodicals as *The Gentleman's Magazine* can enhance cultural history of literature, particularly as eighteenth-century literature and society were perceived by these arbiters of taste.

2. Charlotte Charke, *A Narrative of the Life of Mrs. Charlotte Charke,* 2d ed., intro. Leonard R. N. Ashley (London: 1755; facsimile, Gainesville: Scholars Facsimiles & Reprints, 1969), xxiii. References to the text are noted parenthetically in the essay.

3. Kristina Straub, "The Guilty Pleasures of Theatrical Cross-Dressing and the Autobiography of Charlotte Charke," in *Body Guards: The Cultural Politics of Gender Ambiguity,* ed. Julia Epstein and Kristina Straub (London: Routledge, 1991), 158.

4. *The Gentleman's Magazine,* v. 25 (London: 1755). References to the text are noted parenthetically in the essay.

5. Charke's *Life* can be found in the *Magazine* on pp. 455–59, 495–500, and 537–40.

6. "A brief Account of the Articles contained in Part II of Volume XLVIII, of the *Philosophical Transactions,* just published, beginning with Article *LVIII*" in *The Gentleman's Magazine,* September, October, November 1755 (397, 453–55, 489).

7. Felicity Nussbaum points out the problems of such a reading in "Heteroclites: The Gender of Character in the Scandalous Memoirs," in *The New Eighteenth-Century: Theory, Politics, English Literature,* ed. Laura Brown and Felicity Nussbaum (New York: Methuen, 1987), 144–65. See Lynne Friedli, "'Passing Women': A Study of Gender Boundaries in the Eighteenth Century," in *Sexual Underworlds of the Enlightenment,* ed. Roy Porter and G. S. Rousseau (Chapel Hill: University of North Carolina Press, 1988), 234–60. Lisa Moore's review essay "'She Was Too Fond of Her Mistaken Bargain': The Scandalous Relations of Gender and Sexuality in Feminist Theory," *Diacritics* 21:2–3 (Summer–Fall 1991): 89–101, tends to overstate the homoerotic celebratory possibilities of Charke's book in her review of Felicity Nussbaum's *The Autobiographical Subject: Gender and Ideology in Eighteenth-Century England* (Baltimore: Johns Hopkins University Press, 1989). Cheryl Wanko, on the other hand, discusses as I do the performative aspects of Charke's life, but critiques Charke because her *Life* "does not negotiate the demands of gender performance successfully" (86) in "The Eighteenth-Century Actress and the Construction of Gender," *Eighteenth-Century Life* 18.2 (May 1994): 75–90. However, Wanko does argue—following Nussbaum—that "Charke's refusal to conform to gender norms . . . is a rebellious assertion of a new configuration" of subjectivity (87). See too Sidonie Smith, "The Transgressive Daughter and the Masquerade of Self-Representation" in *A Poetics of Women's Autobiography: Marginality and the Fictions of Self-Representation* (Bloomington: Indiana University Press, 1987), 102–22. Smith argues that "Charke fails to escape her dependency on the father. . . . she remains disempowered psychologically, financially, narratively, ideologically" (122). Up to a point, she is correct; however, the unease that the *Magazine* shows for Charke's representation of her self seems to complicate Smith's conclusion. Also see Pat Rogers, "The Breeches Part," in *Sexuality in Eighteenth-Century Britain,* ed. Paul-Gabriel Boucé (Totowa: Manchester University Press; Barnes & Noble, 1982), 244–58. Rogers writes that Charke "was in all probability homosexual" without really complicating that notion (252).

8. C. Lennart Carlson, *The First Magazine: A History of "The Gentleman's Magazine"* (Providence: Brown, 1938), 58.

9. It is interesting that Charke's *Life* is not noted in the "books published" section in any of the numbers in 1755.

10. *GM,* 214–17, 261–64, 291–94, 349–54, 409–13, 458–61, 499–500.

11. *The Gentleman's Magazine,* v. 21 (London, 1751), 255–57, 390.

12. Ibid., v. 23 (London, 1753), 133–34.

13. Ibid., v. 22 (London, 1752), 199–200.

14. Smith, "Transgressive Daughter," 103.

15. Delarivier Manley, *The Adventures of Rivella* (London: 1714).

16. Ros Ballaster, in *Seductive Forms: Women's Amatory Fiction from 1684 to 1740* (Oxford: Clarendon Press, 1992), discusses the ways in which such women novelists of the late seventeenth and early eighteenth centuries as Behn and Manley use the novel in complex ways to assert their own female power.

17. Nussbaum, "Heteroclites," 150.

18. Armstrong, *Desire and Domestic Fiction,* 5.

19. Nussbaum, "Heteroclites," 146.

20. Rudolf M. Dekker and Lotte C. van de Pol, *The Tradition of Female Transvestism in Early Modern Europe* (New York: St. Martin's Press, 1989), 2.

21. Despite the significance given to Charke's friendship with "Mrs. Brown" in the *Magazine*—and in fact in contemporary criticism—her friend actually plays a small role in the autobiography itself (Charke 192, 224–25, 231, 233, 245, 260, 262). Further, outside of her "affair" with the young gentlewoman, Charke only calls herself "Mr. Brown" one other time in the book (Charke 148). This suggests to me that Charke's drag—while an important aspect of her "character"—is only one way to try and make sense of her "self."

22. Epstein and Straub, "Introduction: The Guarded Body" in *Body Guards: The Cultural Politics of Gender Ambiguity,* 1–28; Randolph Trumbach, "Sodomitical Assaults, Gender Role, and Sexual Development in Eighteenth-Century London," in *The Pursuit of Sodomy: Male Homosexuality in Renaissance and Enlightenment Europe,* ed. Kent Gerard and Gert Hekma (New York: Harrington Park Press, 1989), 407–32.

23. Nussbaum, "Heteroclites," 165.

8

Turning to Men:
Genres of Cross-Dressing in Charke's *Narrative* and Shakespeare's *The Merchant of Venice*

Joseph Chaney

Apologetic Teleology

Current interest in Charlotte Charke focuses, not surprisingly, on the question of her gender identity. In what sense is she subversive of eighteenth-century gender norms, and by what rules may this subversion be measured and given meaning? Although the various identities the author constructs for herself in *A Narrative of the Life of Mrs. Charlotte Charke* seem conventional, what is new—and too disturbing in its ineluctably fragmentary textuality to have been appreciated before the late twentieth century—is the way in which the name Charlotte Charke attaches to so many different and contradictory identities within the narrative. The text is a fabric of performances. However, a reading that emphasizes the performative constitution of gender identity without paying sufficient attention to genre runs the risk of assuming too easily that a subversion of historical gender configurations does in fact take place in the *Narrative,* or that such a subversion could be immediately readable, that it could arrive with its own interpretation, announce its own heterodox significance. Since Charke represents her gender performances without irony and within a moralizing genre that neutralizes their potential subversiveness, we should resist the temptation to view her as an intentionally subversive or consciously feminist figure.

   In this essay I shall examine Charke's representation of her life in order to determine the nature of her motives for cross-dressing. I shall compare her gender performances to an earlier, literally theatrical performance, that of Shakespeare's Portia in *The Merchant of Venice*. Shakespeare's play not only provides an example of a successful subversion and reconfiguration of gender relations by a cross-dressing woman, it also enables us to see in what sense and to what degree any such reconfiguration can be representable. Although the one text is autobiographical and the other dramatic, they present a similar obstacle to the critic who seeks to isolate within them a subversive moment in the history of gender configurations: the teleological genre governing each text threatens to obscure, under an ideological veil of obvious meanings, whatever subversion we might hope to find there. Reading the meaning of cross-dressing in these texts therefore requires a preliminary unveiling, or an understanding of how the texts themselves perform a generic "cross-dressing," occulting the limiting and negating elements of their own apparent truths. Perhaps such a reading is less a matter of undressing the text to reveal the subversive truth beneath the generic disguise, than of determining in what way the genre depends for its very definition upon the unpresentable subversive "content" it formally denies. Conversely, the subversive content is structurally dependent upon its formal disguise and cannot reveal itself except as the effect of a secret. In each text, I believe, the subversive meaning should be sought in the woman's secret motivations for cross-dressing.

Erin Mackie, in her essay "Desperate Measures: The Narratives of the Life of Mrs. Charlotte Charke," distinguishes her reading of Charke's autobiography from those of Felicity Nussbaum, Lynne Friedli, Sidonie Smith, and other critics who, although they may not view Charke as a fully successful feminist, credit Charke with subversive aims. Mackie wants to show that "although [Charke] is transgressive in her momentary effects, she is not subversive in her aims." She reads the *Narrative* alongside Charke's lesser-known works of conventional fiction, and finds that in each text Charke's "impersonation of the masculine, which is often an impersonation of the paternal, seeks to reinforce, reinstate, and maintain the value of masculine, patriarchal conventions" (843). Mackie views Charke as an essentially conservative figure whose aim is to amend patriarchy: "For Charke, trespass and travesty are instruments not for subversion but for representation and reform" (862).

Although I agree with Mackie that Charke's aim in the *Narrative* is conventional, if not exactly reformist, I would nevertheless not wish to dismiss the subversive meaning of what Mackie calls Charke's "momentary effects" of transgression. It is true that such effects are not adequately accounted for by a feminist reading that translates them into signs of subversion; but neither can they be incorporated without contradiction into Mackie's thoroughly conservative interpretation. These effects, which are neither generic nor rhetorical, but mark the limits of the text's conventions, appear only as disruptions in the conventional content of the text. But insofar as these momentary effects, which systematically elude the representational structure that allows Charke to conceive or imagine reality in terms of her genre, they are not accidental effects but systematic elements of a heterodox configuration.

The difficulty lies in the fact that subversive content is not perceptible as such within non-ironic comic genres (in this case, the apology and the prodigal son narrative), whose teleological plot structures predetermine conventional meanings. The genre of apology has as its *telos* the substantiation of a normative subject. By means of a series of self-condemnatory and justificatory gestures, the apologist publicly reenacts the internalization of societal norms. That goal requires that the apologist shape a coherent identity from the fragments of experience. Everything in the apology proceeds as though its writing were the requisite preface to the culminating appendage of a signature. Meanwhile, the fragmentation of self that necessitates the apology resists total suppression. That is certainly the case with Charke's "life." In order to make her public repentance credible, Charke must take account of the many ways in which she has strayed from conventional behavior. But she fails precisely because she is so faithful to her genre. If Charlotte Charke's life is, as she puts it, "unaccountable," it is because she has too much to account for, not because any one of her faults is beyond remedy. She confesses too much. She is too thorough, too sincere. She risks the appearance of glorying in her social faults, not by celebrating them, but by lingering upon them, enumerating them, revisiting so many of them.[1]

At best, cultural subversion may register as a formal disturbance in the discursive conventions of a genre when its logic is forced to its limits. Charke, it seems to me, does unwittingly test the limits of her genre by placing a complete faith in its transformative power. Her attempt to salvage her reputation by means of the conventional program of her genre fails to the extent that the same heterodox desires that motivate her cross-dressing also secretly motivate her narration. It is no accident that she chooses to model her narrative on the parable of the prodigal *son.* In the very gesture by which she renounces her former improprieties, she lays claim to a traditional masculine role. That claim, I believe, arises as an impulse rather than a strategy. Such a claim, and all that it implies about the privileges Charke would wrest for herself as woman and daughter, is unthinkable or "unpresentable" in her society. The subversiveness of Charke's text is readable only as an effect of an "unpresentable" content, a content over which Charke herself exercises no conscious control.

Her conscious strategy, on the other hand, is to submit fully to the authority of London society. Her narrative is a testimony, and everywhere she professes her faith in legal process. She believes that only by a full confession of her faults can she win the pity of her readers. She therefore strives always to defend her honesty as narrator, rather than defend or explain the behavior she is narrating. Toward the end of the *Narrative,* in chapter 6, after describing a long journey she (in the guise of Charles Brown) and her companion, Mrs. Brown, made by foot on very little money (a journey she admits "may be scarce believed"), she defends her accuracy as legally verifiable: "I was questioned, not long since, whether it was possible for me to have run through the strange vicissitudes of fortune I have given an account of, which I solemnly declare I am ready to make oath of the truth of every circumstance, and if any particular person or persons require it, will refer them to hundreds now living, who have been witnesses of every article contained in my history" (172).[2] In the course of (and as though for the sake of) demonstrating her present reputation for honesty, she is ready to forgo any defense of her past behavior: "I have paid so strict a regard to [truth] that I have rather painted my own ridiculous follies in their most glaring lights than debarred the reader the pleasure of laughing at me, or proudly concealed the utmost exigencies of my fate, both of which may convince the world that I have been faithful in my declaration either way, for none, I believe, desire through frolic alone to make sport for others, or excite a pity they never stood in need of" (172–73). Charke wishes to prove the seriousness of her desire to be reconciled to society; she therefore recognizes the right of society to judge her. Her very willingness to represent the facts of her life as foolish and shameful guarantees their social innocuousness. But whereas she manages by such means to negate the ideological subversiveness of her former actions, their illicit value remains evident and still subject to moral accountability.

Charke's apology seems to be modeled partly on her father's work, *An Apology for the Life of Colley Cibber* (1740).[3] Like Cibber, Charke professes to welcome the laughter that her follies may provoke. But Cibber's justificatory strategy is different. If Charke models her persona on the prodigal son (a model that requires her to insist on her sincere conversion from a former life of frivolity), Cibber seems to choose a Falstaffian model and to revel in his frivolity. Unlike Charke, Cibber was able to maintain his image as a frivolous performer and still have hope of winning public approval. The gender definitions of the day made it possible for a man of the theater to represent himself in two distinct modes, as public performer and as private citizen. Cibber's *Apology* is successful precisely in dissociating the singular, inward man from the outward

characters with which he had become associated on the stage. But a woman
player was identified with her roles in a way that a man was not, since, in ac-
cord with the gendered psychological model of the period, her theatrical condition was not unlike her real condition: women were essentially actors, su-
perficial and changeable, and never in fact what they appeared to be. For
instance, in addition to the fact that sexually unorthodox Restoration actresses
were sometimes admired for their resourcefulness in the use of seductive appearances, even those who were famous for their chastity, such as Ann Brace-
girdle, were commonly perceived to be dissemblers who teasingly pretended
to a lewdness they did not have.[4]

Cibber sets out to establish a "true" picture of himself distinct from the roles
of fop and villain for which he was once famous. He imagines his former spectators being curious "to know what he really was, when in no body's Shape
but his own; and whether he, who by his Profession had so long been ridicul-
ing his Benefactors, might not, when the Coat of his Profession was off, deserve to be laughed at himself; or from his being often seen in, the most
flagrant, and immoral Characters; whether he might not see as great a Rogue,
when he look'd into the Glass himself as when he held it to others" (Cibber
6). Cibber realizes that his theatrical roles threaten to claim his identity and
incite public scorn; the *Apology* invites the reader to view him at his private
dressing room mirror before which he will at last remove all his masks. But
even as Cibber sheds his disguises, he manages to reclaim them artistically. He
is not ashamed of them. Many pages later, he explains why he chose to play
the unseemliest characters. In some measure, such roles were forced upon him
because he lacked the voice to play the hero and because other actors didn't
want to be associated in the public mind with low or vicious characters. But
beyond these considerations, Cibber says he did not mind the moral taint. In
fact, he relished the hisses and mocking laughter of his theater audience. He
believes that surely half his auditors, noting the delight he took in performing such roles, assumed he had "a great Share of the Wickedness" of his characters; but Cibber receives the confusion as a compliment: "If this is true, as
true I fear (I had almost said hope) it is, I look upon it rather as a Praise, than
a Censure of my Performance" (124). For such roles more clearly demonstrated
his acting ability, since the real test of talent is in creating characters unlike
oneself (123–25).

This argument enables Cibber to divorce himself from the worst traits of his
characters, while also freeing himself to treat any of his remaining vices as
performances with which he hopes to entertain his readers. He eschews the
role of villain, but that of fop he finds more attractive and useful. At one point

he explains why he does not take offence at Pope's famous satirical attacks: "for my part, I own myself incorrigible: I look upon my Follies as the best part of my Fortune, and am more concern'd to be a good Husband of Them, than of That; nor do I believe I shall ever be rhim'd out of them" (16). Cibber wants his readers to believe that he looks upon his follies with the pride of someone who has staged them for the amusement of others. Recognizing that his own enjoyment of immoral and foolish characters derived partly from his vicarious participation in their improper behavior, he sets about making his readers complicit in his own folly by inviting them to laugh along with him—to take pleasure in his folly, not by identifying with the folly itself, but by conspiring with an abstracted Cibber who is the amused actor of his own ridiculous life. Cibber's apologetic strategy is founded on an assertion of his mastery of performance. So long as he is consciously performing his life, he can act upon his desires with relative impugnity.

Cibber requests only a worldly pardon, a sympathetic recognition of his human frailty. His is no moral tale. In the face of censure, he claims for himself the virtue of cheerfulness ("let them call me any Fool, but an Unchearful one!"), and this one Falstaffian virtue becomes the defining quality of his persona, its stabilizing center.

Of course, as poet laureate and retired patentee of Drury Lane, Cibber was in a position to withstand some censure. Charke's case was rather desperate, and her strategy is more conventional. She is in no position, really, to share a laugh at her own expense. Thus, rather than present herself as the joyous creator of her follies, she attempts always to place herself beyond the target of laughter, as someone who now stands at a distance from her own past morally and shares thoughtfully in the cathartic laughter (and judgment) her former, prodigal self still provokes. She represents her former cross-dressing performances precisely in order to take part publicly in the condemnation and thereby demonstrate her conversion from folly to wisdom, from unconventional behavior to conventional judgment.

The Conversion of the Prodigal

A certain kind of subversiveness is not difficult to locate in Charke's *Narrative*. Judith Butler's recent theoretical work on gender performativity makes it easier to see how the complex layering of identity in Charke's *Narrative* suggests two potential threats to the patriarchal social order of mid-eighteenth-century England. First, Charke's performance of a variety of cross-gender roles in real life and in the theater demonstrates women's potential freedom from

conventional femininity. When a woman performs masculine roles effectively and convincingly, she shows that such roles are not masculine by nature, but
only by convention. Second, her *Narrative,* because it represents real life as
theatrical, threatens to expose the merely performative constitution of all social identity, gender identity included. These threats remain, despite the fact
that Charke is at pains to condemn her own extravagant behavior. But we
should not overlook her self-condemnation, because only by paying attention
to the constraints that Charke herself places upon her account can we hope
to define the limits of a conventional reading of her text in order to remark,
eventually, the breaks and fissures of the narrative's conventionally unaccountable motives.

   In a recent essay partly inspired by the work of Judith Butler, Cheryl Wan-
ko addresses the issue of Charke's subversiveness. She helpfully contrasts the
Narrative with the earlier anonymous biography of an actress, *Life of Lavinia
Beswick, alias Fenton, alias Polly Peachum* (1728). According to Wanko, the
Fenton biography succeeded rhetorically—as an apology for Fenton's life and
as a means of boosting her fame—because it "'perform[ed]' the actress as a
stable gendered identity," satisfying the reader-spectator's desire by reducing
Fenton to her most popular dramatic role in *The Beggar's Opera,* that of Polly
Peachum, "an eighteenth-century happy hooker" (80). Written with the masculine spectator very much in mind, the Fenton biography creates the com-
forting illusion that the actress truly is the fantasy sex object she portrays on
stage and, in effect, no actress at all. But Charke, faced with the same societal
demand for gender stability, Wanko continues, could not represent herself
without calling attention to the constructed nature of gender identity: "Like
an actress on stage, Charke is conscious of her many 'acts,' or roles, and in her
Narrative she attempts to play all roles to satisfy the disparate demands of her
audience(s). But the attempt to perform them all merely accentuates the constructed nature of the performance, rather than convincing readers of a unified character, like Fenton. The *Narrative* shows readers the discontinuous acts
that social custom usually smooths over to produce gender roles" (81). Wanko not only believes that Charke's readers would have noticed, or been made
uncomfortable by, her failure to create the illusion of a unified gender identity, but she also suggests that Charke consciously rebels against the dominant
constructions. Thus Wanko rejects the view, promoted by Sidonie Smith, that
Charke is a failed feminist. Wanko writes:

> Her "failed" gender performance is really a triumph of a sort. [Judith] Butler explains
> how the sustained social performances of gender help to repress "the performative

possibilities for proliferating gender configurations outside the restricting frames of masculinist domination and compulsory heterosexuality": perhaps Charke's refusal to conform to gender norms—even those that were beginning to regulate same-sex desire—is a rebellious assertion of a new configuration. She exemplifies the resistant woman autobiographer Nussbaum identifies: "women's autobiographical writing, organized within prevailing discourses, helped to shape and resist the dominant cultural constructions of gender relations and to substitute alternatives." (87)

Wanko celebrates the fact that Charke's attempted illusion is far from seamless, since her "refusal to conform" is a kind of triumph over conventionality.

The idea of the "refusal," however, seems to contradict the notion that Charke *attempts* to perform the conventional roles—that is, that she tries as narrator to represent those roles convincingly. Surely Charke can't both want to conform to feminine conventions and also refuse to conform. But what would otherwise be a contradiction Wanko permits by allowing her discourse to slide across the formal split that separates Charke-the-narrator from Charke-the-subject of narration. Elsewhere Wanko does call attention to the conflict of subjectivity that splits the culturally resistant autobiographical subject from the desperately conventional autobiographer: "Her appeals to her reading public include adopting conventional feminine personae. She appears as dutiful daughter, afflicted mother, and devoted spouse. Yet her attempts at playing such repertory roles are disrupted by the facts of her outrageous life" (84). Wanko argues, in effect, that what is subversive is not the narration, but the matter of the narrative, Charke's outrageous life.

Wanko's claims that Charke "refuses to conform" and makes a "rebellious assertion of a new configuration" need to be founded on a distinction between the *Narrative*'s genre and the events it fails to incorporate into a seamless representation of the autobiographical subject. But this distinction itself is not very secure, when we consider that those events are already a generic effect. In relation to the *Narrative,* the life itself functions like a secret, veiled by literary convention and not accessible to our direct scrutiny. The "seaminess" of the narrative is certainly one of its most salient features, but it marks the text, first of all, as a failed literary performance, an unsuccessful conventional product. The "facts of her outrageous life" are of the same order as the "conventional feminine personae": both are necessary components of an apology cast as a prodigal son narrative. Thus, when Charke calls herself an "oddity" or her life "unaccountable," she is rejecting and consigning to the past all that might be objectionable about the life she recounts. If Charke is a gender rebel, she does not acknowledge the fact herself. Or, more precisely, she acknowledges her rebelliousness only in order to negate its meaningfulness. She purposely exposes her past self to mockery. And she knows that she can negate the meaning of her rebelliousness simply by representing it, for the mere representation of her former actions calls attention to their imprudence and futility according to the traditional view that rebellion against authority is tantamount to the denial of meaning, even the meaning of the rebellion.

Charke's dedication to the volume, which she addresses to herself as an other and as a new friend, formally marks the end of her resistance to social conventions. The dedication effects a split in her subjectivity, dividing an unwise past self from a reformed present self, but only in order to reconcile the two by the conversion of the prodigal past self. The ideological work of the *Narrative* is already encapsulated in the dedication. Charke represents the prodigal's return as a return to right reason after a period of physical and moral wandering: "Your two friends, Prudence and Reflection, I am informed, have lately ventured to pay you a visit, for which I heartily congratulate you, as nothing can possibly be more joyous to the heart than the return of absent friends after a long and painful peregrination" (2). The movement the passage describes is double: Prudence and Reflection return to the prodigal once the prodigal herself has returned home after her peregrination. The visit paid by Prudence and Reflection marks the very moment at which the composition of the narrative becomes possible, since the *Narrative* will be Charke's prudent *reflection* on her former life as prodigal. That reflection, as though a mirror could steal away the self reflected there, effaces Charke-the-prodigal by the institution of a second, new self in the person of Charke-the-narrator. She looks into the mirror to scrutinize her false self and thereby rediscovers her true self. The *Narrative* is the mirror that reflects the "truth" of this conversion. That is the myth of Charke's text. But "conversion," in this case, can be another term for cross-dressing. The moral conversion effects an impersonation that elides the difference between past and present; it masks the subversive self—whatever that might be—in conventionality.

Charke is always at pains to show that her misfortunes have been the result of foolishness rather than vice. For a very long time, one gathers, she was simply insufficiently reflective to learn from her mistakes. For instance, during her cross-dressing period, after a long sequence of miserable episodes as a strolling player, she takes it into her head to try her hand at farming and pastry cooking. Charke editorializes on this change of life: "Perhaps the reader may think that the repeated rebuffs of fortune might have brought me to some degree of reflection, which might have regulated the actions of my life," but they did not. Even her new endeavors she pursued counter to the prudent advice of a friend. In her later reflections she refers to these doomed pursuits as "my unaccountable farce" and laments the fact that she involved her traveling companion, Mrs. Brown (for whom "I really was the author of many troubles from my inconsiderate folly"), "in the same needless and unreasonable difficulties" (149–50).

In her reflective narrative Charke condemns her past behavior, marking her gender-crossing as either frivolous or forced by circumstances. Although the potential subversiveness of her outrageous life may be hard for us to overlook, that fact doesn't preclude the possibility that Charke herself manages to overlook it—not her life's extravagance or transgressions, but the possibility that these transgressions might be meaningfully subversive, the expression of a new gender configuration in which her heterodox desires could at last manifest themselves socially, could at last become speakable. As narrator and apologist, Charke assumes with conviction the role of penitent prodigal. She clings firmly to this single identity, insisting on its authenticity. Her profession of continuous devotion to her father, to her own daughter, and to her errant husband—her insistence on her fundamentally feminine, familial identity in the midst of her various admitted transgressions—is part of the representational strategy by which she hopes to negate her transgressive identities. She represents her transgressions as inessential features of an otherwise coherent, but often suppressed, feminine character. Any wish we may have to infer a radical consciousness from Charke's reported behavior is undercut by the fact that her role as narrator (which is also to say, the genre of her text) constantly engages her belief and escapes her awareness as performance.

Charke as Prodigal Son

Charke's conventional strategy, her complicity in the culture's denial of her subversive authority, fails to restore the sympathy of her father or society. She seems unaware of how the application of the prodigal son narrative to the adventures of a daughter must doom her in advance. In an attempt to disarm her readers, she adopts a conventionally feminine attitude toward the composition of her *Narrative,* but that is an insufficient measure where her choice of genre is itself so alarming.

Charke opposes her narrative to works of "female poets" that tend to inflame the minds of young readers and offend those of riper years by their excessive attention to romance and sexuality. She assures her readers, "I have paid all due regard to decency wherever I have introduced the passion of love, and have only suffered it to take its course in its proper and necessary time" (3). She announces, in effect, that her recent conversion to conventional behavior is what qualifies her now to be the author of her work. Charke the autobiographer represents herself as humbly standing trial artistically as well as morally. From her readers she seeks pity and encouragement for "one who has used her utmost endeavors to entertain them" (4). Because her history "is the product of a female pen," she worries that people will judge it deficient before having perused it, and she moves "for its having the common chance of a criminal" to stand fair trial (3).

This show of deference establishes her moral (feminine) character for the sake of yet another trial, that in which she pleads for her father's pardon. But here the sword of justice is made to cut both ways:

> Nor was I exempted from an equal share of my father's heart; yet partly through my own indiscretion (and I am too well convinced from the cruel censure of false and evil tongues) since my maturity I lost that blessing, which, if strongest compunction and uninterrupted hours of anguish, blended with self-conviction and filial love, can move his heart to pity and forgiveness, I shall with pride and unutterable transport throw myself at his feet to implore the only benefit I desire or expect—his blessing and pardon. (4)

Charke appears as a contrite former prodigal. Her appeal is public and private at once. The judge is a private reader, Colley Cibber, who must respond (if he will) privately; but a second judge stands over him, namely, the public readership whose opinion Charke tacitly invokes. She attempts to dispel the bad influence of false witnesses (primarily her older sister, Catherine) who may have tainted her father's opinion of her. Public opinion, which has the same function as generic expectation, is invoked to serve as a model for Colley Cibber's emotional response; the model of the prodigal narrative calls upon him, under the gaze of the reading public, to assume the attractive role of the forgiving Christian father who welcomes home his repentant child. The authority of public opinion is implicit in Charke's statement that she hopes not for material gain, but only for "the transcendent joy of knowing that I am restored to a happiness which not only will clear my reputation to the world in regard to former want of duty, but, at the same time, give a convincing proof that there are yet some sparks of tenderness remaining in my father's bosom for his repentant child" (5). In effect, she threatens to expose her father as a hard-hearted parent if he does not comply.

Yet Cibber did not forgive her. His famous reply makes clear that Charlotte's "strange career" deprived him of such an option. A prodigal daughter of the eighteenth century cannot return home to a father's forgiveness, precisely because she cannot properly *be* the traditional prodigal in the first place. Her prodigal condition, unlike the son's, would be considered incapable of reform. When a daughter falls, she falls into irretrievable corruption. One model for such a fall would be Hogarth's six-scene series, "A Harlot's Progress" (1732), which traces the precipitous fall of a country girl, "M. Hackabout," from her innocent arrival in London, through several stages of moral corruption, thence to her death from syphilis at age twenty-three. A young woman is valued for her chastity but defined by her impressionability. The daughter functions as a sign of the father's honor. Because the daughter is not a fully moral creature, but instead partly a cultural object or symbol, she is permanently tainted by any corruption with which she comes into contact. Her prodigality, no matter how slight, can only signify an irrevocable squandering of the soul. The prodigal daughter must be driven away.

Perhaps Charke employs the prodigal son model (and what other narrative model would serve a person who wishes to erase the past?) to free herself by analogy, as though her obvious and faithful reliance on the "logic of desire" by which that essentially comic genre wishes the son into the bosom of his forgiving father might at least impugn the morality of a society that will not wish a penitent daughter the same happiness. But the ideological sticking point of the penitent prodigal strategy is the conversion itself and the impossibility of celebrating the return of the prodigal daughter. Recall that the Fenton biography successfully augmented Fenton's fame precisely because it never presumed to reclaim her from her waywardness. Instead, it constructed for her an acceptably humble and likeable errant persona that actually supported the higher feminine ideals by friendly contrast. Charke, on the other hand, insists on returning home, on crossing back over to the ideal. She practices a kind of gender-crossing even in her appeal to her father. Even as she professes to be the good daughter, she insists on being the son. She seems unaware of the fact that her prodigality is essentially an effect of that insistence.

Charke is a creature of the theater, but she cannot actually stage her performance of the penitent prodigal role. She cannot make her own character come alive, as it were, and reenact, in breeches perhaps, the life she has led, so that a sympathetic audience might applaud her virtue and celebrate her return to the loving bosom of her father. She cannot draw her father onto the public stage, although she tries. Her publication of her suppliant letter to her father, which he returned unopened, is a mark of her frustration in this regard. Her *Narrative* is an attempt to dramatize her plight publicly, but its rhetorical gestures are a poor substitute for a theatrical performance. Charke compensates partly by aligning herself with male characters from drama, such as George Barnwell in Lillo's *The London Merchant*. Charke admires Thorowgood's "beautiful example of forgiveness" as a father-figure to George Barnwell, his wayward apprentice (82). What she doesn't mention about Thorowgood's interaction with Barnwell, although she no doubt recalls it (having herself played the role of the tragically prodigal Barnwell), is Thorowgood's consistent refusal even to hear Barnwell's confession:

> Barnwell: Though I had rather die than speak my shame, though racks could not have forced the guilty secret from my breast, your kindness has.
> Thorowgood: Enough, enough! Whate'er it be, this concern shows you're convinced, and I am satisfied. (2.4.11–15)

Barnwell is never made to explain his failure to return home the previous night. It is enough that the young man has returned in a state of contrition. To the father of the prodigal son, the facts of transgression are not important, because the young man is a fully moral creature and therefore capable of conversion. The father won't hear the story because the details are superfluous to the moral significance of the son's repentant return. To the father of the prodigal daughter, the very fact of transgression is damning, and the details of transgression cannot be represented; they are unspeakable.

Portia's Secret

Charke's self-representation in her *Narrative* and the character of Portia in *The Merchant of Venice* differ with regard to the degree of awareness each has of her own secret motivations for cross-dressing. Portia also exists within a teleological genre that constrains the meaning of her actions, but her subversiveness is nevertheless readable as such. She is a playful and rhetorically astute transgressive woman. Her freedom to cross gender boundaries, however, derives not from realistic social circumstances, but from the socially sanctioned genre of romantic comedy, whose action is directed toward a conventional ending. The requisite final marriages in Shakespeare's romantic comedies resolve the plots to the satisfaction of a generic convention that links emotional fulfillment to social orthodoxy. But because the closure seems assured, the complications and rising action, as well as the very plot devices by which resolution is achieved, may safely exhibit heterodox social tendencies.[5] Within this mutable middle space of romantic comedy the ideological subversiveness of cross-dressing on the Renaissance stage may reveal itself.

In Shakespeare's plays, despite the fact that dramatic production itself depended on cross-dressing (with boys or men playing the female roles), cultural subversion registers primarily, if not exclusively, in secondary cross-dressing, that is, when the female characters put on men's clothing. Insofar as the Renaissance anti-theatricalists did accuse the male actors of effeminacy, they were decrying the showy insincerity of theatrical representation in general. But acting could be an effective art—theatrical representation could be powerful—only because the masses of playgoers, taking for granted the masculine identities of the male players, easily accepted the gender illusion.[6] Men were considered universal subjects, and their acting was an obvious pretense, an aesthetic practice. Women, by contrast, were commonly considered theatrical or false by nature, mere "outward shows" whose apparent identities were always an effect of performance.[7] The feminine ideal, therefore, could not be an essential identity at all, but had to be relational, a function of the woman's value to particular men. And so it remained throughout the seventeenth and eighteenth centuries.

Unlike Charlotte Charke, Portia is able to return to the feminine ideal after a period of masculine empowerment; but just as her impersonation of the lawyer Balthasar is masculinity-with-a-difference, so her return home is a return that reconfigures the home. Portia crosses the gender line with an almost theoretical understanding of her action, a clear perception of its subversive meaning and purpose. Whereas Charke formally separates the female body (as good, repentant daughter) from the masculine disguise (which she represents and rejects as illicit), Portia maintains the doubleness of the cross-dressing figure, thereby preserving the dynamic interaction between genders within genders that threatens to break up the conventional gender configuration.

Portia's conversation with her maid, Nerissa, at the inception of her plan to save her husband's friend from Shylock by means of the cross-dressing device, demonstrates her awareness of the constructed, performative nature of both traditional genders:

> Portia: Come on Nerissa, I have work in hand
>   That you yet know not of. We'll see our husbands
>   Before they think of us!
> Nerissa: Shall they see us?
> Portia: They shall, Nerissa, but in such a habit
>   That they shall think we are accomplished
>   With what we lack. I'll hold thee any wager
>   When we are both accoutred like young men,
>   I'll prove the prettier fellow of the two,
>   And wear my dagger with a braver grace,
>   And speak between the change of man and boy
>   With a reed voice, and turn two mincing steps

> Into a manly stride, and speak of frays
> Like a fine bragging youth, and tell quaint lies
> How honourable ladies sought my love,
> Which I denying, they fell sick and died—
> I could not do withal! Then I'll repent,
> And wish, for all that, that I had not kill'd them;
> And twenty of these puny lies I'll tell,
> That men shall swear I have discontinued school
> Above a twelvemonth. I have within my mind
> A thousand raw tricks of these bragging Jacks,
> Which I will practice. (3.4.57–78)[8]

Commonly the modern actress who plays Portia accompanies her description of the bragging youth with a gestural drag show, and the sixteenth-century actor probably did the same. Portia proposes a game in which the two women will perform in drag for one another. She suggests that gender itself is a performance, for the man who performs "his own" gender, as well as for the woman who imitates masculinity. She calls attention to the symbolic cut, the sign of gender difference that marks the woman as a figure of "lack"—both in the phrase, "accomplished / With what we lack" (i.e., a penis), and in the description of the shift from a woman's "mincing steps" to a "manly stride"; but the "mincing" that traditionally characterizes the woman's behavior also applies to the behavior of the "bragging youth," who fabricates masculine traits in a desperate attempt to convince his auditors of his manhood, as though he ran the constant risk of revealing his lack. The feminine, in Portia's representation, is precisely what cuts up and cuts through the masculine identity, exposing its makeshift constitution and denying its essentialist claim.

Portia mocks the expressive model of gender. Judith Butler, in her book *Gender Trouble,* says of drag that it "fully subverts the distinction between inner and outer psychic space and effectively mocks both the expressive model of gender and the notion of a true gender identity":

> The performance of drag plays upon the distinction between the anatomy of the performer and the gender that is being performed. But we are actually in the presence of three contingent dimensions of significant corporeality: anatomical sex, gender identity, and gender performance. If the anatomy of the performer is already distinct from the gender of the performance, then the performance suggests a dissonance not only between sex and performance, but sex and gender, and gender and performance. As much as drag creates a unified picture of "woman" (what its critics often oppose), it also reveals the distinctness of those aspects of gendered experience which are falsely naturalized as a unity through the regulatory fiction of het-

erosexual coherence. *In imitating gender, drag implicitly reveals the imitative structure of gender itself—as well as its contingency.* (Butler 137)

Portia unravels gender unity in just this way, defusing its power for the sake
of reconfiguring her own specific relationship to masculine authority in the
person of her husband, Bassanio.

The work of gender reconfiguration takes place, first of all, in language.
When Nerissa asks, following Portia's presentation of the cross-dressing strategy, "Why, shall we turn to men?" (3.4.78), Portia hears the sexual innuendo
in the word "turn" (which Shylock earlier used in its sexual sense: "the ewes,
being rank / . . . turned to the rams" [1.3.79]) and answers with mock horror:
"Fie, what a question's that, / If thou wert near a lewd interpreter!" (79–80).
Portia's response projects a prurient intention onto her interlocutor. The point
of such interpretation, however, is not to decide a singular meaning, but to free
multiple meanings from a superficially univocal discourse. Thus, Portia follows Nerissa's double entendre with one of her own, a play upon the word
"near," which could be either an adverb ("if you were *virtually*—or anything
like—a lewd interpreter yourself") or a preposition ("if you were *in the vicin-
ity of* a lewd interpreter"—which is indeed the case, as Portia's reply shows).
Concealed beneath Portia's mock horror is her awareness of the difference
between a rhetoric of intention and a rhetoric of reception (of the nearly lewd
and the nearby lewd). Not only is Portia not bound by an innocent reading,
but she realizes that rhetorical power consists in the ability to hear and to speak
double, the ability to draw from words the full range of possible signification.

In rhetorical terms we could say that Portia recognizes that cross-dressing
is structured like a quibble, or pun: the improper meaning—or improper gender—is substituted for the "proper," but not in the obvious manner of a metaphor. Here the rhetorical effect of the double structure, like that of the pun,
may go undetected: the cross-dresser may "pass" with many viewers. The fact
of transgression, of the crossing itself, may be known only to the transgressor
or may be the shared secret of a few.

Portia's pointing up of the double-entendre—which marks the close of act
3, scene 4, and the turning point of the drama—reveals a characteristic turn
of thought. This same interpretive tendency toward multivalence lies at the
foundation of her inspired legalistic quibble on "pound of flesh" as signify-
ing "no jot of blood" (4.1.304). There the strategy is really the reverse of the
punning strategy of cross-dressing, for she intentionally cuts out the multiple significations associated with the word "flesh." The gesture saves Bassanio's friend Antonio from Shylock's knife, but it also mocks the masculine ten-

dency to reduce doubleness to singularity (for example, to reduce the subtlety of a woman's meanings to the bluntness of a man's, her two steps to his one stride, or the doubleness of the romantic couple's desire to the singularity of the man's will). When Portia becomes Balthasar, what she represents to the world of men is the masculine decisiveness of a judge; what she conceals by means of this persuasive presentation is her own will as a woman to influence the affairs of men, to turn men to her purposes. In this sense, gender is a trope; it is always a matter of "turning"—in imitation of the other, in submission to the other, toward the other as an equal; and, in various ways, toward and with one's own traditional gender. The turning point, the place of gender-crossing, indicates a lack at the center of gender identity, an absence betrayed by—and necessitated by—performance.

What does this strategy gain for Portia? Portia's father has, from beyond the grave, made her the object of a contest in which young noblemen from around the world compete for her hand and rich inheritance. In effect, they compete for the father's favor, since the casket trial, whose terms have been dictated in the dead father's will, makes the father the ghostly judge of Portia's suitors. The choice of the three caskets effectively eliminates any influence Portia might have exercised over a living father. By that rule, Portia herself is rendered as though dead and must be resurrected from one of the caskets by a savior-husband (in fact, her portrait, "fair Portia's counterfeit" [3.2.115], is to be found in the correct casket; and Bassanio thinks it so life-like that he says it sees and breathes). Once Bassanio has chosen correctly, Portia nevertheless faces the prospect of welcoming a substitute father in her dead father's place, since the rules by which authority is transferred treat Portia as an object of masculine ownership. This fear is perhaps allayed by the news that Bassanio, worse than penniless, stands indebted to his friend Antonio. The formerly rich merchant Antonio has seen his ships lost at sea and is now bankrupt himself and imprisoned (they soon learn) for his unpaid debt to Shylock. That debt was incurred for Bassanio's sake, to finance Bassanio's (essentially financial) romantic venture. Portia can now offer to pay Antonio's forfeiture and at the same time liberate herself from the oppressive gratitude she might otherwise feel toward Bassanio. The offer of assistance becomes a means of bestowing her wealth upon Bassanio and underscoring his dependence upon her gift, upon herself *as* gift.

Portia disguises herself as a young lawyer, Balthasar, and gets herself appointed by her relative, Bellario, to judge Shylock's case against Antonio. Her cross-dressing, therefore, seems motivated by a desire to save her husband's friend. But her even more secret intention is to test the depth of her husband's love; and beyond that, to convert her authority as judge into a new authority within her marriage. Thus, at the successful conclusion of the trial, Portia-as-Balthasar asks Bassanio for his ring, her first gift to him that he has sworn never to part with. It is helpful to recall the language she uses in originally bestowing her ring on her betrothed. The terms of her speech reveal something of the ring's symbolic meaning beyond its romantic value. First she tells him that her "gentle spirit" commits itself to him to be directed, "As from her lord, her governor, her king" (3.2.163–65). Then she adds, by way of wedding ceremony:

> Myself and what is mine to you and yours
> Is now converted. But now I was the lord
> Of this fair mansion, master of my servants,
> Queen o'er myself; and even now, but now,
> This house, these servants, and this same myself
> Are yours, my lord's. I give them with this ring,
> Which when you part from, lose, or give away,
> Let it presage the ruin of your love
> And be my vantage to exclaim on you. (3.2.166–74)

This performative speech act effects Portia's conversion, not only from freedom to subjection, but also from the masculine roles of "lord" and "master" to the feminine role of wife. We learn that (despite the fact that she has been subject to the will of her father regarding her marital fate) she has grown accustomed to exercising, in most respects, a freedom like her father's own former freedom. She has replaced her father as guardian of the family estate. The threat implied in Portia's speech constitutes a defense measure that stands in lieu of the masculine power she is formally abdicating: she threatens, in addition to reproaching him for his infidelity, to exercise her "vantage" over him. If he loses the ring, he must abdicate the husband's traditional authority.

After the trial, Bassanio initially offers to reward Balthasar-Portia with the money formerly owed to Shylock. When she refuses payment and demands the ring instead, he balks. But after she has gone Antonio persuades him to send the ring after her: "My lord Bassanio, let him have the ring. / Let his deservings and my love withal / Be valued 'gainst your wife's commandement" (4.2.447–49). Portia knows, without having to hear this speech, that Bassanio's action implies a judgment against her love and in favor of Antonio's supposedly stronger emotional claim. She understands that Bassanio has chosen to reduce her gift to a legal technicality. The judicial interpretation by which she has elevated blood above flesh, spirit above letter, is lost on Bassanio, who now views the ring as an object devoid of spiritual significance. This loss of the ring-as-gift threatens to place Portia again in the position of the oppressed daugh-

ter, as the subject of a formal power-relation lacking even the sign of reciproc-
ity. When Bassanio gives the ring to Balthasar, it is immediately devalued as a
symbol and becomes—with Portia herself—a mere token in the masculine
exchange of property. But Portia saves herself by reclaiming the ring in the
person of Balthasar. Thus, a symbol that represented her willing submission
to Bassanio's authority returns to her as the symbol of her free will. Portia in
possession of her ring is always a kind of Portia-Balthasar. When a woman's
desire is her own, her very gender is a double entendre, for those who have ears
to hear it.

Bassanio is not true to his word; in losing his ring and his word, he reveals
himself to be less than the manly ideal. In the final scene of reconciliation, he
must beg Portia for the return of the ring, which suddenly appears more clearly
to be the symbolic supplement of his deficient masculinity. The woman's will,
always officially written out of the marriage contract, now inscribes itself there
where it had always invisibly endorsed the man's authority. In that unpresentable inscription, Portia-Balthasar, Portia's identity assumes, for a moment, the
uncanny property of self-sufficient doubleness, a self-othering that is yet the
secret propriety of all identity.

Before revealing to Bassanio the facts of her cross-dressing adventure, Portia proclaims her sexual independence. Speaking of Balthasar, the supposed
possessor of her ring, she tells Bassanio:

> Let not that doctor e'er come near my house.
> Since he hath got the jewel that I loved,
> And that which you did swear to keep for me,
> I will become as liberal as you:
> I'll not deny him anything I have,
> No, not my body nor my husband's bed.
> Know him I shall, I am well sure of it.
> Lie not a night from home. Watch me like Argus;
> If you do not, if I be left alone,
> Now, by mine honor, which is yet my own,
> I'll have that doctor for my bedfellow. (5.1.223–33)

The point seems to be not only that Portia feels free to give herself to whom-
ever she pleases, but also that she is now her own secret lover. She has regained
her freedom, but in her newfound doubleness, she is now husband to herself.
Her honor is her own. She owns her own desire, as only a man can claim to
do in her society, and she chooses to desire herself.

The play ends with Gratiano, Bassanio's counterpart and husband to Nerissa, joking about his commitment to "keeping safe Nerissa's ring" (5.1.307),

playing on the double meaning of "ring" as *vagina*. His fantasy would be to short-circuit the symbolic relation by once again reducing the woman to the symbol; but now it is not the easily portable ring that substitutes for the woman, but the woman, her bodily presence, that stands in for a ring that was not, after all, so easy to keep safe. This fantasy of control, in which the woman is always literally at hand, betrays its source in the masculine anxiety that a woman is not at all like a ring, she cannot be the possession the ring traditionally symbolizes.

Portia has shown that she comprehends both senses of the word at once. Her double impersonation of the heterosexual couple, the performance of Portia-Balthasar, stands for a fundamental truth that the romantic conventions of her society are designed to conceal. The revelation within the revelation of cross-dressing in *The Merchant of Venice* is that heterosexual coupling is secretly modeled on the self-difference of the homoerotic pair. In this case, the woman is her own "other" first, prior to alienating her desire in the service of heterosexuality. The man who puts her ring on his finger takes the place of the other woman.

The new gender configuration embodied by the two cross-dressing women of *The Merchant of Venice* emerges partly as the result of Portia's displacement and decentering of the masculine ideal image. The new configuration keeps always both sides of the cross-dressing double-image in play in order to insist on the self-difference that defines the gift. The gift is precisely that which stands between, belonging to neither side of the romantic couple; it is the hyphen or the coupling itself—the copula, if you will, of the metaphorical phrase that defines marriage and cross-dressing alike: "Portia is Balthasar"; "Portia is Bassanio"; they are one. In the course of the ring plot, Portia transforms the secretive, punning structure of impersonation into the open, metaphorical structure of travesty. She "comes out," if you will. Her power becomes manifest. Rather than an institution, gender is a source of creation for Portia, gender is generative. She manages to weaken the homosocial bond between Bassanio and Antonio and, at the same time, shatter the specular relationship subsisting between father and son-in-law whereby the son-in-law inherits the woman from the father and thus becomes a new father to her, a new embodiment of the Law. The play's "happy" ending only confirms the efficacy of Portia's strategy, as Bassanio (along with, unfortunately, the vast majority of spectators and readers over the centuries) is mystified by the transformation and reconciliation Portia devises. Bassanio remains blissfully unaware of the "turn" his wife has achieved in the realm of marriage, but is altered by it nevertheless. When Bassanio humbly accepts the ring anew, he receives it from the hand of a lordly Portia: the second exchange underscores the secondarity of his authority.

Charke's Secret

At the point of crossing genders, Portia and Nerissa free their own desires. Insofar as they perform for one another, they travesty traditional masculine roles. Charlotte Charke's attitude toward impersonation (outside of her theatrical roles per se) is invariably devout rather than ironic. The difference between an ironic travesty and a devout impersonation is that a travesty calls attention to the incongruous identity of the performer and treats that incongruity as a focus of the performance itself. On the other hand, the devout impersonator hides behind the mask, letting the mask substitute for the self, without remainder. In her youth, Charke truly believes she is a hunter and a groom and a gardener. She takes seriously her career as a physic. Her effort is always directed toward learning the script, perfecting the appropriate gestures. Even as a young actress, what she most enjoys is the idea of being an actress. She strolls around admiring her name on the playbills and enjoys watching others read it.

All of her over-serious tradesman-like activities betray a desire to be "taken for" a man. That is the source of her pleasure, not the trade itself—a fact Charke-the-narrator acknowledges when she speaks of her "natural propensity to a hat and wig" (188). The pleasure of the costume, the immediate relation to the material signifiers of the masculine body, supersedes the necessity of disguise in her motivation for cross-dressing. This illicit pleasure is partly what renders Charke's life "unaccountable." But Charke's retrospective assessment of these activities paints them as invariably ridiculous and even shameful. Her genre requires the trivialization of her pleasure.

Cheryl Wanko suggests that Charke asserts a new gender configuration—in her life, if not in her *Narrative*—but does not define the configuration or locate it precisely. Such a configuration, of course, is necessarily indescribable, unnameable, in conventional terms, since it would imply or enact a deconstruction of those terms. If the rebellious assertion is possible, if a certain kind of deconstruction does occur in Charke's text, then where is that irruption readable? It has no place in the narration (that is, as a verbal assertion or description), which is constructed precisely to deny it a place. On the other hand, with regard to the events of Charke's life, we may remark that *something* new is happening, something "outrageous," whatever it is that makes her life seem an "oddity" even to herself. But terms like "oddity" only serve to mark the place of an absence, of the culturally "unpresentable."

I propose that we look for the site of this gender irruption in the childhood narratives, both because they take the form of unrationalized myths that may program her later behavior, and because her childishness in those stories renders her actions forgivable in her own eyes. This latter factor is important, because whereas Charke is constantly seeking either pardon or sympathy for her adult adventures and is thus careful to represent them in moral terms, she is less guarded in her narratives of childhood.

Charke's childhood stories describe the formative conflict between her own childish person and her idealized image of her father, which she has not yet internalized. We have already seen how the narrative frame of Charke's text, the prodigal son model, determines the shape this conflict takes in later life. The prodigal daughter transgresses *especially* when she seeks forgiveness. But by presenting her case publicly and acting the part of the son, Charke is also taking revenge on her father, in effect.

Charlotte's early cross-dressing episodes are marked by this same deep ambivalence toward her father. She makes her first attempt at age four, believing "that by dint of a wig and a waistcoat I should be the perfect representative of my sire." More than cross-dressing attempts, they are explicitly attempts to impersonate Cibber. The process is one of concealment and self-cancellation. Young Charlotte's head and body are "entirely enclosed" by her father's tie-wig, which she calls a "covert of hair." She hides in her father's identity. She is creating an illusion she herself must ultimately believe in; that is her goal. But she will recognize its truth only in the approving eyes of her adult observers. Under their gazes she walks herself "into a fever," a kind of delusional state, because her own gaze is focused inward on a "happy thought," that of "being taken for" her father. In her imagination the laughing crowd forms not a theater audience come to applaud her performance in the role of Mr. Cibber, but an everyday crowd of her father's presumed admirers. Charlotte the performer dissolves in the pleasure of "being" her father. Hers is a devout impersonation, a form of worship, not a conscious travesty. Hence her subsequent "shame and disgrace" at being carried off on the footman's shoulders as though she were a child, and the need of being "forced into my proper habiliments" (6).

The concluding scene calls our attention to the psychological origin of her impersonation, namely, her sense of inadequacy vis-à-vis her father's image. By virtue of the footman's intervention, she is finally forced to admit the difference, whereas her desire was to erase it. The footman, in effect, lifts her out of her desired role and removes her from its pleasure, at the same time marking that pleasure as transgressive. This early experience, which links the pleasure of an imagined successful impersonation to the subsequent pain of a retributive unmasking, is formative. However, the economy of the prodigal narrative—in which moral judgment, remorse, and penitence follow hard on the heels of transgression—does not yet govern Charlotte Charke's life; for it is important to note that, just as the cross-dressing performance in these earliest episodes is motivated by a serious and deep pleasure, and not by necessity or mere fun, so also the response she will later represent as remorse originally expresses itself as rage.

The rage manifests itself most clearly in the second childhood narrative. In the first incident she must be "forced" into her proper clothing, an action that implies a vigorous resistance on her part. The following summer, Charlotte is once again made to feel the sting of disgrace, and her response is likewise not at all regretful and penitent. In this incident the five-year-old Charlotte manages to enlist some local peasants, probably young adolescents, in a scheme to bridle the foal of an ass she wishes to ride into town: "One of the small crew, who was wiser than the rest, proposed their garters being converted to that use, which was soon effected, and I rode triumphantly into town astride, with a numerous retinue, whose huzzas were drowned by the dreadful braying of the tender dam, who pursued us with agonizing sounds of sorrow for her oppressed young one." Charlotte's mother is quick to correct Charlotte:

> But, alas, how momentary are sometimes the transports of the most happy? My mother was not quite so passive in this adventure as in that before related, but rather was, as I thought, too active, for I was no sooner dismounted than I underwent the discipline of birch, was most shamefully taken prisoner in the sight of my attendants, and with a small packthread my leg was made the sad companion of a large table.
>
> 'O! fall of honour!'
>
> *It is not to be conceived* the violent indignation and contempt my disgrace raised in my infant breast, nor did I forgive my mother, in my heart, for six months after, though I was obliged to ask pardon in a few moments of her, who, at that time, I conceived to be most at fault. (8, emphasis added)

What Charke represents as unrepresentably mad and childish here is her "violent indignation and contempt," an emotional response founded on a sense of rightful superiority. The young Charlotte reacts like an insulted gentleman. A major source of her sense of disgrace lies in the subordination to her mother's will, whereas Charlotte had conceived of herself as the perfect image of her father. The punishment symbolically corrects her gender transgression. Like a woman, she is now effectively chained to the domestic space. Her fall of honor is a descent through the gender hierarchy.

What most interests me in this early narrative is the way the "not to be conceived" (in this case, Charlotte's rage against gender constraints) may be linked to the fundamental motive of her *Narrative,* namely, the need to belittle, veil, or dismiss her transgressive impulses. The very impulses that comprise her central motivation in life are precisely what must be suppressed in her *Narrative.* The complement of these positive impulses, equally suppressed except in the childhood narratives, is her rage against the social conventions that prevent her from openly pursuing her desires. Like her life, which is "unaccountable," her behavior, which is "strange," and she herself, who is an "oddity," her rage is "not to be conceived." In this sense, her *Narrative,* no matter what else it is, is the record of her evasion of an unspeakable truth about herself and her society.

In small but important ways, this rage escapes her control in the narration of her adult adventures. Not surprisingly, her rage, like her desire, focuses indirectly on the image of her father. For instance, Charke refutes two rumors that represented her as having attacked her father's person. Charke repeats the rumors in order to vindicate herself, but in each case the retelling makes possible a vicarious reenactment of the alleged crimes. The first rumor describes an explicit act of revenge against her father. The following was alleged:

> I hired a very fine bay gelding and borrowed a pair of pistols, to encounter my father upon Epping Forest (where I solemnly protest I don't know I ever saw my father in my life), that I stopped the chariot, presented a pistol to his breast and used such terms as I am ashamed to insert; threatened to blow his brains out that moment if he did not deliver, upbraiding him for his cruelty in abandoning me to those distresses he knew I underwent when he had it so amply in his power. I would force him to a compliance and was directly going to discharge upon him, but his tears prevented me, and asking my pardon for his ill-usage of me, gave me his purse with threescore guineas and a promise to restore me to his family and love, on which I thanked him and rode off. (78–79)

To retrace the bare outlines of such a story is already to affront Cibber. But Charke goes so far as to paint in the more humiliating details. Moreover, she *publishes* the story, disseminating it far beyond the circle of London gentry. Why does she do so? The story pleasingly reverses the power relation and the direction of the request for pardon. Throughout her text Charke represents herself as humbly seeking her father's pardon, but here she has the pleasure of at last representing the scene she really desires. The story enacts a conversion: she becomes the father, the judge of a prodigal Cibber; or in the figure of a rebellious son, she demands the transfer of wealth and masculine authority from a contrite and newly effeminate father.

In her subsequent act of revenge against the rumor's author, Charke repeats this gesture. She discovers the man and designs to catch him in the act. When she hears him retelling the story, she rushes out from behind a screen and thrashes the slanderer with an oaken stick. Having been prevented from killing the man, she inquires into his motives: "the only reason he assigned for his saying it was he meant it as a joke, which considerably added to the vehemence of my rage. But I had the joy of seeing him well caned and obliged to ask my pardon on his knees" (79). Charke is again attempting to defend Cibber, but to do so she must represent herself as just the sort of "highwayman" the slanderous tale made her out to be. And again she has the joy of hearing another beg for her pardon. Taken as a tableau, the scene so confuses the roles of Charke and Cibber as to make them symbolically interchangeable. By taking revenge against her own representative, the man who has harmed her father, Charke plays her father avenging himself against her, the frivolously destructive child; simultaneously, she plays herself in the reverse role of wronged daughter avenging herself on her father.

The second malicious rumor tells of a time when Charke is selling some flounders (a trade she never pursued) "and, seeing [her] father, stepped most audaciously up to him, and slapped one of the largest [she] had full in his face" (103). It's hard not to feel a violent satisfaction at the loading up and releasing of that descriptive sentence. In such instances, the rage and pleasure are so intimately joined as to give the impression that nothing would please Charke more than to make herself, by direct violence, the sufficient cause of her father's apparent disdain. What the father withholds from her is not simply, or even primarily, his pardon, but instead his identity—in which she would gladly share in the manner of a faithful son, or of a *daughter* who could freely assume the traditional role of a son. The numerous Charlotte Charkes of the *Narrative* may signify this one absent possibility.

Although her precise gender identity must remain a matter of speculation, Charke's heterodox desire is constantly intruding upon her narration and disrupting the conventions of her chosen genre. Whether Charke's longtime traveling companion, Mrs. Brown, was a lover remains a secret. What cannot remain so easily secret, however, but strains at the chains of its own concealedness, is a rivalry with her father that is equal parts admiration and resentment. Throughout her life Charke impersonates her father insofar as she continues to perform masculine roles in a theatrical manner and for the sake of worldly respect. There is something touching about her persistence. But the same performance entails a desire to replace the father or even put him to death. In sudden, bright flashes, we witness in Charlotte Charke the pure rage of a soul wronged by history, born centuries before the steady light of liberation shone.

Notes

1. In ascertaining the success of Charke's *Narrative,* we need to distinguish between its relative popular success (fueled by curiosity) and its evident rhetorical failure. The publication seems not to have improved the public reception of her person in London, as she herself records in the latter part of the *Narrative,* and it did nothing to soften her father's heart.

2. All quotations from *The Narrative of the Life of Mrs. Charlotte Charke* are taken from the text edited by Fidelis Morgan in *The Well-Known Troublemaker: A Life of Charlotte Charke* (London: Faber and Faber, 1988). As of this writing, there is no standard, readily available edition of the *Narrative.*

3. Viewing the *Narrative* itself as another example of Charke's tendency to impersonate her father, Erin Mackie argues that "Charke's formal imitation of Cibber's *Apology* . . . is a gesture, perhaps an unconscious one, of imitation and appropriation of her father's life. This appropriation may be read as a first step towards Charke's rewriting of that life. Imitating Cibber's autobiography, Charke continues it towards its correct conclusion: his generous absolution of his daughter" (847). Although my analysis of this textual relationship concurs with Mackie's on several points, I don't believe that Charke's text is essentially imitative of Cibber's or that Mackie's thesis that "emulation of the father is the origin and end of Charke's self-representations" directs our attention to every crucial quality of this relationship.

4. See Katherine Eisaman Maus, "'Playhouse Flesh and Blood': Sexual Ideology and the Restoration Actress," 602–3.

5. For an extended discussion of the teleology of romantic comedy, see my article, "Promises, Promises: *Love's Labor's Lost* and the End of Shakespearean Comedy."

6. The boy actor does not, strictly speaking, perform drag, since his impersonation is meant to be seamless. The fact that Shakespeare on rare occasion does call attention to the body of the actor for ironic effect (see, for example, Cleopatra's speech in *Antony and Cleopatra,* 5.2.219–21) would seem to support this view.

7. See Maus's discussion of this problem in "'Playhouse Flesh and Blood,'" especially 603–6.

8. Quotations from *The Merchant of Venice* are taken from the Bantam edition, edited by David Bevington.

Works Cited

Butler, Judith. *Gender Trouble: Feminism and the Subversion of Identity.* New York: Routledge, 1990.

Chaney, Joseph. "Promises, Promises: *Love's Labor's Lost* and the End of Shakespearean Comedy." *Criticism* 35 (1993): 41–65.

Cibber, Colley. *An Apology for the Life of Colley Cibber.* Ed. B. R. S. Fone. Ann Arbor: University of Michigan Press, 1968.

Lillo, George. *The London Merchant.* Ed. William H. McBurney. Lincoln: University of Nebraska Press, 1965.

Mackie, Erin. "Desperate Measures: The Narratives of the Life of Mrs. Charlotte Charke." *ELH* 58 (1991): 841–65.

Maus, Katherine Eisaman. "'Playhouse Flesh and Blood': Sexual Ideology and the Restoration Actress." *ELH* 46 (1979): 595–617.

Morgan, Fidelis, with Charlotte Charke. *The Well-Known Troublemaker: A Life of Charlotte Charke.* London: Faber and Faber, 1988.

Shakespeare, William. *The Merchant of Venice.* Ed. David Bevington. New York: Bantam, 1988.

Wanko, Cheryl. "The Eighteenth-Century Actress and the Construction of Gender: Lavinia Fenton and Charlotte Charke." *Eighteenth-Century Life* 18 (May 1994): 75–90.

Afterword:
Charke's "Variety of Wretchedness"

Felicity A. Nussbaum

> And on her crooked shoulders had she wrapped
> The tattered remnant of an old stripped hanging,
> Which served to keep her carcass from the cold,
> So there was nothing of a piece about her.
> Her lower weeds were all o'er patch'd
> With different coloured rags, as black, red, white, yellow,
> And seem'd to speak variety of wretchedness.
>
> *Thomas Otway,* The Orphan

Charlotte Charke, a catalyst for theoretical debate, continues to spark intense discussions on vital and timely issues. Much of the debate centers on the disquieting relationship between Charke's lived experience and her autobiographical representation in *A Narrative of the Life of Mrs. Charlotte Charke (Youngest Daughter of COLLEY CIBBER, Esq.) . . . Written by Herself.* How can we "know" Charke, her attitudes and intentions, in spite of the actress's obvious posturing in her writing and her commercial motivation? Is the narrative written to contest her father's authority, or does Charke instead succumb to her veiled desire to imitate masculinity? Can her renegade activities be made intelligible within the modern spectrum of sexual proclivities and identities?

The essays in this volume energetically engage these and other matters. Yet the "meaning" of Charke's life remains elusive. For example, as Philip Baruth notes, Charke's sealing the secret to her cross-dressing allows all interpretive possibilities of her sexuality to remain in play. Charke forever obscures her motivation for masquerading as a man: "The original Motive proceeded from a particular Cause; and I rather chuse to undergo the worst Imputation that can be laid on me on that Account, than unravel the Secret, which is an Appendix to one I am bound, as I before hinted, by all the Vows of Truth and Honour everlastingly to conceal" (114–15). Her inscrutability both magnetically attracts the reader to the *Narrative* and thwarts the reader's impulse to elucidate conclusively its meaning. The essays gathered together here, then, testify to the fact that readers cannot simply reduce Charlotte Charke's life to her autobiographical account, and that contradictory explanations of its significance are not easily reconciled.

For Charke, as for any individual subject, the question of whether she is resisting patriarchy or complicit with it, whether she is homophobic or lesbian, can simply reduce her, like other politically sensitive historical personages, "to a bone of contention among conflicting groups" (Pathak and Rajan 273). What is at stake, we ask, in this or that particular reading of submerged voices in history? Whether Charke's flaunting convention is a conscious act of resistance is debatable, but one effect of her life and writing is to allow other women, in the eighteenth century and after, to create imagined alternatives to traditional understandings of femininity. "Resistance," writes contemporary feminist Rajeswari Sunder Rajan, "is not always a positivity; it may be no more than a negative agency, an absence of acquiescence in one's oppression" (12). The secret at the textual center of Charke's *Narrative* violates accepted sexual norms in its negation and in its refusal to expose the heart of the matter, and it exceeds any discursive construction that attempts to mold it into something fixed and coherent. Rather than the blush of modesty that we might expect from her more decorous sister authors, a surprising reticence permeates the narrative and contrasts to her seemingly reckless posturing. Her integrity, Charke seems to maintain, paradoxically requires evasiveness and camouflage rather than revelation. Charke's subjectivity is less a monolith, a reified and knowable self, than a knotty intertwining of identities that yield multiple and often contradictory material effects that are as varied and heterodox as the roles she performed in public and private. Modern critics have largely concurred with the epigraph to Charke's *The Lover's Treat*: there was "nothing of a piece about her."

As readers, then, we have to acknowledge that *we* are reading with vested interests. At the same time, such motives, even when explicitly articulated, are themselves subject to contest since our constitution of Charke's subjectivity is always an approximation of the real rather than a transcription of it. Rajan's formulation of the problem of situated knowledges is relevant here: that "whether the subaltern historian/feminist critic celebrates resistance or privileges the ultimate authority of the dominant will depend largely on the strategic, political or corrective purpose that underlines her interpretation and intervention" (5). Assessing Charke's affinities to the collective female subject through history, to an "ontologically grounded feminist subject" (Butler and Scott xiv) that is nevertheless provisional and contingent, is an interpretive act fraught with all the pitfalls of identity politics. The practice of reading is firmly located within culture, history, and ideology as much as we might be tempted by the compelling nature of a personal testimony that seems to convey unadulterated truth.

Yet in spite of the apparent undecidability of Charke's motivations, her narrative benefits from historically specific understandings. To some extent Charke adapts her lived experience to various ideological grids dominant in the mid eighteenth century—spiritual autobiography, travesty, tragicomedy, and apologia. Charke seeks her birthright through the *Narrative* in a public act of self-defense rather than through the more familiar model of female victimization and its suffering heroine. In an essay included in this volume, Joseph Chaney is among those who posit the generic model of the penitent prodigal, a figure prevalent in spiritual autobiography of the period, as most appealing to Charke, whose ironic conformity to that type he believes to be muted by her studied impersonation of various male roles. Chaney finds Charke to be most frequently engaged in imitating her father rather than parodying him, though he acknowledges that she sometimes disrupts generic conventions. But, as Madeline Kahn reports, generic expectations vary depending on the historical location of the readers. Women college students of the 1990s who interpret the autobiographical narrative often attempt to shape Charke into a contemporary heroine, flagrantly defiant, with whom they find an easy identification. Such students yearn to fuse her fractured self-representation and her attempt to usurp public space into an inspiring and reassuring narrative that leaps across centuries of women's attempting to claim legitimacy in both spheres.

Other critics have emphasized the extravagant spectacle of Charke's life as it conflicts or blends with the paradigm of a spiritual quest. Sidonie Smith among others identifies Charke's "flair for dramatic posturing, and energetic preoccupation with theatrical entertainment and self-fabrication" as they compete with the predominant mid-eighteenth-century types of "sentimental heroine and female rogue" (103–4). Kristina Straub also emphasizes the theatricality of Charke's identity, and her wishing to *live* the roles that she played. Actress and person meld together, and Charke toys with that blurry margin between art and life to attract readers and spectators. What makes Charke's identity so intriguing, not unlike modern audiences' identification of film stars with their characters, is the slippage between life and theater. Jean

Marsden also demonstrates that this performance of the self further muddies the uncertain boundaries between public and private life. That Charke broadly applies dramatic roles to her daily life and conceives of subjectivity as theater was characteristic of her performing family, whose members were always the object of curiosity, alternately praised and reviled, as Marsden observes. Yet her brother Theophilus's idealized portrayal of the Cibber family contrasts sharply to Charke's version of family misery.

Performance theory as developed by feminist critic Judith Butler has been especially fertile in its application to Charke since it conceptualizes identity as something constructed and enacted, "*produced* or *generated*," rather than essential. Performance theory, Butler argues, "opens up possibilities of 'agency' that are insidiously foreclosed by positions that take identity categories as foundational and fixed. For an identity to be an effect means that it is neither fatally determined nor fully artificial and arbitrary" (147). Performativity effectively loosens anatomy from identity, and sexual behavior from an essential self. For Butler, agency consists of the capacity to fabricate a coherent gendered identity through reiteration, through the repetitious performance of a culturally recognizable standard, but neither as a knowing instigator nor simply as a constructed self. Yet as useful as performance theory proves in elaborating on the nuances of gendered subjectivity and in allowing readers to escape the traps of essentialism, it also threatens to dissolve identity into a ludic indeterminacy that neglects the historical and economic conditions of its production within patriarchy. Teresa Ebert has launched a piercing critique of the dislocated subject of performance theory: "But for historical materialists, ideological interpellation . . . places the [individual] in the relations of production, in the social division of labor, according to gender, sexuality, race, nationality. Butler's theory of performativity eclipses this dialectical relation between ideology and the economic" (219). Arguing for Charke's widely diffused identity, as many recent critics have done, usefully unsettles sexual coherence and questions the concept of a primary identity, a fixed gender, from which all deviations are judged to be aberrations. At the same time, however, it also allows that identity to defy tracing and to escape the assignment of meaning. Further, it jeopardizes a historically nuanced feminist politics that assumes the existence of "woman," an especially pertinent category during the century that witnessed the emergence of feminism culminating in Mary Wollstonecraft's *Vindication of the Rights of Woman* (1792). The emphasis on performance theory in Charke might, I suggest, be tempered with greater attention to the material conditions of its production, and in particular the economic circumstances that induced Charke to write and to mold her life history into a commodity.

Materialist feminists posit that the performing body, its representation in text, its relation to identity and sexual behavior, are embedded within systems of gendered oppression that are often concealed. The purpose of the kind of critique that assumes that knowledges are situated rather than perpetually displaced is to bring the systemic aspects of ideological interpellation as "woman" to the foreground. In particular, the consequences of a female anatomy may be unpredictable, uncalculated, and culturally various. The "performing" body still succumbs to rape or clitoridectomy; it becomes pregnant, lactates, menstruates, or not. In short, female anatomy has particular effects; but the terms of its significance vary widely within history and culture. Charke's *Narrative*, an especially pertinent example, makes manifest the extraordinary difficulty of holding steadfast the category of woman, of a female subject, in the eighteenth-century context of a life devoted to public mimicry, pretense, and theatrical display.

In the 1750s, the decade in which Charke's *Narrative* was published, women writers such as Sarah Fielding, Charlotte Lennox, and even Eliza Haywood wrote domestic and sentimental novels whose adventurous heroines reform their errant ways or bring their lives into congruence with cultural expectations. This brand of femininity, equated with virtue and chastity, is on the ascendancy in the fictions of the period. The mid eighteenth century is also marked by the celebration of a national female genius that exudes respectability in George Ballard's *Memoirs of Several Ladies of Great Britain, who have been Celebrated for their Writings* (1752), John Duncombe's *Femniad: or, Female Genius* (1754), and Thomas Amory's *Memoirs of Several Ladies of Great Britain* (1755). During the same period, John Brown's much reprinted *Estimate of the Manners and Principles of the Times* (1757) launched a diatribe against unmanly English soldiers that inspired heated public debate on the nature of masculinity and its connection to nationalism. The Jacobite rebellion of 1745, Brown laments, had encouraged a *"vain, luxurious, and selfish EFFEMINACY,"* and its Cavalier heroes deserved to be quashed.[1] Brown also claimed that England was in danger of losing the Seven Years' War (1757–63) because men had sunk into "effeminacy," and women had advanced toward "boldness." As various cultural factors encouraged a particular kind of femininity, the emphasis on a particular brand of national manliness also intensifies. Hans Turley's study of the periodical press at midcentury, included in this volume, might also be understood in the context of an imperiled English masculinity. Turley places Charke's autobiographical writing within the 1750s to argue that the *Gentleman's Magazine* published during that decade reduced her sexual ambiguity and transgressive gender to an essential manliness, while clarifying the important distinction between cross-dressing and homosexual activity.

Recent critical work has reminded us that it is inadvisable to associate too closely the masculine with the public, the feminine with the private, even at the moment when the structural transformation of the separate spheres for men and women is believed to have emerged. Midcentury also brought new consciousness of the constructedness of gender, and of its production within cultural circumstances. Modern notions of sex, of incommensurable differences between women and men, increasingly solidify at the same time that England expands its interests into emerging world markets of mercantile capital. Writing at a crux in the formation and definition of sexual difference, Charke seems to worry little about public virtue, though she protests that she writes for moral purpose and claims that she never engaged in prostitution, no matter how destitute she became. Charke's failure to conform to a public respectability *or* a private domesticity made her unaccountable life especially threatening to stable notions of femininity and masculinity. Kristina Straub acutely remarks that even the masculinity that Charke impersonates is compromised because of Colley Cibber's reputation as a fop, and curiously Charke becomes an emblem of impotence, a threat to virility, and a symptom of the constructed nature of male sexuality. This apparently idiosyncratic eccentricity, then, is indicative of larger social and cultural conditions at a time when the nation feared effeminacy as a threat to its security and worried over the ramifications that an emasculated national character might bring. In short, Charke threatens to reveal that patriarchy and masculinity at midcentury, like femininity, are highly permeable and malleable categories. These contradictions in prevailing notions of gender at midcentury work "both to destabilize gender definition, and to reconfirm the central importance of sexual difference"(Guest, "Neuter Somethings"). They make ludic readings attractive even though, in fact, specific historical circumstances delimit the range of possible meanings that we can assign to Charke's life as readers constitute her identity.

Charke would not, of course, identify herself as a feminist, and she carefully dissociates herself from at least one tradition of women's writing, amatory poetry. In spite of her claim that she is unfairly deprived of her father's support, she does not call upon a community of women for validation or upon a collective gendered identity that recognizes its oppression. Charke's representation of gender, however, seems consonant with midcentury feminist tracts that assert that custom and patriarchal interests rather than biology confine women. "All the researches of Anatomy," contends the much reprinted "Sophia" pamphlet, "have not yet been able to shew us the least difference in this part between *Men* and *Women*"[2] (*Beauty's Triumph* 23). "It is a known truth," the pamphlet continues, "that the difference of sexes regards only the body, and that merely as it relates to the propagation of the Species. But the soul, concurring to it only by consent, actuates all after the same manner; so that in *this* there is *no sex* at all." Though most women think that they deserve inferior treatment, it is simply founded in custom: "In this Respect, the Conduct of Men is so analogous in all Ages, and in every Part of the Globe, that one would be inclined to imagine they have entered into an hereditary and universal Combination against us.—'Tis, indeed, the Opinion of many, that they are prompted by instinct to oppress us" (33). *Female Rights Vindicated* (1758), a later revision of the tract, also argues that, just as custom once maintained that the sun revolved around the earth and the Julian calendar was supplanted by the Gregorian, a female general or statesman might at first seem odd (31). The world, however, would soon accustom itself to the change since male superiority is simply instituted by habits of thought and action. Charke would have taken heart from the assertion in these polemical tracts that the theater allows women who are natural orators a public venue: "When I mention a *Cibber* or a *Pritchard* as public Orators (for such are Actresses to be consider'd, as the Stage is the only Place where we can display our Talents that Way) perhaps I shall be excused citing any private Personages" (37). The *Narrative* resonates within this context of assertions of women's equality, though Charke's actual ideas and intentions, as postmodern theories of authorship make clear, remain subject to conjecture. By violating midcentury expectations of proper femininity, the effect of Charke's life, no matter what her intention, effectively interrogates the legitimacy of patriarchy. The mystery at the core of the *Narrative* affords a tempting means of keeping multiple significations in view without regard for the material consequences that arise from reading in one way rather than another. In spite of the difficulty in formulating a female "character" in mid-eighteenth-century England, Charke insists on her own agency in producing an identity: "I THEN WAS WHAT I HAD MADE MYSELF." Resistance, then, is realized within particular historical boundaries, and identifying the material effects of the decision to read Charke's *Narrative* in one way or another allows us to escape the morass of intentionality or the equally unproductive indeterminacy of keeping all possible meanings in play.

As a cross-dressed woman, Charke does not embody the fashionable adornments and commodified virtue associated with her sex that would make her a female object of masculine desire. Robert Folkenflik demonstrates the pervasive fascination with Charke's iconographic representation, and it is not surprising that a bookseller would mistake that other famous "*Man-Woman*," Daniel Defoe's Roxana, for an image of Charke. Yet Charke's cross-dressing, as several essays included here point out, is not a certain indicator of her sexual identity or gendered performance. Part of her reason for being a male impersonator may well have been to escape her creditors. In addition, it afforded her freedom of movement in places women did not frequent, in seeking work, and in moving about at night. But Charke also allows the reader to entertain the possibility that she and "Mrs. Brown" are lesbians. Marrying twice, once to Richard Charke, the other in 1746 to John Sacheverell, she joined her actress friend as Mr. Brown by 1747. Given the sketchy evidence and the historical context, perhaps it would be more accurate to speculate that Charke was bisexual, even though we cannot definitively ascertain her erotic inclinations.

There has been some suggestion that love relationships between women in the mid eighteenth century were simply "romantic friendships," or that women's sexual liaisons, if they might have occurred, would not have been deemed scandalous. The preponderance of evidence now seriously disputes this claim.[3] Lesbianism and cross-dressing have too often been conflated when discussing Charke in the context of her historical moment, and whether Charke and her partner Mrs. Brown engaged in genital sexual activities is the subject of endless speculation. Definitions of "lesbian" are, of course, various. *Webster's Ninth,* as Terry Castle has pointed out, defines a lesbian as a woman "characterized by a tendency to direct sexual desire toward another of the same sex" (15). Castle applies this definition to the present moment as a woman who *prefers* women to men, but who may also make love to men. These contemporary sexual categories are finally not very useful in regard to Charke, who gives us insufficient grounds to make a determination, but the merest hint of genital activity between eighteenth-century women, I suggest, potentially threatened economic structures of patriarchal property and diverted heterosexual desire in troublingly illicit ways. While I do not think we can close off the possibility that Charke was "lesbian," we also cannot claim certain knowledge that such an assumption would mean that she prefers women as erotic objects, that they engaged in same-sex genital activity, or that her identity rested primarily on her sexual preference.

Even the attitude that Charke's characters display toward homosexuality in *The History of Henry Dumont, Esq; and Miss Charlotte Evelyn Consisting of Variety of Entertaining Characters, and very Interesting Subjects with some Critical Remarks on Comick Actors* (1756) may not in fact be indicative of her attitude toward lesbian activities. In *Henry Dumont* Charke defers criticism of homosexuality by making it a joke and by allowing a character to issue a vitriolic attack. The sentimental hero Dumont challenges Billy Loveman, an apparent homosexual who has sent him a comically illiterate love note that reads in part, "Permet me lusty objeckt, to meet you this evening at the fish-pond, vher I may be happy in paeing my rispex to the divine charmur of my soul" (59). Dumont is appalled at the sexual advance and thinks that Loveman must instead intend the billet-doux for Miss Evelyn, who mocks his naive heterosexism. When Dumont grudgingly acknowledges that he has heard of "a set of unnatural wretches, who are shamefully addicted to a vice," he determines to make an example of the "detestable brute" (60). Thus the gentle Dumont feels compelled to prove his manliness by fighting his suitor. Loveman's gender and that of his attendant valet (who appears to be a young wench in boy's clothes) are ambiguously portrayed, and Loveman's sexual orientation is at the very least the subject of debate. But the farcical scene of confrontation with Dumont makes Loveman seem to be a monster in the midst of an otherwise civil society, who deserves his ducking in the fishpond: "This odious creature in a female rich dishabille; who running to Mr. Dumont, cried out, 'I come, I fly, to my adored Castalio's arms! My wishes lord!'—stopping here, with a languishing air, said, 'Do my angel, call me your Monimia!' Then with a beastly transport, kissed him with that ardour, which might be expected from a drunken fellow to a common prostitute" (65). After Dumont canes Loveman, the "male-madam" along with his jealous wife-like lover Mr. Turtle, retreat to a remote country as "shepherdesses." While Mrs. Evelyn expresses compassion and makes it possible for the reader to share such an attitude, Miss Evelyn adds her homophobic note: "no punishment was sufficiently severe for such unnatural monsters" (69). In these passages Charke certainly seems to treat same-sex love as the object of ridicule (147), but it is not very remarkable that she attacks male homosexuality in *Henry Dumont* as typifying the monstrosity that she herself would not wish to be accused of being.

Nor are such sentiments particularly surprising in the years just preceding the Seven Years' War, when giving evidence of effeminate masculinity would have been tantamount to national disloyalty. The narrator of *The History of Henry Dumont* gently chides the English as a people for failing to be generous to less fortunate beings. Dumont combines English bravery, French politeness, and an Irish benevolence that the narrator wishes were more prevalent among the English populace: "I think a national gratitude incumbent on all who have the least regard to humanity; and were the lower people here, more kind to strangers, or their near acquaintance in distress, I am apt to believe two very great evils would be by that means avoided, the first of which is an inhuman deprivation of that power to do good, which the great Ruler of the world has for our own advantage bestow'd upon us; the next is thro' pinching want and dire necessity, reducing by our cruel parsimony a hapless wretch to barter his honesty to support a miserable life, which too often brings it to a shameful period" (31). The novel repeatedly cautions readers to avoid despising people for being poor. The narrator, in a move designed to avoid being accused of treason, openly apologizes for seeming to voice anti-English sentiment by favoring the Irish.

Dumont, which saw two editions in the year of its first publication, was written in abject poverty, and it offered Charke her sole hope of economic survival. Charke's poverty, however, may well have had an effect on the content of *Henry Dumont* beyond its preoccupation with getting and spending and their relationship to virtue. By at least one account, revisions in the novel were not her original idea, and the extent of the changes cannot be known. According to Samuel Whyte in *The Monthly Mirror,* "The work was read, remarks made, alterations agreed to, and thirty guineas demanded for the copy," and she was paid only ten and fifty personal copies (187). Perhaps the section on Billy Loveman was among those subject to her editor's changes.

There is, however, no reason to assume that gay practices and lesbian practices would have evoked identical sympathies in Charke or, for that matter, in any other eighteenth-century reader.[4] The histories of sexual preferences in the early modern period, only now beginning to emerge, suggest asymmetrical developments between male and female homosexuality. The cultural climate at midcentury is perhaps best exemplified in John Cleland's *Memoirs of a Woman of Pleasure* (1748–49), where Fanny Hill's same-sex induction into prostitution is erotically satisfying to her: "But this I know, that the first sparks of kindling nature, the first ideas of pollution, were caught by me that night, and that the acquaintance and communication with the bad of our own sex, is often as fatal to innocence, as all the seductions of the other" (12–13). In the *Memoirs,* however, a male homosexual incident (later censored) evokes extreme revulsion in the heroine. Fanny swoons and falls to the ground senseless when she views two country boys engaged in sodomy through a chink in the wall and Cleland, himself accused of homosexuality, makes his character Mrs. Cole launch a homophobic diatribe. Charke's sexuality cannot be definitively determined by her fictional portrayal of male homosexuality within the subtly nuanced context of eighteenth-century attitudes.

In another central example of the limits imposed upon our understanding, Charke's provisional identities and their performance regularly collide with the fact that she is, as the title of the *Narrative* testifies, Colley Cibber's daughter. In particular, the text delineates the unrelenting control, even neglect, that Cibber exerted over his daughter's economic situation. A notorious gambler, he had mercenarily claimed the thousand pounds per annum willed to his daughter Elizabeth by her maternal aunt Rose Shore, and he squandered the profits from *The Non-juror,* a play produced to benefit Charlotte in 1719 (Morgan 24–25). His ill-treatment of his wife and children was public knowledge. Charke's father, however, assisted her in regaining work at Drury Lane in 1735 after serious disagreements with Charles Fleetwood. Charke obviously felt considerable ambivalence toward her father, acting the part of Lord Place in Henry Fielding's *Pasquin,* a part that satirized Colley Cibber in his position as poet laureate. Further, Cibber publicly embarrassed Charke by ignoring his own daughter's desperate financial straits while bailing out another memoirist of dubious virtue, Laetitia Pilkington. An obituary, published in the *British Chronicle,* April 16, 1760, identifies Charke as a gentlewoman, a social status that she assumed to be her birthright but could not achieve without her father's financial support: "died, the celebrated Mrs Charlotte Charke, in the Haymarket, daughter of Colley Cibber Esq; the poet laureate; a gentlewoman remarkable for her adventures and misfortunes."

The economic inducement for Charke's professional decisions, including her decision to write her *Narrative,* cannot be overestimated, though recent criticism has paid insufficient attention to it. Charke's inexplicable life is partly explicable because of her lack of money. The threat of debtor's prison was very real. Having created difficulties for herself at Drury Lane, Charke came on hard times with the Licensing Act of 1737, and she turned to other less lucrative and stable pursuits, including producing puppet shows. Her attempts to earn her living as a provincial strolling player were plagued with problems of licensing and potential arrest as a vagrant. Though she could not trade on her virtue (the one certain commodity that mid-eighteenth-century women possessed) her public display of a titillating private life in the *Narrative* yielded economic value. In an important way, Charke uses the commercial system that would trade on her misfortunes to her own economic advantage. She seems bold and even vulgar, but she cannot be accused, as can most eighteenth-century women who aspire to a certain social class, of personifying the prevailing notion of consumption that expected her to wear the spoils of commercial gain. Business is not simply funneled through her; she initiates it and claims its profits while she insists (perhaps aware of the common collapsing of the distinction between lesbian and prostitute) that "I did not prostitute my person" (*Narrative* 15). Charke's vulgar public appearance, outside fashionable society, testifies to her inability and perhaps unwillingness to compete with displays of femininity as fashion or luxury. Instead, Charke wears men's clothes.

In short, emphasizing Charke's performance, her perpetual reconstruction of herself, tends to understate the material effect of Cibber's evacuation of any

responsibility for his daughter. Cibber's means of power over an obstreper-
ous daughter was both emotional *and* economic, depriving her of class privileges, of her expectations as his daughter, and of his affection. His searing letter
relating this withdrawal of support survives: "The strange career which you
have run for some years (a career not always unmarked by evil) debars my
affording you that succour which otherwise would naturally have been extended to you as my daughter. I must refuse therefore—with this advice—try Theophilus. Yours in sorrow, Colley Cibber."[5] The family and its affective economy were denied to Charke because Cibber violated family ties and assigned
his daughter little value. Here as elsewhere the line between emotional and
economic "succour" seems very thin.

The economic thoroughly preoccupies Charke in her writing as well as her
life. *The History of Charley and Patty; or, The Friendly Strangers,* published after *The History of Henry Dumont* but without a publication date, is a simple
tale of misery engendered by poverty. To the best of my knowledge, no one
has recognized that this little thirty-two page novella, most interesting because
of a brief cross-dressing incident, is extant. Since the hero Charley's name
echoes that of Charlotte Charke and it was the first name she adopted as Mr.
Brown, it provides another example of Charke's interest in gender fluidity. In
the moral tale, two close friends from "very good families in the West of England" (3) are each orphaned. Forming "a plan of future happiness by an hon-
orable conjunction, when their years should permit 'em to enjoy a happy
union" (4), Charley and Patty taught themselves a smattering of French and
Latin, shared their most intimate thoughts, and consoled each other in their
destitute situation.

Though Patty "had a blooming complexion with a set of features that might
reduce the heart of a savage to a tenderness and delicacy of thought only incidental to a generous sense of the softest passion of refin'd love" (23), the narrator repeatedly attests to the virtue of the two friends. When the rich but "very
crooked and extremely ugly" (6) daughter of Charley's guardian falls in love
with him, the young couple flees to a country inn to avoid his having to marry her. Patty's aunt and Charley's guardian conspire against the penniless run-
away pair, causing Charley to be imprisoned for allegedly committing a rob-
bery. In a parallel series of adventures, after Patty escapes a wealthy gentleman's
debauchery, she is falsely accused of stealing some silver plate and is sent to
jail. In an instance of cross-dressing that recalls Charke's own experience, Patty
escapes from the inn by exchanging clothing with "a virtuous young man"
(title page) who befriends her.

Charke's moral tale, like Sarah Fielding's *David Simple* (1744), is a testimony to the value of true friendship, since Charley and Patty, "destitute and friendless" (26), encounter numerous loyal friends who assist them. Further, Patty's behavior is exemplary when, rather than succumb to a rich lecherous man, she pawns her mother's diamond ring. The act shames her landlady, a bawd, into "promising this poor innocent virgin never more to expose her in public" (24). Vindicated, Charley and Patty form a community of sociability with Mr. Goodwill and a benevolent doctor. Finally, Patty's aunt restores her to her fortune: "The story of these two persons is an evidential proof that heaven is ever careful of those who repose their confidence in that power;—though several afflictions surround us for a time, we may by these occurences be convinc'd we ought not even in the most extream distress be excited to despair" (32). In *The History of Charley and Patty*, virtue withstands strong economic incentives to yield to temptation, and friendship and community, familiar midcentury themes, permeate the tale. A far remove from the amatory fiction popular earlier in the century, this novella provides testimony to the endurance of heterosexual love based on companionship rather than passion, though the pair could as easily be imagined as a same-sex union. Written to escape her own dire economic straits, Charke achieves here the happy ending that eluded her in reconciling to family and restitution of her birthright.

In another of Charke's fictional pieces, *The Mercer, or Fatal Extravagance: Being a True Narrative of the Life of Mr. Wm. Dennis, Mercer, in Cheapside, London* (1755?), family strife is also rooted in the economic, and its moral politics quickly yield to the vicissitudes of family fortune. *The Mercer* asserts that nothing is worse than living beyond one's means. Young Dennis, the silk mercer of the title, earns a large fortune and surrounds himself with the accoutrements of wealth, servants, and equipage. His tutor, Mr. Arnold, lectures him on his excessive spending as he becomes tired of business and fond of pleasure. Unable to keep his creditors at bay, Dennis is "basely and luxuriously waste in needless and unwarrantable pleasures, and unnecessary grandeur" (12). Turning highwayman and murderer, Dennis fails in a suicide attempt. Later he discovers that his debts have been paid by his sister's lover, but he is eventually hanged. The moral of the tale criticizes the mercantile economy as interfering with blood ties: "the presumptiae [*sic*] Vanity daily increasing and prompting many Persons in Trade to live up to the State of those, whose Birth and Fortune might justifie the running into such Expences, as must naturally terminate in the Ruin of Trading Families, and be the unhappy cause of Multiplying the numerous Indigent, who but for this failing in Parents might live comfortably to themselves and be generally beneficial to the world" (31). *The Mercer* links greed and poor money management to the dissolution of families.

Similarly in *The Lover's Treat; or, Unnatural Hatred* (1758?), Charke narrates another tale of bitter family discord. Written shortly after Colley Cibber's death and Charke's discovery that she had been left only five pounds, while her sister Catherine was awarded the bulk of the estate, this story tells of a wealthy grazier who loved all his children equally. The grazier's son Anthony, a "Monster of Inhumanity and Falsehood" (10), spurs his father's hatred for his twin siblings George and Jenny (the name of one of Theophilus Cibber's daughters) in order to gather all his father's money to himself. Anthony is a misogynist as well, who believes that "Women are dangerous Things to encounter" (11). Jenny's intended husband, also George's master, replies, "you have met with some Disappointment, but that should not urge you to an open War with the rest of Womenkind, but be it as it may, I'm fully persuaded that your Sister is intirely exempt from any of the Follies or Imperfections, which are I own too incidental to Females, and till I find her wrong 'tis my Duty and my Interest to believe *her* in the Right." Anthony, continuing his unmitigated evil, entraps her in a house of prostitution so that her husband-to-be questions her virtue. Her fiancé "expired raving," and Jenny is cut off without a shilling from her father (28). The twins wander the world seeking a subsistence, "outcast of our Families and cut us off from a very good inheritance" (38). When Anthony's evil is revealed to their father, he advertises "in case *they* are living that if *they* will return to You *they* will find all that can be wish'd for to make them *happy*" (39). The family reconciled, they retire to the country in prosperity. *Lover's Treat* depicts a family's treachery against itself over economic resources, and like *Charley and Patty* provides this dark tragedy with the happy ending that Charke unsuccessfully aimed to achieve in her life.

In short, what hinders Charke's agency in her own behalf is her financial predicament; but it also paradoxically encourages her seeking activities beyond the usual restrictions for women. As a number of the essays published in this volume point out, Charke played Macheath in Gay's *The Beggar's Opera*, Lord Place in Fielding's *Pasquin*, Captain Plume in Farquhar's *Recruiting Officer*, Bevil in Steele's *The Conscious Lovers*, and many other breeches roles with extraordinary vigor. The freedom from gendered restrictions she seeks in her early masquerading as a boy and in avoiding education in domesticity provides her with childhood training in refusing to acquiesce to the economic and social relations of patriarchy.

In Charlotte Charke's writing and her life, then, she seeks alternatives to the traditional patriarchal family, ingeniously circumventing both the Licensing

Law and compulsory heterosexuality, though her public authority clearly never equals her father's. The profoundly ambivalent subjectivity of Charlotte Charke constituted in her *Narrative* does not result in an easy or comfortable unity, and the stories that we weave about her measure our own cultural and political commitments. Charke's textuality serves as a means of preserving herself as a property, yet her cross-dressed pen bespeaks contradictions internal to subjectivity and in excess of the "whole self." Charke performs her captivating identity, but economic, historical, and cultural factors inevitably produce narrative constraints on the range of possibilities for action and for interpretation. These constraints, while vulnerable to our temptation to conflate lived experience and its textual representation, also remind us of the efficacy of resituating the narratives that we compose about Charlotte Charke beyond performativity, beyond contingency, and within the historical conditions of their production.

Notes

The last three lines of the epigraph that opens this essay serve as an epigraph to Charlotte Charke's *The Lover's Treat.* The passage spoken by Chamont, a soldier of fortune and brother to Monimia, describes a wrinkled beggarly hag who forecasts doom in Otway's *The Orphan,* a popular tragedy of rape and incest (act 2:31).

1. For a discussion of the exchange of gendered characteristics, see Nussbaum, "Effeminate Men."
2. This tract, *Beauty's Triumph,* is one of the several versions of Francois Poullain de la Barre's *The Woman as Good as the Man* published during the eighteenth century.
3. See especially Terry Castle, Emma Donoghue, Martha Vicinus, and Felicity Nussbaum (*Torrid Zones*).
4. Tom Yingling clearly identifies this problem in contemporary criticism: "As my own prose demonstrates, lesbian and gay studies slips all too easily and all too often into simply 'gay studies,' yet never into 'lesbian studies'" (157).
5. This letter appears in the Enthoven Collection, British Theatre Museum, and is cited in Fidelis Morgan's biography.

Works Cited

Amory, Thomas. *Memoirs of Several Ladies of Great Britain. Interspersed with literary reflexions, and accounts of antiquities and curious things.* London, 1755.
Ballard, George. *Memoirs of Several Ladies of Great Britain, who have been Celebrated for their Writings.* London, 1752.

Beauty's Triumph, or, the Superiority of the Fair Sex invincibly proved. 3 parts. London, 1751.

Brown, John. *Estimate of the Manners and Principles of the Times*. London, 1757.

Butler, Judith. *Gender Trouble: Feminism and the Subversion of Identity*. New York: Routledge, 1992.

———— and Joan W. Scott, eds. "Introduction." *Feminists Theorize the Political*. New York: Routledge, 1992.

Castle, Terry. *The Apparitional Lesbian: Female Homosexuality and Modern Culture*. New York: Columbia University Press, 1993.

Charke, Charlotte. *The History of Charley and Patty; or, The Friendly Strangers*. London, [1760?].

————. *The History of Henry Dumont, Esq; and Miss Charlotte Evelyn Consisting of Variety of Entertaining Characters, and very Interesting Subjects with some Critical Remarks on Comick Actors*. 2d. Ed. London, 1756.

————. *The Lover's Treat; or, Unnatural Hatred. Being a True Narrative as deliver'd to the Author by one of the Family who was principally concern'd in the following Account*. London, [1758?].

————. *The Mercer, or Fatal Extravagance: Being a True Narrative of the Life of Mr. Wm. Dennis, Mercer, in Cheapside, London*. London, [1755?].

————. *A Narrative of the Life of Mrs. Charlotte Charke*. 2d. ed. London, 1755. Ed. Leonard R. N. Ashley. Gainesville: Scholars' Facsimiles & Reprints, 1969.

Cleland, John. *Memoirs of A Woman of Pleasure*. Ed. Peter Sabor. Oxford: Oxford University Press, 1985.

Donoghue, Emma. *Passions between Women: British Lesbian Culture, 1668–1801*. London: Scarlet Press, 1993.

Duncombe, John. *Femniad: or, Female Genius*. London, 1754.

Ebert, Teresa L. *Ludic Feminism and After: Postmodernism, Desire, and Labor in Late Capitalism*. Ann Arbor: University of Michigan Press, 1996.

Female Rights vindicated: Or The Equality of the Sexes Morally and Physically proved. By a Lady. London, 1758.

Guest, Harriet. "'These Neuter Somethings': Gender Difference and Commercial Culture in Mid-18th Century England." Paper delivered at Huntington Library, December 1995. Forthcoming in *Re-Thinking Revolution*, ed. Keven Sharpe and Stephen Zwicker. Berkeley: University of California Press.

Morgan, Fidelis. *The Well-Known Troublemaker: A Life of Charlotte Charke*. London: Faber and Faber, 1988.

Nussbaum, Felicity A. "Effeminate Men, Manly Women: Gender and Nation in Mid-Eighteenth-Century England." Forthcoming in *Genders* (1998).

————. *Torrid Zones: Maternity, Sexuality, and Empire in Eighteenth-Century English Narratives*. Baltimore: Johns Hopkins University Press, 1995.

Otway, Thomas. *The Orphan*. Ed. Aline Mackenzie Taylor. Lincoln: University of Nebraska Press, 1976.

Pathak, Zakia, and Rajeswari Sunder Rajan. "*Shabano.*" *Feminists Theorize the Political.* New York: Routledge, 1992. 257–79.

Poullain de la Barre, Francois. *The Woman as Good as the Man, Or the equality of Both Sexes.* Trans. A. L. Ed. Gerald M. MacLean. Detroit: Wayne State University Press, 1988.

Rajan, Rajeswari Sunder. *Real and Imagined Women: Gender, Culture and Postcolonialism.* New York: Routledge, 1993.

Smith, Sidonie. *A Poetics of Women's Autobiography: Marginality and the Fictions of Self-Representation.* Bloomington: Indiana University Press, 1987.

Vicinus, Martha. "'They Wonder to Which Sex I Belong': The Historical Roots of the Modern Lesbian Identity." *Feminist Studies* 18 (Fall 1992): 467–97.

Whyte, Samuel. *The Monthly Mirror.* London, 1760.

Yingling, Tom. "Fetishism, Identity, Politics." *Who Can Speak? Authority and Critical Identity.* Ed. Judith Roof and Robyn Wiegman. Urbana: University of Illinois Press, 1995.

Contributors

PHILIP E. BARUTH is an assistant professor of English at the University of Vermont. His work on autobiography and biography has appeared in *Modern Language Quarterly, Biography,* and *The Age of Johnson.* Most recently, he has been involved in work on eighteenth-century connections to the film tradition and has coauthored an essay with Nancy West—"The History of the 'Moving Image': Rethinking Movement in the Eighteenth-Century Print Tradition and the Early Years of Photography and Film"—to appear in *Questioning History: The Postmodern Turn to the Eighteenth Century,* ed. Greg Clingham.

JOSEPH CHANEY is an assistant professor of English at Indiana University–South Bend. He has written articles on Shakespearean drama and Renaissance rhetoric. He is currently writing a book on the teleology of Shakespearean comedy.

ROBERT FOLKENFLIK is a professor of English at the University of California at Irvine and the author of *Samuel Johnson, Biographer* and *The Culture of Autobiography: Constructions of Self-Representation.* His essay "Gender, Genre, and Theatricality in the Autobiography of Charlotte Charke" will appear in *Life-Writing in the Age of Reason.*

MADELEINE KAHN is an associate professor of English at Mills College in Oakland, California. She is the author of *Narrative Transvestism: Rhetoric and Gender in the Eighteenth-Century English Novel* and of articles on pedagogy, eighteenth-century English literature, and the twentieth-century porno-graphy debates.

JEAN I. MARSDEN is an associate professor of English at the University of Con-necticut. She is the author of *The Re-Imagined Text: Shakespeare, Adaptation, and Eighteenth-Century Literary Theory,* the editor of *The Appropriation of Shakespeare: Post-Renaissance Reconstructions of the Works and the Myth,* and has published widely on Restoration and eighteenth-century drama. She is currently working on a study of women and the eighteenth-century stage.

FELICITY A. NUSSBAUM is a professor of English and women's studies at the University of California at Los Angeles. Her recent publications include *Tor-rid Zones: Maternity, Sexuality, and Empire in Eighteenth-Century English Nar-rative* and *The Autobiographical Subject: Gender and Ideology in Eighteenth-Century England,* which was the co-recipient of the Louis Gottschalk Prize for 1989 given by the American Society for Eighteenth-Century Studies. She is cur-rently working under an NEH grant to complete a book on gender, race, and monstrosity in mid-eighteenth-century England.

SIDONIE SMITH is a professor of English and comparative literature at SUNY Binghamton. She is the author of *Where I'm Bound: Patterns of Slavery and Freedom in Black American Autobiography, A Poetics of Women's Autobiogra-phy: Marginality and the Fictions of Self-Representation,* and *Subjectivity, Iden-tity, and the Body: Women's Autobiographical Practices in the Twentieth Centu-ry;* and coeditor, with Julia Watson, of *De/Colonizing the Subject: The Politics of Gender in Women's Autobiography* and *Getting a Life: Everyday Uses of Au-tobiography.*

KRISTINA STRAUB is an associate professor of English at Carnegie-Mellon University. The author of books on Frances Burney and eighteenth-century actors and their role in the history of sexuality, she recently finished work on an edition of Burney's *Evelina* and is writing a book on guilt, innocence, and bodily excess in eighteenth-century British criminal biography.

HANS TURLEY is an assistant professor of English at Texas Tech University. He is the author of *Rum, Sodomy, and the Lash* and the coeditor of *The Eighteenth Century: Theory and Interpretation.*

Index